Military Trains
and Railways

Military Trains and Railways

An Illustrated History

Jean-Denis G. G. Lepage

McFarland & Company, Inc., Publishers
Jefferson, North Carolina

Library of Congress Cataloguing-in-Publication Data

Names: Lepage, Jean-Denis, author.
Title: Military trains and railways : an illustrated history /
Jean-Denis G.G. Lepage.
Description: Jefferson, North Carolina : McFarland & Company, Inc.,
Publishers, 2017 | Includes bibliographical references and index.
Identifiers: LCCN 2017032529 | ISBN 9781476667607
(softcover : acid free paper) ∞
Subjects: LCSH: Military railroads—History. |
Military railroads—Pictorial works.
Classification: LCC UG345 .L47 2017 | DDC 355.8/3—dc23
LC record available at https://lccn.loc.gov/2017032529

British Library cataloguing data are available

ISBN (print) 978-1-4766-6760-7
ISBN (ebook) 978-1-4766-2764-9

Cover illustrations, clockwise from top left (all by author): German concrete
flak car; Russian BP Nr. 77 armored locomotive; Russian Zaamurets rail-cruiser;
German Steyr scout car; German Krupp K5 (E) 28 cm railroad gun; British armored train;
Austro-Hungarian Motorkanonwagen with 70 mm Skoda cannon; U.S. 14-inch railroad gun.

Printed in the United States of America

*McFarland & Company, Inc., Publishers
Box 611, Jefferson, North Carolina 28640
www.mcfarlandpub.com*

Acknowledgments

The author wishes to express his gratitude for the friendly support provided by Jeannette A. à Stuling, Eltjo de Lang, Ben Mercato, and Jan à Stuling, and to Edwin A. Pratt, Keith J.K. Davies, David Bishop, Christian Wolmar, and Steven J. Zaloga for their useful and instructive work.

Table of Contents

Part 6. Post-1945 Military Use of Railroads   183

Preface

This book tells of the adventures, achievements and failures, triumphs and tragedies that constitute the dramatic history of railways in war from the 1830s until the Cold War. The book is set up chronologically, starting with the earliest records of military railways and encompassing and discussing the major conflicts in both the 19th and 20th centuries in which railways were involved.

Military trains remain one of the less-explored subjects of vehicle history, and their use at war is especially neglected. While books on tanks and armored vehicles are countless, works on military trains in English are rather few and generally cover only one facet of the subject, for example, the transport trains of a particular nation in a specific war (e.g., the U.S. Civil War), or the popular armored trains, and more specifically the post–1917 Russian Civil War trains, or World War II German Panzer trains. Many authors focus on narrow aspects and specific details of the story that are geared toward train enthusiasts rather than general readers. This book's principal contribution is that all aspects of military trains are described, including: transport and logistics; rail-borne artillery; armored trains; and draisines. It covers such well-known topics as the American Civil War (1861–65), the Boer wars (1880–1902), and both world wars of the 20th century (1914–18 and 1939–45), but also lesser-known conflicts such as the Austro-Prussian War (1866), the Franco-Prussian War (1870–71), the Russo-Turkish War (1877–78), the Finnish Civil War (1918), the Spanish Civil War (1936–1939), and the French Indochina War (1946–1954). The cause, the key battles and the outcome of each war are outlined as well. Attention is also given to the role of railways in colonial wars in Africa and Asia, as well as to rolling stock, materials and equipment, uniforms, and weapons.

It is intended that this volume should appeal to rail fans, train modelers and historians, military historians, and anyone interested in military history and warfare in general.

Introduction

Within a few decades after its appearance the railroad became the most importance means of long-distance transportation. The railroad brought life to even the remotest small village, just as the automobile did after World War II. The development of the railroad necessitated extraordinary economic efforts and enormous investment in capital. Its construction moved tens of thousands of workers and, once built, its maintenance, management and operation created numerous jobs. Because of the railroad, the production and consumption of coal, steel, and iron skyrocketed. The development and industrial employment of the Bessemer converter and the improvements made on puddling furnaces in the 1860s and 1870s by Siemens and Martin enabled increased steel production. At the International Exhibition of 1867 held in Paris, bridges, ships, lighthouses and many other architectural elements made of steel were displayed.

After the Napoleonic wars ended in 1815, the early part of the 19th century saw a period of peace in Europe with prodigious industrial and commercial expansion. By the middle of the 19th century, however, tensions were increasing, and an intense rivalry gradually developed again between European powers, partly as a result of nationalism, partly as a result of the revolutionary change from sail to steam in the navies, and partly because of colonial expansion. On land the development of yet more powerful weaponry and the introduction of the railroad brought other significant changes. The construction of the first railway lines was stimulated by peaceful purposes—the carriage of freight and passengers—but it was not long before some military officers realized the potential for moving troops and supplies. However, the steam railroad was not invented for military use, and at first its impact on warfare could only be guessed. Military use followed the development of the railroad itself. When their use was fully understood, transport, communications and logistics were completely transformed by the steamship, the telegraph and the railroad. Construction programs were largely intended for civilian passengers and transport of freight, but soon at the back of many governments' minds was the consideration that the railroad could also be used for war. As soon as the new technology evolved in the second part of the 19th century, military use was adopted.

The railroad made it possible to carry out administrative work in areas ten times as large as any that had hitherto been workable under one administration. In military terms, the railroad revolutionized strategic geography, increased the pace and power of tactical maneuver, made armies more massive and more mobile, and stimulated a whole new science: logistics. The principal features of strategy—time and space—were fundamentally altered. For the first time, an army could put its whole strength against the enemy. The debilitating long marches of the past, which so often had wasted an army's strength before it even went into battle, were largely reduced. Once the track was laid, there existed a method of transport that would not become bogged down in the mud, however heavy its load. Speedy mobilization and great concentration of force along frontiers, even in advance of war, were now possible. In the 18th century it was generally admitted that armies in excess of 80,000 men could not be properly supplied in the field. This limit was transcended by the French armies of the Revolution and Napoleonic era (1790–1814). The collapse and doom that overtook Napoleon's Grande Armée (600,000 strong) in the Russian campaign of 1812 was mainly caused by problems of communication and lack of supplies. With the introduction of the railroad, these limits were broader, mass armies were rendered possible and practical, and this further increased the move towards the concept of a nation-in-arms based on the total mobilization of a country's resources in war involving all sections of society. For a time it almost seemed that a war could be won by advance planning, or decided by the first few battles. Nations with the greatest industrial resources, particularly in railroad, seemed to have a great advantage over their neighbors.

Rail became a unifying force as the tracks expanded across various countries. It also contributed to the escalation in the scale of warfare. As a strong stimulus to unification, development of nationalist feelings, and economic growth, the railroad also encouraged expansion and imperialism, and consequently aggressive intent towards neighboring countries. The wars of the pre-industrial era in the 18th century generally included short battles, invariably conducted in the spring and summer months to ensure that men and animals could live off the land, and interspersed with lengthy periods of respite before other operations would be launched. By contrast, the railroad gave rise to a new style of war, particularly in the 20th century, with long, bloody,

and devastating campaigns between countries lasting several years and involving entire populations. Railroads also permitted the development of colonialism and the establishment of dominance by force over countries and people all over the world.

It is no coincidence that the heyday of the railway age was also the era of total conflicts and world wars.

These attitudes developed late in the 19th century, but it took time for military authorities to realize the potentialities offered by the railroad and to learn how to use them effectively at war. Once the railroad became operational, the nature of warfare changed and conflicts increased in intensity, length and destructiveness.

Three distinct railway roles gradually appeared: transportation of men and supplies; armored trains; and heavy railroad artillery.

The first and most obvious military use of railroads was troop and supply transport. Instead of marching, large armies with supplies, cavalry and artillery could now be moved quite rapidly. As a comparison, in 1805 Napoleon's army of 200,000 men took forty-two days to march the 700 kilometers (435 miles) from France to Ulm on the Danube. In his invasion of Russia in 1812, Napoleon's losses in men who succumbed to the fatigue, exposure, ordeals and trials they experienced on their way far exceeded the casualties due to actual fighting. Transport by rail resulted in much less fatigue. Furthermore, in all ages the feeding of troops in enemy territory had always been one of the gravest problems a military commander had to solve. Although, in some instances, vast armies succeeded in drawing sufficient support from the land they had invaded, there have been many others in which armies intending to live upon the country failed to get the food they needed. History is full of armies of thousands, depleted, defeated, and annihilated as the result of sheer starvation. From ancient times until today an army moves more upon its belly than upon its legs, as a happy combatant is a well-fed soldier. Horses and pack animals, too, were out of condition for want of proper and sufficient fodder. The equation between mobility and ability to access supplies, as well as all adverse conditions, were changed by the introduction of the railroad. When the military authorities understood how and when the railroad was fully incorporated into military logistics, an army could now draw its supplies from the whole of the interior of the home country, provided, of course, that the lines of communication could be kept open. Under these conditions the feeding and supplying of an army in the field could be assured, regardless of the possible scanty resources of the country in which it was engaged or its distance from one's own base of supplies.

Railroads enabled a quick mobilization, a large deployment of forces, the forwarding of reinforcements, provisions, clothing,

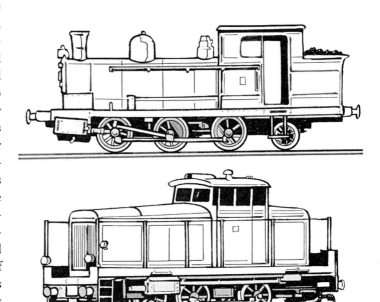

Top: *Steam locomotive. A locomotive or engine is a powered rail transport vehicle that provides the motive power for a train (a series of vehicles that runs along a rail track). A steam locomotive is powered by an external combustion engine. Basically it works as follows: By use of a coal- or wood-fueled fire, water is heated and transformed into steam within a boiler operating at a high pressure. The steam from the boiler is piped to cylinders, where it moves reciprocating pistons. The pistons are mechanically connected to wheels by driving rods and shafts, which transmit rotating energy to the wheels. A locomotive usually has no payload capacity of its own, but both fuel and water supplies are carried along with the locomotive, either on the locomotive itself or in a tender (a trailing vehicle closely coupled with the locomotive). Cargo and/or passengers are transported in vehicles called carriages, wagons or coaches (British English) or railroad cars (U.S. English). Locomotives are commonly designated by their wheels' arrangement, using a three-digit system devised in 1900 by the mechanical engineer Frederick Methven Whyte (1865–1941). The first digit indicates the number of (generally small) leading wheels at the front of the locomotive; the second is the number of larger and powered driving wheels under the main body of the machine; and the third is the number of small trailing wheels at the rear. For example, 0-4-2 indicates no wheel at the front, four in the middle and two at the rear; 2-6-4 indicates two wheels at the front, six in the middle and four at the rear; 0-6-0 indicates no wheels at the front, six in the middle and none at the rear; 2-8-2 indicates two wheels at the front, eight in the middle and two at the rear. The depicted locomotive is 0-6-2. There are other systems of classification, though. For example, the French system counts axles rather than wheels. A locomotive is then designated by three digits corresponding to its axle configuration: The first digit is the number of leading unpowered axles; the second digit is the number of powered axles; the third digit is the number of trailing unpowered axles. So 0-6-0 corresponds to 030, with 2-6-0 to 130, and 0-6-2 to 031.*

Bottom: *Diesel locomotive. A diesel locomotive is powered by a compression ignition engine–developed by engineer Rudolf C.K Diesel (1858–1913).*

munitions, supplies and stores to the front in enormous quantity. In the other direction, railroads allowed a steady flow of sick and wounded, prisoners of war, and matériel no longer needed at the front, followed by the final return of the troops back home by the end of the campaign.

However, the use of railroads for transporting armies had a double-edged impact. It hampered political considerations and last-minute diplomatic interventions, and could reduce strategic and tactical mobility by putting too many forces into the field too rapidly to be effectively wielded. Both problems were compounded by an understandable human failure to appreciate the full effects of this evolution.

Although many years were to pass before an efficient system of railroad ambulance service finally evolved, transport of casualties greatly benefited from the introduction of railroads. For centuries, the wounded after any encounter were left on the battlefield, and many remained there for days and nights before survivors could be removed in carts and wagons—at least, when these were available for the purpose. Within days, even hours, many wounded had died from lack of proper medical attention. To the sick and wounded among the troops, prompt removal by rail and distribution among hospitals in the interior meant that they avoided the risks to which they would have been subjected in the overcrowded dressing stations and pestilential improvised hospitals near the fighting line. There, slight injuries readily developed dangerous infections, and contagious diseases further increased the risk of fatality. On the whole, the railroads offered the wounded soldiers a better chance for a speedy recovery, and of saving both life and limb than before. Fast medical evacuation by train was thus a fantastic boost for the morale and pugnacity of the troops. Rail, as part of the Industrial Revolution, helped intensify war's terrible carnage, but also served at least to relieve warfare of a few of its horrors.

The second military use of the railroad was the armored train. Quicker transport and evacuation were important considerations, but other, more specific uses of the railroad by the military were developed to make them genuine instruments of warfare, for both defensive and offensive roles.

Inevitably, as the railroad became increasingly important for troops and supply transport, to appropriate and make use of the enemy's own rail system was often the aim of attacking forces. Railroad lines were fought over as prized possessions, a system of great value to whomever controlled it. Railroad lines, stations, junctions, bridges

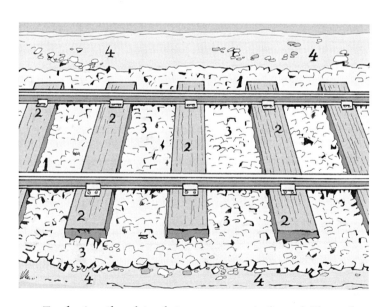

Track. A railroad track is a permanent, dependable surface enabling trains to run. The structure consists of two parallel rails (1) that are strongly fastened on ties or sleepers (2) lying on ballast (3) generally made of crushed stones, and a compact subgrade (4)—a flat prepared earth surface. The distance between the two rails is called gauge.

and hubs thus became major targets. Consequently, blowing up a railroad link, destroying a station or a bridge, blocking a tunnel, and sabotaging a switch were favored tactics in every conflict, since to do so was to cut off, disturb, or slow down the enemy's lifeblood. An attempt to counter this was the use of rail patrol and heavily armed and armored trains. These were used by most combatants in one form or another during the late 19th and first half of the 20th centuries. Indeed, armored rolling fortresses offered an innovative way to quickly move large amounts of firepower into position, to facilitate scouting missions, patrol and protect ordinary traffic trains, tracks and railroad installations, and to provide support for offensive actions in enemy-held territories. During World War I (1914–1918), armored trains were developed alongside armored cars and tanks, and they played an important role in the Russian Civil War (1917–1922) and in China in the 1920s. They were used in World War II (1939–1945), but by then their heyday had passed; they were replaced by the more versatile tank (armored fighting vehicle). In the second half of the 20th century, armored trains were only sporadically used, mostly in anti-guerrilla warfare.

Finally, another elaborate adaptation of railroads for military use was heavy artillery mounted on trains. This consisted of artillery pieces placed on rail cars towed by locomotives, being moved from point to point along the battlefield to meet, as far as the network made it possible, the needs of the military situation. This method was developed by all major industrial powers from the end of the 19th century onwards. Heavy cannons were

Tender. Many steam locomotives pulled an attached rail vehicle called a tender or coal-car, which carried the large quantities of water and fuel (wood, coal, or oil) needed when the machine was running over long distances. A steam locomotive that carried all its fuel and water on board instead was called a tank locomotive.

progressively placed on special carriages with standard fitting gauge, carefully designed suspension and specific pieces of equipment. Railroad-mounted artillery presented many advantages. It often consisted of heavy guns (sometimes, large discarded naval pieces) with a long range that could not possibly be transported by road. They had a formidable range, allowing gunners to fire behind enemy lines from a relatively safe distance. Also, railroad guns enjoyed great mobility, particularly in Europe, owing to the dense rail networks. A large rail-mounted gun could indeed do the job of many smaller ones.

All industrial nations realized the necessity of having an organized and well-regulated system of forwarding men, weapons, ammunition and supplies, in order to both avoid congestion of stations and lines and to ensure the punctual arrival of the right supplies in the right quantities, at the right spot, and at the right time.

Between 1814 and 1914, the development in communication strategy was transformed, and the revolution in weapons technology radically changed tactics. In the second half of the 19th century, the "romantic heroism" of the Napoleonic era, which had flourished in the small colonial campaigns where adventurous officers had made their mark, was steamrolled into oblivion by a system which made war a matter of scientific calculation, administrative planning, and professional logistics expertise.

Previous military reference books have concentrated on military transportation, armored trains, or railroad-mounted artillery. This book has been compiled in an attempt to cover all three subjects, plus other aspects equally essential to a complete understanding of the railroad at war. This includes the historical background in which it was used, as one cannot adequately describe how wars were fought without giving some general idea of what they were fought for—or alas, often the total absence of clear purpose.

Conversion of imperial measurements to metric:

1 mile = 1.6 km
1 yard = 0.9 m
1 ft = 0.3 m
1 in = 2.54 cm or 25.4 mm
1 gal = 4.5 liters
1lb = 0.45 kg
1 U.S. ton = 0.9 tonnes
1 hp = 0.745 kW

PART 1

Early Military Use of Railroads

THE CONCEPT
OF MILITARY RAILROADS

Britain was the first nation to adopt railroad. Richard Trevithick put a steam locomotive to work in a Welsh coal mine as early as 1804. This was the first time a steam engine operated on rails. Hosts of designs for steam locomotives were drawn up between 1804 and 1820, but the first truly practical one was designed by George Stephenson, who not only built the locomotive but also the track line. Construction on this line, running between Stockton and Darlington, was started in 1822, and it began operations in 1825. It caught the attention of the world, and soon new railroad lines appeared. In 1830, the opening of the Liverpool and Manchester Railroad marked the birth of the Railroad Age, for it combined for the first time the characteristics of a train, including: a specialized track (two parallel rails, which could be used only by vehicles having wheels of appropriate shape at the right distance apart); accommodation of public traffic; conveyance of passengers and freight; and mechanical traction.

Military thought in Britain at that time looked upon the railroad primarily as a valuable adjunct in the preservation of internal order, and in the second place as a link in the chain of transport to overseas stations. Indeed, both the British and French authorities were initially interested in railroads as a means of transporting troops to quell riots in their large cities. In 1830 a British infantry regiment (about 1000 soldiers) was conveyed over the 46 km (34 miles) between Manchester and Liverpool in two hours, a journey which would have required two days to accomplish on foot. The idea that railroads might be used in actual military operations would not easily occur to British officers, but gradually far-seeing men became still more impressed, and began to realize that there had, indeed, been introduced a new factor destined to exercise a powerful influence on the future conduct of war.

The difference between the geographical conditions of the British Isles and those of the principal countries in continental Europe led to an original organization of rail transport for military purposes. In Britain, there was no question of building lines of invasion or lines to facilitate the massing of troops on a neighbor's frontiers. The employment of railroads focused both on resisting invasion and on the conveyance of expeditionary forces to ports of embarkation for oversea operations. In the 1860s and 1870s, William Bridges Adams (1797–1872), an authority on railroads, and several military engineers (e.g., Lieut. Arthur Walker and Colonel E.R. Wethered) suggested the utilization of armored trains and heavy artillery mounted on railroad cars for defending the shores of Great Britain against invasion instead of expensive static fortifications. These rolling fortresses would constitute a strong line of mobile defense along the whole coast, as they could quickly bring troops and artillery to threatened places of landing. More especially, for the defense of London, the employment of armored trains was also advocated as the most efficacious and the most economical line of defense London could have. A strategic circular railroad line would form a complete defensive cordon around the capital at a distance of fifteen miles from the center. These suggestions were not followed, and military funds were employed for the improvement of static coastal defenses, notably the fortifications of Portsmouth and Plymouth.

At a time when military aviation did not yet exist, the concept of replacing static fortifications with mobile armored trains and heavy artillery mounted on train cars was after all not such an absurd idea. In 1891, in Italy a distinguished officer raised the question in the Italian Parliament as to whether Sicily should be defended by means of a coastal railroad network and armored trains.

In Germany, keen minds were also busy with the issue of military railroads. As early as the 1830s, the Germans were amongst the first to perceive its military implications. The German economist and journalist Friedrich List (1789–1846) foresaw and advocated the use of trains for military purposes. Friedrich Wilhelm Harkort (1793–1880), a Westphalian staff officer and a veteran of the Napoleonic Wars, advanced the first definite proposals for the use of railroads in Germany for strategical purposes. As an industrialist and engineer, Harkort had subsequently shown great energy and enterprise in the development of steam engines, hydraulic presses, iron making, and other important industries in Germany. Harkort had been the first writer in that country to give an account (already in 1825) of the progress England was making in respect to railroads and steamships. He also had placed a working model of a railroad in the garden of the Elberfeld Museum in 1826. Following these various efforts, Harkort brought for-ward in the Westphalian Parliament a project for the building of a railroad to connect the Weser and Lippe Rivers in 1833. He also published a book in which he advocated a line from Minden to Cologne in order to thwart a French invasion. With the help of such a railroad, Harkort argued, it would be possible to concentrate a large army at a given point much more speedily than if soldiers had to march on foot by road. He made calculations as to what the actual saving in time, as well as in physical strain, would be in transporting Prussian troops from various specified centers to others.

Harkort's efforts and suggestions were followed by those of Karl E. Pönitz, who published a treatise in 1842 pointing to the advantage that German railroads would confer if France and Russia attacked at the same time. Pönitz's work was translated into French in 1844, and some French military and parliamentary leaders discussed these matters a good deal. As a countermeasure, the construction of a line from Paris to Strasbourg was advocated, predicting that any new invasion of France by Germany would obviously be attempted between Metz and Strasbourg. But the French did not build as many railroad lines as the Prussians. In the 1840s Germany had nearly 3,300 miles of railroad, while France was operating only a little over 1,000 miles. By 1850 the French system was still fragmentary—only 1,870 miles with many gaps, against 3,735 miles in Germany and 6,621 in the United Kingdom. By 1848 Belgium had 450 railroad miles in operation and over 2,500 by 1900. The Dutch were slow to adopt railroad; by 1860 they had only 211 miles and 1,628 in 1890. The same applies to Scandinavia with 995 miles in Denmark in 1880. Italy was another slow starter with 4,000 miles in 1870.

In 1846, Prussia moved over 12,000 men to Cracow by rail upon two lines together with horses, guns, road vehicles and ammunition, a force intended to quell a nationalist uprising.

It took only two days to transport this force over 300 km. From that date down to the outbreak of the First World War in 1914, the whole subject of rail transport received an ever-increasing degree of attention from the German military authorities, and also from many military thinkers considering the question of German expansion.

By the middle of the 19th century most leading countries of Europe were engaging in military use of the railroad. In 1849 a Russian army of 30,000 men, with all its equipment, was transported by rail from its cantonments in Poland to Goding, Moravia. Also there were movements of German troops by rail to Schleswig-Holstein during the troubles of 1848–50. But of greater importance than these instances was the transport of an Austrian army of 75,000 men, 8,000 horses and 1,000 vehicles from Vienna and Hungary to the Silesian frontier in the early winter of 1850. These comparatively minor demonstrations went to show that the great land empires would be able to use existing lines to make concentrations of troops at required points behind their frontiers in a relatively short time.

Together with the train, which enabled armies to be transported to the front with unprecedented dispatch, the electric telegraph allowed speedy communication between headquarters and commanders in the field. Increasingly, war became no longer a remote affair about which the civil population learned only from brief governmental announcements or soldiers' tales long after the event. Yet such technological advances were slow to transform 19th-century armies from essentially Napoleonic-styled entities into recognizably modern forces.

CRIMEAN WAR (1853–1856)

Historical Background

The Crimean War was fought between the Russian Empire on one side and an alliance of France, Great Britain, the Kingdom of Piedmont-Sardinia, and the Ottoman Empire on the other. The war was part of a hazy and long-running contest between the major European powers for influence over territories of the declining Ottoman Empire. Some roots of the war lay in the existing rivalry between the British and the Russians in other areas such as Afghanistan, and conflicts over control of holy places in Jerusalem. Although Britain and France attacked targets in the Baltic, and launched minor operations in the Arctic and the Pacific to blockade Russia, Crimea (located south of Ukraine) was their primary objective. Their steamships moved a substantial army to the peninsula and besieged the city-port of Sevastopol, home of the Tsar's Black Sea Fleet and the associated threat of potential Russian penetration into the Mediterranean. The Allies failed to take into account the sophistication of the fortifications of Sevastopol; moreover, their supply system broke down amid the harsh winter. The port was captured on September 9, 1855, after an appalling year-long siege.

The Crimean War was notorious for military and logistical immaturity by the allied armies. Uniforms were inadequate; rations, when available, proved inedible; and an incompetent medical service further exacerbated the troop's misery. In the terrible winter of 1854–55, the French and British had engaged some 56,000 men, of whom nearly 14,000 ended up sick in hospitals. In spite of some primitive health care and nursing techniques, pioneered and introduced by Florence Nightingale (the famous "Lady with the Lamp"), many sick and wounded died because of the appalling lack of care.

The Crimean War was in many respects an old-fashioned conflict in the 18th century tradition with professional armies led by generals who had been brought up in the strategic and tactical schemes of the Napoleonic era. Yet it is often considered to be the first "modern" conflict, in which technical innovations were introduced (e.g., railroad, telegraph, trench warfare, blind artillery fire, the use of the Minié bullet coupled with the rifling of barrels, and new naval weapons such as the torpedo, floating mine and armored gunship). Unlike previous wars, reporters and war correspondents (e.g., William Howard Russell working for the British *Times*) were present on the scene. They sent their copy to London and Paris by telegraph, and thereby allowed the British and French public (increasingly literate, urbanized and politically aware) to follow the campaign in far greater detail, and as a result with far greater critical interest. These technical changes, which were to affect the future course of warfare, greatly increased lethality and damage.

In the end, the futile Crimean War had little geopolitical impact. It only temporarily halted Russian ambitions in the Balkans and postponed to another century Ottoman Turkey's collapse. The war was a pointless and costly affair, with the Russians losing some 256,000 men and the French and British between them about 252,000.

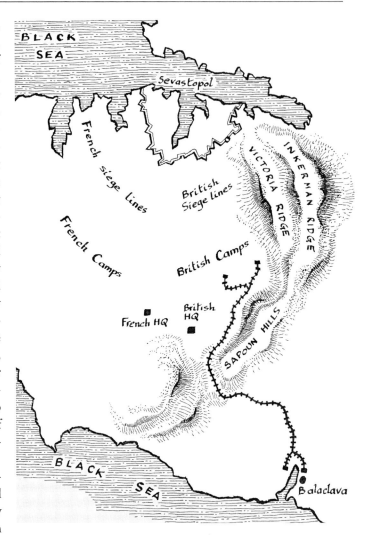

Map of Balaclava railroad.

Balaclava Railroad

By the time the Crimean War broke out, western nations had already experienced about 25 years of railroad building. Yet governments and military authorities had made no really serious attempt to use it until then. The earliest instance of a purely and solely military railroad being constructed to serve the purpose of a campaign occurred at the siege of Sevastopol during the Crimean War. At the time it was looked upon as a remarkable innovation in warfare. It was the Balaclava Line (eight miles long), established between the siege camps of the allies at Sevastopol and their rear base of supplies at the harbor of Balaclava. Amid the bungling chaos of the Crimean War, the line was, however, extremely primitive and not much of a railroad. Its operation was a cumbersome process. It was a single track with a 4-foot 8-inch gauge. For the first two miles from the harbor, supply cars were moved by conventional steam locomotives imported from Britain and operated by soldiers of the Royal Engineers. Then the trucks (wretched second-hand vehicles) were drawn up an incline, eight at a time, by a cable operated by a stationary engine due to a steep gradient. Next, six horses drew two trucks at a time up another incline. After this came a fairly level piece of track, followed by two gullies, where each car was detached in succession and made to run down one side of the gully and up the other by its own momentum. Then horses were

Balaclava railroad.

again attached to the trucks and so drew them, finally, to the end of the line on the upland to the camps. The return journey of the trucks to the Balaclava harbor was largely by force of gravity, at times a dangerous procedure, which caused a lot of accidents and derailments when brakes failed. The quantities of ammunition and supplies that could be carried were far below the requirements of the troops engaged in the siege operations. At first the track was not fully operated, and activities ceased from 5:30 p.m. to 8 a.m. the following morning. But during the last period of the siege in April 1855, it was operated day and night by a staff increased to about 1,000 men. The volume of transport rose from 200 tons a day, the limit attained under operation by the navvies, to 700 tons of ammunition. While the Balaclava railroad might appear to have been a modest little line, its importance should not be underestimated. It was used to evacuate injured and sick soldiers, and also did excellent work on the re-embarkment of the supplies at the end of the campaign. The track was dismantled right after the war, and it was its lessons for the future (more or less well drawn) that were just as important. The Balaclava

track can now be seen to have faced the basic problems and perennial questions with regard to military railroads: whether technicians are to be employed in the construction and operation of lines under military supervision; how far the railroad can be kept free from interference by other branches of the Army; and how the loading and forwarding of vehicles can be kept under control. In every war since 1855, staffs have had to grapple with these issues, and it seems that the lessons painfully learned in the Crimean War had to be picked up all over again. If these lessons had been learned more quickly, several wars would have been finished sooner.

FRANCO-AUSTRIAN WAR (1859)

Historical Background

The Franco-Austrian War was a conflict opposing Emperor Napoleon III of France and the Kingdom of Piedmont-Sardinia on one side to the Austrian Empire on the other. In the 1850s, Italy was still a deeply divided land made of several kingdoms, small duchies, principalities, and free cities. These independent states included Sardinia-Piedmont, as well as Lombardy and Venetia (both occupied by

Austria since 1814), Tuscany with its capital Florence, the tiny duchies of Modena, Parma and Lucca, the Papal State (the hereditary possession of the Roman Catholic See), and in the south the large kingdom of Naples, also called the Two Sicilies, ruled since 1735 by a branch of the French Bourbon dynasty. The local rulers and governments were generally content with their own separate independence but Italy was a powerless country. Some people wanted *Risorgimento* (rebirth) for unification and establishment of a central power.

Fought in 1859 in Northern Italy the Franco-Austrian War was directly linked to the Italian unification process, and also called the *Second Independence War*. It followed the failed 1848 *First Italian War of Independence* when the Piedmontese had been defeated by Austria. This time, well aware that Italy needed a great power at her side, the leading figure in the movement toward Italian unification and Prime Minister of the Kingdom of Piedmont-Sardinia, Camillo Benso Cavour (1810–1861), established a secret alliance with France. The dictator and Italophile Napoleon III who wished to weaken Austria, decided to support Piedmont-Sardinia. War broke out between Piedmont and Austria on April 23, 1859 after Cavour had provoked Vienna by ordering a series of military maneuvers close to the border between the two lands. As agreed the French intervened to support their Piedmontese ally. The conflict was short, and marked by a first battle at Montebello (May 20), and two extremely bloody clashes at Magenta (June 4) and Solferino (June 24).

In spite of his military success, Napoleon III was shaken by the enormous casualties of Solferino. He was alarmed by the progress of revolution in Italy, and particularly anxious about the reactions of French Catholics to the threats weighing on the Papal State. He also worried about Prussian reactions, which became a major power in northern Europe. Napoleon III began to negotiate independently with the Austrians, and on July 7, 1859,

an armistice was concluded bringing an end to this pointless and bloody war. He abandoned Piedmont, his ally, which obtained Lombardy but not Venetia. As an honorarium, France acquired in 1860 the southern Alpian province of Savoy and the border city of Nice on the Riviera where plebiscites disclosed enormous majorities for annexation to France. The 1860 Italian campaign paved the way to the emergence of a united Italy. After complicated moves and alliances, the unity of Italy was completed in 1870.

Railroads in the Franco-Austrian War

In the late 1850s, military railroad was still in its infancy, and many experts of the time thought that the railroad would give the advantage to the nation on the defensive, but this conception was shattered in the Italian campaign of 1859. It was in this war that railroads first played a conspicuous part in actual offensive warfare, both strategically and tactically. Thousands of French soldiers were transported daily by train from Paris through France to Toulon and Marseille, where they embarked on ships to the Italian port of Genoa. Some troops went by train to the foot of Mont Cenis in the Alps, and there had to disembark for crossing the mountain pass on foot. Once in northern Italy, troops were hastened up to the battlefields by train again, and many casualties were brought swiftly back to hospitals. Therefore railroad cuttings, embankments, stations, bridges and other facilities in northern Italy presented features of importance equal or superior to the natural features of the terrain, and their possession was hotly contested (e.g., the Magenta hub).

The initial concentration by the French from Paris to the Piedmontese frontier in the Alps was well executed. In eighty-six days (from April 19 to July 15, 1859), the French transported some 600,000 men and over 125,000 horses, including nearly 228,000 men and 37,000 horses sent to Culox, Marseille, Toulon, Grenoble and Aix-en-Provence. The greatest movements took place during the ten days from April 20 to April 30, when the Paris-Lyon Company, without interrupting the ordinary civilian traffic, conveyed an average per day of 8,421 men and 512 horses. On April 25, a maximum of 12,138 men and 655 horses was attained. During the eighty-six days there were run on the lines of the same company a total of 2,636 trains, including 253 military specials. It was estimated that men and horses transported by rail from Paris to the Mediterranean or to the frontiers of the Kingdom of Piedmont-Sardinia between April 20 and April 30 would have otherwise taken sixty days to make the journey by road.

The advantages gained by the transport of the French troops to the battlefields were, however, thwarted by serious defects in administrative organization caused by poor comprehension and coordination between the military and the railroad officials. Troops were there but supplies did not follow, although they had a fully working railroad communication system behind them. When the soldiers got to the end of their rail journey, there was some prolonged waiting for food and supplies. On June 25, the day after the Austrian defeat at Solferino, the French troops had no provisions at all for twenty-four hours, except some biscuits, which were so moldy that no one could eat them. Their horses also were without fodder. In these circumstances it was impossible to follow up the Austrians in their retreat in good order to strong defensive positions beyond the river Mincio.

As for the Austrians, they improved but little on their admittedly poor performance in Bohemia in 1850, in spite of the lessons they appeared to have learned as the result of their experiences on that occasion. Government and railroads alike were unprepared. Little or no real attempt at organization in time of peace had been made. As a result, trains were delayed or blocked when stations got congested with masses of supplies, which could not be forwarded. At Vienna there was such a deficiency of rolling stock, accelerated by great delays in the return of empty trains, that many of the troop convoys for the south could not be made up until the last moment. Besides, between Innsbruck and Bozen the railroad line was still incomplete, and troops had to proceed by foot between these two points on their journey from Prague to Verona, a considerable distance in a difficult mountainous terrain. On average it took fourteen days for troops to travel from Vienna to the north Italian theater of operations in Lombardy.

In the Italian War of 1859 both the French and the Austrians made use of the railroad for the withdrawal of their sick and wounded. However, no arrangements for their comfort on the journey had been made in advance, and the changes in the military situation were so rapid, when hostilities broke out, that no special facilities could be provided then. All they could do was to lay down straw on the floor of the cargo or cattle trucks used for the conveyance of some of the more serious cases. Interestingly, the large-scale butchery at the Battle of Solferino resulted in the creation in 1863 of the Red Cross at the instigation of the Swiss businessman Henri Dunant. This international, impartial, neutral and independent organization had (and still has today) an exclusively humanitarian mission to protect the lives and dignity of prisoners and victims of war and to provide them with assistance.

Both the French and the Austrians might have made better planning to avoid mistakes in the movement of their armies by rail. Rail transport had proved crucial, but its use was still very basic and unsophisticated. One of the earliest and most obvious criticisms advanced against the use of railroad in war was the vulnerability of the track, more particularly in enemy territory. The destruction of a bridge, the tearing up of a few rails, or the blocking of a tunnel would, it was argued, suffice to cause an interruption in the transport of troops or supplies. That was absolutely true, and as a result all army forces employing railroad eventually developed patrol and protection units as well as quick emergency repair services. The Italian War of 1859 marked a further stage in the early employment of railroads for the purpose of warfare, but their use indeed remained rather primitive. Far greater results in the same direction were brought about shortly afterwards during a conflict that raged in the United States: the American Civil War.

American Civil War (1861–1865)

Historical Background

The American Civil War ranks as one of the most important conflicts of the second half of the 19th century because two opposing governments harnessed the popular enthusiasm for industrial technology. The war was admittedly caused by fundamental disagreement between two entities, in fact two civilizations, each with its own way of life, North and South, and about the place of chattel slavery in the Union. The root cause was also the profound difference of character in the Northern and Southern citizens of the United States. Although the following is a rough generalization, it may explain the profound difference between North and South. The Northerners were on the whole eager and businesslike, often the descendants of men who, dissatisfied with their lot, had left Europe to seek a new life of liberty in America. The Southerners, heirs to an old tradition of colonial prosperity, were more "aristocratic," easy-going and self-assured. The South was almost entirely agricultural, and depended on black slave labor, while the North was expanding industrially and commercially. The issue of slavery became so acute that eleven Southern slave states declared their secession from the U.S. and formed the Confederate States of America (also known as the Confederacy). Led by President Jefferson Davis, they fought against the U.S. federal government (the Union), which was supported by all the free states and the five border slave states in the North.

In the presidential election of 1860, the Republican Party, headed by Abraham Lincoln (1809–1865), had campaigned against the expansion of slavery beyond the states in which it already existed. Propaganda, passion and emotions ran high. The Republican victory in that election resulted in seven Southern states declaring their secession from the Union even before Lincoln took office on March 4, 1861. Both the outgoing and incoming U.S. administrations rejected secession, considering it pure rebellion. From the start, the contending sides staked out positions that brooked no compromise: unconditional restoration of the Union for the North; total independence for the South. The war started on April 12, 1861, when Confederate forces attacked Fort Sumter in the harbor of Charleston in South Carolina. Lincoln responded by calling for a volunteer army from each state, leading to declarations of secession by four more Southern slave states. The Union assumed control of the border states early in the war and established a naval blockade of Southern ports. As with many wars, it was expected that the conflict would be short, and the powerful and industrialized Union confidently expected to gain victory easily. However, the Confederate Southerners proved more resilient than expected, the result being hard determination and ruthless battles. In September 1862, Lincoln's Emancipation Proclamation made ending slavery in the South a war aim, and dissuaded the British from intervening.

Both the Union and the Confederacy faced daunting problems in creating effective military forces out of nothing or very little before they deployed large numbers of men. For the predominantly agricultural Southern Confederacy, war demanded additional efforts to develop an industrial economy to challenge the far greater manufacturing potential of the Northern Union. Despite its efforts at industrialization, the mobilization of 75 per cent of its white male population, and unprecedented participation by white women and black people in industry and agriculture, the Confederacy was doomed to defeat by the superiority of the Union's numbers and resources.

The Confederate commander Robert E. Lee won several battles in the east, but in 1863 his northward advance was turned back at Gettysburg. On the same day, in the west, the Union gained control of the Mississippi River at the Battle of Vicksburg, thereby splitting the Confederacy. Long-term Union advantages in men and matériel were achieved in 1864 when General Ulysses S. Grant fought several battles of attrition against Lee, while Union General William Sherman captured Atlanta, Georgia, and made a decisive offensive to the sea. Confederate resistance collapsed after Lee surrendered to Grant at Appomattox Court House on April 9, 1865.

The American Civil War was the deadliest war in American history, causing an undetermined number of civilian casualties and around 625,000 soldier deaths, both sides included—a figure equal to the total of all other American wars up to and including the Vietnam conflict. The legacy of the war included ending slavery in the United States, restoring the Union, and strengthening the role of the federal government. The social, political, economic and racial issues of the war decisively shaped the Reconstruction era that lasted until 1877, and brought important changes that helped make the United States of America a superpower that was to play a crucial role in the 20th century.

Railroads in the U.S. Civil War

There was once a tendency to view the American Civil War largely in terms of its military developments and to focus upon such innovations as clashes of armored warships, the first loss of ships to mines and submarine torpedoes, extensive use of the telegraph, and so on. In fact, the largely amateur armies fought the war on the battlefield as if it were the last Napoleonic encounter rather than the "first modern war," at least in the early phase of the war. The American Civil War began with the assumption by both sides that after just a few battles the war would end with either the Confederacy collapsing or achieving their independence. No one could have envisioned a war that lasted four years and took about 625,000 lives. At the start of the conflict, both armies were manned for the most part by untrained militia. Early battles were simply clashes between armed mobs, resulting in appalling casualties.

After the initial phase of the war, logistics, strategy, field fortifications and training were developed, and it is now widely recognized that the Civil War was truly modern in terms of its impact upon society. The industrialization dramatically increased the destructive capacity of armies by providing them with weapons of increased range, accuracy and rate of fire. Without the use of the railroad, it is doubtful whether the Civil War could have been fought at all. The area of military operations, from first to last, was as large as the whole of Western Europe. Many regions where the war was fought were covered with huge pathless forests and crossed by broad rivers. The then partly unexplored Appalachian Mountains formed a significant obstacle between the flat Atlantic Coastal Plain and the broad Mississippi Valley. Everywhere, except in the towns, territories were so thinly populated that an advancing army could not live off the country—that is, by pillaging. Roads and tracks were few, mostly indifferent or bad, and if rivers were navigable, it was obvious from the start that the railroad was to play a central role. It was indeed the American Civil War that demonstrated to the world that the railroad had become a strategical factor of the first importance, and that it could on occasion have a significant bearing on the tactical handling of a large battle. Until then, the railroad had been an ancillary. It had assisted armies to fight where the generals had decided the battles should be fought. But now the railroad junction (e.g., Atlanta, Georgia, or Chattanooga, Tennessee) became a military objective in its own right, as important as a mountain pass or a river crossing. The war was saved from becoming even more bogged down because of increased mobility provided by the railroad, and because intelligence, information, news, and orders could be quickly transmitted through the telegraph.

The Civil War also produced one real-life story of adventure on the rails that has never since been surpassed, or even approached— a fact illustrated by many factual and fictional books, tales, epics, songs, and films like Buster Keaton's wonderful silent masterpiece movie *The General* (1927), probably one of the greatest films ever made. The first railroad in America was built in 1829, and development had been constant ever since. Between the 1830s and the 1850s, railroad building boomed enormously in the United States of America— about 30,000 miles by 1860, more than the rest of the world put together. The railroad even replaced canals and rivers as a primary mode of transportation. It changed the whole way of life in the USA. With the advent of the railroad, a money economy developed, a new social class of merchants and dealers appeared in fast-growing cities, and a machine industry started the production of equipment that greatly increased efficiency.

Out of the 30,000 miles of railroad, only 9,000 lay within the Confederate States. The North had three east-west railroad systems, plus tracks leading south to Washington and radiating out from Kentucky into Tennessee, Mississippi, and Georgia. In the Confederacy, one line ran from Richmond to Wilmington, North Carolina, and another linked Richmond with the east-west line running from Charleston to Memphis. These lines joined at Chattanooga, a Unionist area open to Northern attack down the valleys of the Tennessee and Cumberland Rivers. During the war the Confederates finished a second east-west line from Vicksburg to Charleston. There were a few short lines across the Mississippi, but none linking with Texas or Florida.

The U.S. track network at the time of the Civil War was indeed impressive; however, it was comparatively a lightly and poorly laid system, without any of the solidity of the early European lines. Railroad in North America displayed activities on a very much larger scale than in Europe, but it had also been submitted to social and more particularly economical pressure. Because of the strong belief in states' rights, centralized and coordinated control of railroads was not adopted until far later, so that most railroad development remained in the hands of many private companies, particularly in the Confederacy. Railroads in the USA had been constructed as quickly and cheaply as possible by these private companies in order to keep costs down and instead satisfy immediate needs and make fat, short-term profits. The lines were mostly single tracks following the contours of ridges, hills and valleys to avoid the construction of expensive bridges and tunnels. They were often resting on ill-made roadbeds and poor ballast; they had sharp curvature and meandering traces. They were frequently constituted of light iron rails of poor quality laid on rough local timber ties, which were rather easily breakable. Many bridges and viaducts were built of wooden trestles, not strong masonry. Locomotive speeds were determined by track conditions rather than by engine capacity. On a good track a light train could make 60 mph, and 40 mph if laden with 20 freight cars. Wood, not coal, was the fuel, and communications and signaling were of the most elementary sort, if indeed any were supplied at all. Railroad lines were nevertheless in many cases the only existing connection between centers of production and settlements of population. As a result, many Civil War battles were fought for the control of tracks, for the safeguarding of communication, or for the possession of important railroad junctions.

Another great disadvantage of the American railroads at the time of the Civil War lay in their differences of gauge, which greatly complicated military transport and caused delays. The various companies had built their lines with gauges chosen either to suit local conditions or according to the views of their own engineers, with little or no consideration for connecting with other lines. There were at that time gauges ranging from 6 feet to 4 feet 8 inches. Between Philadelphia and Charleston, for example, passengers and freight had to change cars eight times because of variations in gauge. These adverse conditions prevailed until 1866, when the companies adopted a standard uniform gauge of 4 feet, 8 and a half inches. Finally, in the first phase of the war, the insufficiency of engines and rolling stock hampered the movements of both Southern and Northern combatants. A certain Colonel R. Delafield had published a report in 1860 in which he called the attention of the U.S. Congress to the development of military railroads in Europe. Nevertheless, neither the Federal nor the Confederate army was quick to organize its railroad campaign successfully. The Civil War was the story of military improvisation, and both sides had to learn the hard way on the battlefield. From the start, the railroad proved crucial in the first major battles of the war. It is no exaggeration to compare U.S. Civil War railroad with American helicopters in the Vietnam War.

Two skilled men created the United States Military Railroads (USMRR), without which it is arguable that the Confederacy might have proved unconquerable: Daniel C. McCallum and Herman C. Haupt.

Daniel Craig McCallum (1815–1878) was a Scottish immigrant, a versatile man, a poet and architect who had held for many years the position of general superintendent of the Erie Railroad, and was one of the ablest and most experienced railroad engineers in the United States. In January 1862, McCallum was appointed Military Director and Superintendent of Railroads in the United States with the rank of colonel. Having virtually total power over the Union's railroads, McCallum created two

U.S. Military Railroad Engineer 1863. The engineer has a civilian straw hat, a dark blue sack coat with brass buttons, a civilian shirt, and dark blue trousers (white in summer). By the time of the Civil War, the railroads had made such advances as to allow the movement of large numbers of troops. However, railroads had not yet matured into a truly integrated transportation system, as gaps between lines, incompatible track gauges, and other vexing impediments remained. Nonetheless, engineers met these issues with skill and utilized the rail system to its fullest potential. All in all, the railroad was an essential ingredient for the Union's ultimate victory.

distinct services: the Transportation Department, embracing the operation and maintenance of all the lines brought under use by the army of the North; and the Construction Corps, which was to repair the damage done by enemy wrecking parties, maintain lines of communication, and reconstruct, when necessary, railroads captured from the enemy as the Federals advanced. The Construction Corps was headed by Herman Haupt (1817–1905), trained at West Point, a brilliant civil railroad engineer who had distinguished himself more especially as a bridge builder. The extremely capable and hardworking but also stubborn Herman Haupt dictated two important principles. First, the military was not allowed to interfere in the operation of the train service. Indeed, any delay in one part of the network invariably caused hold-ups elsewhere. So trains must be run with precision in order to avoid chaos. Second, the rolling stock should be returned quickly for immediate re-employ, and not used as warehouses or as offices in the field.

Transport

The role of the railroad was all-important, even essential, since the land frontiers between the belligerents were close to 2,700 miles long. In the beginning, neither side was in position to fully mobilize their potentialities over such tremendous distances. Many mistakes were made, and traffic organization was so primitive that at times there were more supply trains waiting in sidings than convoys on the move. Gradually improvements came and allowed the development of a war of movement on a scale absolutely unprecedented. Owing to McCallum and Haupt, prodigies of improvisation were wrought to span rivers and gullies, to keep trains rolling in order to supply armies up to 300 miles from their bases. At Bull Run in July 1861 occurred the first-ever tactical delivery by rail of troops to the fringe of a battlefield. The arrival of 1,900 Confederate soldiers by rail at Manassas Junction from the Shenandoah Valley initiated a rout, as Federal troops ran like wildfire to the outskirts of Washington.

Soon the Civil War was fought by armies of ever-increasing size, ever-mounting firepower, and ever-improving command with skilled generals. After General Rosecrans's disaster at Chickamauga, the Union moved by rail some 23,000 reinforcements from the Army of the Potomac to Nashville, Tennessee, a journey of 1,192 miles (twice the distance from Paris to Berlin), in seven days. In December 1864, General Schofield's corps of 15,000 men transferred from the valley of the Tennessee to the banks of the Potomac, moving by river and rail down the

U.S. Civil War locomotive (4-4-0). This particular design of locomotive was extremely successful in North America—performing most of the work between 1850 and 1900. The legendary type was built by Baldwin Locomotive Works, Philadelphia; Canadian Engine and Machinery Company, Kingston, Ontario; Danforth Locomotive and Machine Company, Paterson, New Jersey; the Hinkley & Williams Works, Boston; the Portland Company, Portland, Maine; Rhode Island Locomotive Works, Providence, Rhode Island. The 4-4-0 was not really well suited for heavy military work, but it could burn wood, so fuel was never short. The 4-4-0 played a major role in the development of rail transport in the U.S.

Front view locomotive. For the most part, locomotives burned wood and emitted huge clouds of smoke through their turnip-shaped stacks. Some experiments had been made with coal as a fuel, but its use did not become general until after the Civil War.

Tennessee, up the Ohio and across the snow-covered Alleghenies, a distance of 1,400 miles, accomplished in the short space of eleven days. General W.T. Sherman's celebrated march to Atlanta in the summer of 1864 would have been impossible without the use of water and rail transportation. In the struggle for Atlanta, which preceded his still more famous March to the Sea, Sherman used his trains to carry supplies from the railheads to his force of 100,000 men and 23,000 animals. His base of supplies, when he approached Atlanta, was 360 miles distant. The continuance of his communications with that base depended on what he afterwards described as "a poorly-constructed single-track railroad" passing for 120 miles of its length through the country of an extremely active enemy. Yet Sherman is said to have made his advance in perfect confidence that, although subject to interruptions, the railroad in his rear would not collapse. This confidence was fully warranted by the results accomplished. Food, clothing, fodder, ammunition and every other requisite came to the front, while sick and wounded, refugees, freedmen and prisoners were transported back to the rear. The rail-

U.S. 4-6-0 locomotive. The 4-6-0 Ten Wheelers type with an extra set of driver wheels was a significantly more powerful locomotive than the 4-4-0. It became the standard freight locomotive after the Civil War in the 1880s.

road, in fact, contributed greatly to the brilliant success of Sherman's campaign, and hence also to the final triumph of the Northern cause. In the last year of the war, the Federal military railroad, with 365 engines and 4,203 cars, delivered over 5 million tons of supplies to the armies in the field.

Some historians have argued that the South made its attempt at secession ten years too late. In 1850, with only a few disconnected railroads at its command, the North could not have mounted those massive attacks in Tennessee and down the Mississippi that ultimately defeated the Confederacy. In 1850, secession could probably have been achieved, and the map of North America might well have come to be as variously colored as Latin America's. In 1860, the South had, at first sight, a favorable position. It had a seaboard and only a small navy, but could look to supporters overseas. Its economy was separate from the North's and independent of it. There were able leaders and an immensely strong patriotic emotion to sustain its very considerable war effort. Yet in spite of all this, the railroad enabled the North to bring its ultimate superiority to bear and prevail. Separatists in all parts of the world might take note. Owing to the railroad, power could now be wielded by determined governments over great distances with complete effectiveness.

A tactic that developed on both sides consisted of destroying railroads by fast and punchy cavalry detachments raiding deep into enemy-held territory. The U.S. Civil War saw indeed both the destruction and repair of railroad lines

become efficient. Expeditions and swift cavalry incursions were undertaken with no other object than that of burning down bridges, blocking tunnels, tearing up and bending rails, making bonfires of ties and telegraph poles, wrecking stations, rendering engines, trucks and carriages unserviceable, and cutting off the water and fuel supply for locomotives. This was a leading feature in the strategy of the South. The last two years of the conflict, 1864 and 1865, saw feverish activity of the USMRR, which built and reconstructed as well as operating and maintaining railroads. Confederate raiders were highly efficient in destroying, but the Union's Construction Corps, directed by Herman Haupt, achieved equally astonishing results in reconstructing. For example, the Potomac Creek bridge near

Potomac Creek Bridge. This bridge was built by the U.S. Military Railroad from 204,000 feet of standing timber in nine days.

A foreign observer noticed: "The Yanks rebuild tracks as quickly as the Rebs destroy them."

Armored Trains and Rail Artillery

In the American Civil War of 1861–65, the railroad provided logistical support, but also for the first time performed a few tactical missions and close combat.

The conflict saw the appearance of armored-protected gun-carrying trucks in modern warfare. At first these trains were just common locomotives towing flat cars with field guns placed on them. The next step was to increase survivability and protection by reinforcing walls with sandbags and covering cars with iron

Fortified bridge on Cumberland River at Nashville, Tennessee, created in 1864. The traffic on the bridge could be interrupted by closing heavy doors, while watchtowers allowed for observation, control and defense. Indeed, garrisoned blockhouses and fortlets to protect key points became common features of the Civil War.

Richmond (414 feet long with an elevation of 82 feet above the water) was destroyed in 1862, and restored in only nine days. In May 1862, five bridges over Goose Creek, destroyed by Southern raiders, were reconstructed in a day and a half. One especially remarkable feat accomplished was the rebuilding, in four and a half days, of the Chattahoochee bridge, near Atlanta—a structure 780 feet long and 92 feet high. On the Nashville and Chattanooga Railroad the Construction Corps, from February 1864 to the end of the war, re-laid 115 miles of track and put in nineteen miles of new sidings, eight miles apart and each capable of holding from five to eight long freight trains, and erected forty-five new water tanks.

U.S. Civil War armored car. This early armored car was designed in 1861 by the Union. It was a normal car clad with metal plates and fitted with gun ports. It was originally intended to protect workers of the Philadelphia & Baltimore Railroad Company from attacks by Confederate raiders.

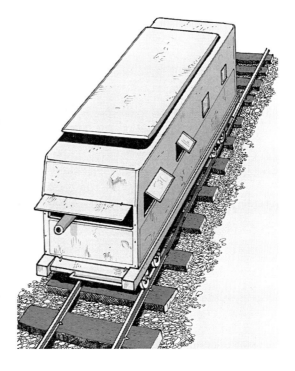

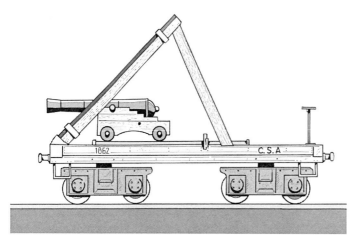

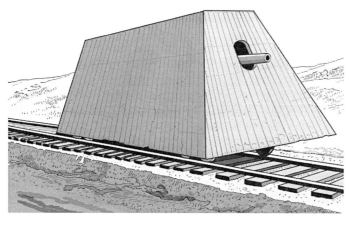

plates with openings made for small arms. Finally, typically armored cars and locomotives were designed especially for military use to decrease vulnerability to sharpshooters and snipers who might perforate a boiler or shoot a crewman.

Trains could transport heavy guns to the battlefield, and soon commanders took the idea a step further by using the train as a mobile gun platform. Of the few armored cars which were in use in the Civil War, one was formed by heavy timbers built up on a flatcar. The armor consisted of old rails spiked on the outside of the planking composing the sides and front of the car. Along the sides there were portholes for musketry fire, and at the front end there was an embrasure covered with a shutter behind which a gun was mounted. Another car was similarly constructed, but was armed with a naval howitzer. The cars were run ahead of the engine, and were used in reconnoitering along the railroad line west of New Bern, North Carolina.

A primitive form of early railroad-mounted artillery consisted of a low truck with, at one

Top: *Profile view of a CSA railgun.*

Middle: *U.S. Civil War railgun. This Confederate improvised railroad-mounted artillery piece, one of the earliest on record, was designed by Lieutenant John M. Brooke of the Confederate Navy. It was first used at Savage Station, Virginia, in 1862. It was intended to be pushed in front of a locomotive to a point from which it could fire at the enemy. It saw little if any effective service. Rail artillery was not yet really useful.*

Bottom: *Confederate railgun. This kind of railgun was actually of limited use since it was confined to the track and had only a restricted field of fire.*

end, a sloping armor plate coming down almost to the rails; this shield featured an aperture through which the gun placed behind it on the truck could be fired. The sides of the truck were protected from the top of the sloping armor downwards, but the back was open. Also, plans were adopted to protect the locomotives of ordinary troop or supply trains with armor plating and bulletproof cabins as a precaution against attack and snipers. Rifle cars resembled ordinary boxcars, but their sides were reinforced and fitted with small apertures allowing infantrymen's firing. Some carried additional light artillery pieces fired from hatches cut in the hull. These cars could guard key railroad features, protect repairmen, escort supply trains, patrol tracks, and conduct reconnaissance missions.

While armor protected from projectiles, explosive devices planted in the roadbed posed a serious threat to military trains. Therefore trains often pushed flatcars called control cars over the rails in order to detonate mines before the train passed over them. The pioneering arrangement of armored locomotive (often placed in the center of the convoy) and various ironclad artillery and rifle cars marked the origin of the armored train, which proved a prominent weapon in numerous subsequent conflicts, including the Second Boer War and the later Russian Civil War.

Ambulance Trains

The U.S. Civil War was a bloody and prolonged conflict that clearly showed how the railroad allowed a major increase in the scale of warfare, the numbers of men involved, and the level of logistical support needed. Rail made possible frequent and intense offensives, thus causing many more casualties than in earlier wars. Fortunately the railroad also enabled medical evacuation. In the early days of the Civil War, the arrangements for the conveyance by rail of the sick and wounded from the battlefields of the eastern states to the hospitals in the large cities were still distinctly primitive. Ordinary freight cars were used, with a thick layer of straw or hay on the floor. In overcrowded and badly ventilated cars, it's easy to imagine the suffering and discomfort endured by the wounded on the journey. In June 1863,

Telegraph and train. Telegraphic communication consisted of transmitting electric signals over wires from location to location by using pulses of current to deflect an electromagnet, which moved a marker to produce written code consisting of dots and dashes on a strip of paper. It was first demonstrated in 1838 by K.A. von Steinheil and developed by Samuel F.B. Morse (1791–1872) in 1844. Land telegraph systems were rapidly developed in the second half of the 19th century. The contemporary telegraph was an important innovation. However, it was an instrument with encryption and decryption procedures necessary at both ends of the line. Despite the inflexibility inherent in fixed cable routes, the telegraph made contact possible at long distance, and news which had hitherto traveled slowly from one point to another became much quicker. The railroad system could only be operated to maximum effect if the trains' movements were carefully coordinated. For the sake of maintenance, rail tracks and telegraph wires tended to run together in parallel.

over 9,000 casualties of the Federal disaster at Chancellorsville were taken by the single-track Aquia Creek railroad from Aquia Creek to Washington. After the Battle of Gettysburg (July 1–3, 1863), more than 15,000 wounded were sent by rail from the battlefield to hospitals in Baltimore, New York, Harrisburg or Philadelphia. The predicament improved owing to the efforts of a government agency, known as the Sanitary Commission, which developed special ward trains. As an improvement on primitive methods of transport, the plan was adopted of fixing two or three tiers of wooden bunks, with a central passage through the coach car. Next, converted passenger cars were used, and in place of the uncomfortable fixed bunks came an arrangement by which the tiers of patients' stretchers were suspended by strong India-rubber rings and resting on brackets attached to the sides, to protect against jolting, jerking and shaking. Also, doors were widened for ease of access. The first car so arranged was capable of accommodating about fifty patients and two attendants. Other innovations introduced on the ambulance cars were ventilation pipes, a stove to make meals, soup and tea, as well as a water tank and a locker. An ambulance train generally consisted of ten ward-cars, an ordinary passenger car for sitting-up patients or convalescents, a dispensary car (in which an ample supply of medicines, instruments and appliances was carried), a food supply and kitchen car (able to feed from 150 to 200 persons daily), and quarters-cars for surgeons and orderlies. The cars were heated and lighted in winter, and special attention was paid to ventilation. The ambulating, self-contained hospital-train, capable of carrying in relative comfort both stretcher cases and sitting-up patients, and able to supply all their needs on the journey, thus became an established institution in modern warfare. Three of these trains were ready by the spring of 1864, and they ran regularly, each taking a section of the journey between Atlanta and Louisville, a distance of 472 miles. Ambulance trains, of course, were never available in sufficient numbers to ensure that all casualties could be taken care of. Nevertheless, the combined effect of all the provision made for the care of the sick and wounded and their speedy recovery was to ensure for the Federals the retention of a force equal in itself to an army of 100,000 men. No single fact could show more conclusively the strategic as well as the humanitarian value of railroad ambulance transport.

As a conclusion, one may perhaps say that the American Civil War was a byproduct of railroad technology, which exacerbated the scale, length and intensity of the conflict. To this might be added that a few years after the end of Civil War, in 1869, when the transcontinental line joined the Atlantic and the Pacific coasts, the railroad was feted for bringing the United States together. During the U.S. Civil War, military officials from Europe had crossed the Atlantic Ocean in order to observe and witness the operation. Regarding the use of the railroad, all military attachés were unanimous: indeed, transport by rail played an increasingly important role, but many lessons were not yet learned about how to organize it.

AUSTRO-PRUSSIAN WAR (1866)

Historical Background

The Austro-Prussian War or Deutscher Krieg ("German War") was a short conflict fought in 1866 between the Austrian Empire and its German allies on one side and the Kingdom of Prussia with its German allies and Italy on the other. The war arose through Austria's determination to block Prussia's growing power and influence in central Europe. It was marked by a few clashes at Trautenau and Nachod, and above all by a Prussian crushing victory at the battle of Sadowa (Königgrätz) in Bohemia on July 3, 1866. This decisive battle of the Austro-Prussian War was followed by an armistice signed at Prague three weeks later.

The victorious war was highly beneficial to Prussia. It provided a great opportunity for Prussian statesmen by clearing a path toward North Germany's unification. Indeed the major result of the war was a shift in power among the German states away from Austrian and towards Prussian hegemony, and impetus towards the unification of all of the northern German states. It saw the abolition of the old Napoleonic German Confederation and its partial replacement by a North German Confederation, in a *Klein Deutschland* ("Lesser Germany") that excluded Austria and the South German states such as Bavaria.

Railroads in the Austro-Prussian War

Prussia had sent observers to the United States during the Civil War and had obtained detailed information about Haupt's successful organization of the USMRR. As a result, directly influenced by the developments of the Civil War in North America, Prussia took a further step in 1864 by forming a railroad section of her general staff. This new body was actively employed in the furtherance of Prussia's interests in the Danish War of the same year, and the organization was further developed by Prussia in the campaign of 1866 against Austria. The railroad system of Prussia was indeed more extensively developed than that within Austria, as the nature of the Prussian strategy relied upon rapid mobilization and operations based on surprise and speed provided by transport on rail. Railroads made it possible to supply larger numbers of troops than had previously been possible, and also allowed the rapid movement of troops within friendly and conquered territories. The better Prussian rail network therefore allowed the Prussian army to concentrate more rapidly than that of the Austrians. The scheme was, however, far from being perfect. At the Battle of Sadowa, the Prussians attempted to bring three armies together for the battle, but problems with sending orders by telegraph, lack of rolling stock, and disorganization in moving men and supply by railroad meant that only two of the three armies had arrived in time.

In the Austro-Prussian War of 1866, the principle of punishing a hostile civilian population for attacks on the military railroad lines underwent a further development. The Prussians increased the number and strength of guards posted along the tracks in hostile territories, and threatened civilian saboteurs with the terror of harsh reprisals.

The conditions in regard to the care of the sick and wounded in the campaign of 1866 were deplorably defective. The Germans did not follow the improvements achieved by the U.S. ambulance trains. After the Battle of Sadowa, thousands of wounded were left unattended on the battlefield. Those taken to hospitals in Dresden and Prague in ordinary passenger carriages or cargo vans were detained for days on the journey owing to the congestion of traffic on the lines. Some of them, also, were in the trains for days before their wounds were dressed.

The fighting in the Austro-Prussian War of 1866 was over so soon that the aspects of military rail transport, which become obvious only in a prolonged campaign, showed nothing new. Immediately on the close of the war, a mixed committee of staff officers and railroad authorities was appointed, under the supervision of general Helmuth von Moltke the Elder (1800–1891), to inquire what steps should be taken to organize the Prussian military transport services on such a basis as would avoid a repetition of the faults already experienced. An elaborate service was constructed by the Great General Staff, and the scheme was to be tested in the war with France for which it had been designed.

FRANCO-PRUSSIAN WAR (1870–1871)

Historical Background

In the 19th century, Germany was still a profoundly divided land comprising many duchies, kingdoms, principalities, bishoprics and free cities. It would become a powerful sovereign state in 1871, after a series of aggressive wars, backed by brilliant diplomatic moves, largely due to the skills and efforts of the Prussian Chancellor Otto von Bismarck (1815–1898). The French Emperor Napoleon III had always defended the principle of nationality and encouraged German unity but soon he had to face up a dangerous and aggressive Prussia. Germany was gradually Prussianed, and provided with sound finances and a very strong army allowing an aggressive policy. The Danish province of Schleswig-Holstein was annexed in 1864. The powerful and rival Austria was defeated at the battle of Sadowa in 1866. These resounding victories allowed Prussia to carve out a position for itself as a great military power and preparing for German unity with itself at the core. The final obstacle, which appeared to stand between Bismarck and his ambition was France. To the Prussian Chancellor and his military clique it was clear they could not reckon on completing the half-finished German unity without a violent clash with France. Strenuously, seriously and methodically they pushed on the work of military preparation. In spite of Napoleon III's early sympathy for Prussian ambitions, the German victory of 1866 suddenly gave rise to misgivings in France. As a result, tension increased between France and Prussia when a quarrel broke out with regard to the Spanish throne to which a Hohenzollern, a relative of the king of Prussia, had laid claim. France obtained full satisfaction in the matter, and the affair would have ended there, but France was so resentful that she demanded that Prussia pledge herself not to accept similar offers in the future. Anger at the Prussian court resulted in the sending of the famous "telegram of Ems", purposely written in a provocative, abrupt and impolite manner. Everything happened with extraordinary celerity, and within a fortnight, a wholly unanticipated quarrel came to a sudden climax, and convulsed two of the most civilized people of the world with savage hatred before reason or mansuetude could gain a hearing. The French felt humiliated, Napoleon III attempted to recover his waning prestige and fell into the trap designed by the German Chancellor. Napoleon III—now fearing Prussia as the leader of a united Germany—made the foolish mistake of declaring war on Prussia on July 19, 1870. This was the war that Bismarck had long dreamed of, as war with France was seen as an opportunity to rally all Germans to his program of national unity.

The Prussians quickly seized the initiative of operations and invaded northeast France. Marshall François-Achille Bazaine—put at the head of the most powerful French army—soon found himself blockaded in the city of Metz with a force of 173,000 men. French defeats followed in quick succession at Wissembourg, Froeschwiller and Forbach. General Mac-Mahon, with another army, received order to relieve Bazaine's forces and concentrated his troops around the fortress of Sedan. The battle of Sedan ended on September 1, 1870 with a catastrophic outcome for the French. Bazaine and MacMahon's troops—about 83,000 soldiers—were forced to surrender, and—supreme humiliation—Napoleon III himself fell prisoner and signed personally the act of capitulation. After a short custody in Germany, the destitute Emperor finished his life in exile in England where he died in 1873.

After Sedan, the Prussians had the way open to Paris where important events had happened. Indeed the defeat and capitulation of the Emperor had great political consequences. As soon as news of the capture of Napoleon III and the capitulation of Sedan reached Paris on September 4, 1870, crowds overran the Palais Bourbon, the siege of the Assembly. The Republican statesman Léon Gambetta made a speech at the City Hall proclaiming the fall of the Empire and the creation of the Third Republic. An emergency republican government of national defense was formed, and presided over by Léon Gambetta, Jules Favre and general Trochu. Military defeat had annihilated a regime which had never been popular in hearts and minds.

The new French republican government decided to continue the war. Gambetta proclaimed a national war, with Paris as the symbol of national and republican resistance. The capital of France was soon besieged by the Prussians and surrendered after an appalling siege that lasted from September 1870 to January 1871. Ten days before the surrender of Paris, in the Hall of Mirrors at Versailles, Wilhelm of Prussia was proclaimed Emperor of Germany by the assembled German princes; the greatest of the wars of nationality of the mid-19th century had achieved its goal; the creation of the Second German Reich (empire) marking the culmination of the movement for the national unity of Germany. Peace between the French Republic and the new German Reich was signed with the Treaty of Frankfurt on May 10, 1871. The lost war with Prussia was a disaster. The two rich and industrially developed north-east provinces of Alsace and Lorraine were transferred to Germany; the annexion of Alsace and Lorraine—against the will of the inhabitants—created an abyss between France and Germany. This hatred was one of the causes of the two world wars of the 20th century (1914–1918 and 1939–1945).

The French Railroads

In its conduct, the 1870 Franco-Prussian War mixed the weapons, tactics and methods of an earlier era with new military science (notably the use of rifled artillery, early machine guns, and railroad) and a new political attitude.

The most impressive achievement of Napoleon III's Second Empire was the increase of the mileage of railroad, with over 11,000 miles by 1870. However, when France went to war with Germany in 1870–71, the shortsighted

and foolish Napoleon III had made neither adequate military preparation, nor diplomatic efforts to get allies on his side, nor clear objectives. France embarked on this hazardous conflict with ill-organized military forces. France's military rail transport was still governed by obsolete regulations adopted as far back as 1851 and 1855, the very same out-of-date and wholly defective regulations under which her troops had already suffered in the Italian War of 1859. The French railroad system itself was developed on principles that practically ignored military strategic considerations. Being operated by private companies, it was mainly based on short-term economical profit, political and local interests, and was not designed for purposes of national defense. Paris was regarded as the common center from which all main lines radiated in all directions. Communication was thus established between the capital and the principal inland towns, important points on the frontiers, and on the coasts of France. As a result, there was an inadequate number of lateral or transverse lines linking up and connecting these main lines. This caused great difficulty for communication between the provincial centers themselves other than via Paris.

The Eastern Company performed prodigies of operation between July 16 and July 26, 1870, when 594 troop trains were dispatched, conveying 186,620 men, 32,410 horses, 3,162 guns and road vehicles, and 995 wagonloads of ammunition and supplies. During the thirty-five days preceding the investment and siege of Paris, the Western Railroad Company alone delivered 72,442 tons of provisions and 67,716 head of cattle. But for these supplies, the capital of France could not have endured so long a siege. After the siege, in the re-victualing of Paris, the railroads, though much restricted by the German requisitions, brought into the starving city 155,955 tons of provisions and 42,580 head of cattle in the course of twenty days. All this activity on the part of the railroad companies was, however, neutralized more or less by the absence of any adequate organization. Confusion and delays at the stations during the entraining of the troops were rendered the more complete because the railroad staffs failed to get an adequate degree of support from the military authorities. The overworked railroad people did what they could; troops were transported and ill-fated battles were fought in the summer of 1870. But in the end, the results of poor preparation, confusion, and lack of cooperation were soon predictable: delays, bottlenecks with frightful traffic jams, and inextricable chaos, leading to collapse, defeat and surrender of the army, followed by the civil war known as *la Commune* in 1871. These tragic events are poignantly described by Emile Zola in his 1892 novel *La Débâcle* (*The Downfall*).

The Franco-Prussian War of 1870–71 saw a development of improvised armored and artillery trains by the newly created French Republic. Guns mounted on four armor-plated trucks, fitted up in the workshops of the Orleans Company, under the supervision of M. Dupuy de Lorme, engineer-in-chief for naval

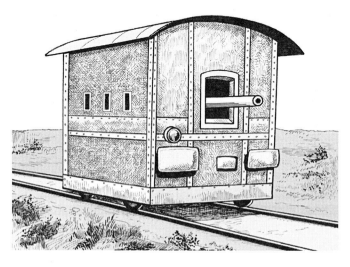

French armored railcar 1870. A very early use of armored train, this military car was a standard freight boxcar reinforced with thick planks and metal plates. It included rifle holes on the side and a small gun at the front of the car.

construction, were taken into action on four occasions during the siege of Paris: at Choisy-le-Roi, for the sortie preceding the one from Champigny; near Brie-sur-Marne, to support the Champigny sortie; at Le Bourget, for one of the attempts to recapture that position; and at La Malmaison, to support the Montretout sortie. The locomotives and wagons were protected by a covering, which consisted of plates of wrought iron, each two inches thick. Some of the wagons and locomotives were struck by field-gun shells without sustaining further damage than the denting of their plates. On going into action, the armored trains were followed by another bulletproof engine conveying a party of men with tools and materials to repair any interruption of the lines that might interfere with the return of the trains. These daring counterattacks, however, did not prevent the fall of Paris in January 1871, total defeat and the occupation of Northern France until 1873.

The German Railroads

No European nation utilized the railroad as effectively in war as Prussia, whose rail network had been designed with an eye to its use in future wars. The experience of the U.S. Civil War had been studied, the Prussian General Staff had a translation of McCallum's report on the work of the U.S. Military Railroad, and by the late 1860s Prussian rail strategy had become a highly developed and complicated art. So far as the mobilization of the German troops and their concentration on the frontier were concerned, the plans worked, on the whole, remarkably well. Small rural stations at the border with France were equipped with platforms a mile long, so that several troop trains could disgorge whole divisions in a single visit. In July and August

1870, some 1,200 trains conveyed to their assembly areas 350,000 men, 87,000 horses, and 8,400 guns or road vehicles, yet with delays. In September, on five different lines, there was a total of 2,322 loaded wagons, containing 16,830 tons of provisions for the Second Army, sufficient to keep it supplied for a period of twenty-six days.

Complete success and totally smooth running were, however, not attained, notably in the efforts of forwarding supplies and troop provisioning. The position of the Prussian supply railroad became bad, even chaotic, when the retreating French destroyed the lines behind them, increasing the difficulties of the invaders in maintaining their communications with the fatherland. Lines were choked and a large block of wagons full of supplies lay between Cologne and Frankfurt, while the troops in France were short of food. Difficulty in feeding the army was especially experienced during the investment and siege of Paris between September 1870 and January 1871. This obliged the Prussians to resort to highly unpopular requisitions, and to live off the land by pillaging in the French territory they occupied. It was not until the end of 1870 that any approach to regularity in supplying the wants of the German forces was finally secured by repairing and employing over 2,000 miles of French rail lines. In addition, the Prussians built two purely military railroad lines, distinct from civilian commercial use, which were completed in October 1870. First a track, twenty-two miles in length, connecting Remilly, on the Saarbruck Railroad, with Pont a Mousson on the Metz-Frouard line; and second a loop line, three miles long, bypassing the tunnel at Nanteuil-sur-Marne, blown up by the retreating French.

Altogether some 4,200 men were employed on the improvement of the German military rail network: 400 belonging to two field railroad companies; 800 forming four fortress pioneer companies; and about 3,000 miners from the colliery districts of Saarbrucken. The building corps had at their disposal a park of 330 wagons and other vehicles. A squadron of cavalry performed patrol, requisition duties, and protection against guerrillas.

The Franco-Prussian War of 1870–71 also confirmed what harm could be done to deny use of the railroad to an advancing enemy. The so-called *francs-tireurs* were volunteering irregular partisans fighting the Prussian invaders, harassing and obstructing them in their requisitions. They carried out guerrilla warfare, attacked convoys, cut roads and railroads, and destroyed bridges. Some 57,000 volunteers were raised, who, like all other irregular guerrilla fighters, had the advantages of offering mobility, ease of dispersal, local knowledge, and support from the local population. Francs-tireurs were able to cause many interruptions of the invaders' transport service by destroying miles of tracks and rolling stock, and even by direct attack. For instance, a spectacular attack occurred in October 1870 near the village of Lanois near Metz when francs-tireurs placed a bomb that wrecked a Prussian train and inflicted about 400 casualties. Francs-tireurs' operations and sabotages, and consequently Prussian counter-guerrilla actions, increased in the winter of 1870–71 with mounting terror and retaliation. The Prussian Chief of Staff General Helmuth von Moltke the Elder denied them the status of legal combatants and ordered captive francs-tireurs taken red-handed to be summarily shot. The Prussians had adopted an especially elaborate system for safeguarding their lines of communication with Germany during the time they occupied French territory. Many troops were diverted for protection purposes only. At each station they placed a guard formed of detachments of the Landwehr, while small detachments were stationed in towns and villages in the neighborhood. In each signal-box a detachment of troops was stationed, and the whole line was patrolled from posts established along it at distances of every three or four miles. The

Prussians also introduced measures of retaliation against the civilian populations. At localities where sabotages and attacks had occurred, inhabitants were fined or imprisoned, their belongings confiscated, the local authorities arrested and held hostage, and some people shot and some villages actually burned down. Both French guerrilla activity and German reprisals, however, should not be exaggerated. There was never anything like the systematic slaughters that followed the Paris Commune (a short but extremely bloody French civil war in 1871).

Although still primitive and spartan, and although medical trains were not always given the priority which the suffering of their passengers merited, the ambulance service of the Germans worked relatively well during the 1870–71 war. They had twenty-one ambulance trains, fitted up more or less as complete traveling hospitals (including feeding, nursing and general comfort). The total number of casualties evacuated by rail is estimated at over 89,000.

Aftermath

In the war of 1870–71, Prussia and the North German Confederation deployed 1,200,000 soldiers against France—twice the number of men Napoleon I had led into Russia in 1812. Thanks to the railroad's ability to transport numerous armies, the Franco-Prussian War was extremely bloody with more than 180,000 dead, a very high casualty rate, given that combat lasted only for ten months. This conflict, a striking example of mass multiplied by impulsion, had clearly demonstrated that the Prussian Railroad Corps, even when under heavy pressure, could operate with relative success. However, the Prussian victory was also the result more of French errors and incompetence than German brilliance. The lessons of the Franco-Prussian War were studied with great attention, not only in the two countries immediately concerned, but also by other nations. The lessons drawn from mistakes of the 1870–71 War certainly laid the basis for sound military use of civilian railroads in subsequent wars.

The French started to put their house in order on the Prussian model, creating organizational connections between the military and the civil authorities. After the disastrous war of 1870, France created coordinating organs—the Directions Militaires des Chemins de Fer de Campagne (Military Field Railroads Committees), and the two-battalion 5th Engineering Regiment, which specialized in military railroad warfare. In 1887 the line Chartres-Orléans was entrusted to the army engineers who would exploit and train troops on that stretch.

In 1876–1879 Bismarck worked to bring the German railroads under state ownership in order to control and to provide preferential rates for freight shipment within Germany—to benefit German industries. State railroad ownership increased from 6,300 km in 1879 to 31,000 km by 1900.

As for the British, they took an interested note of what happened in the Franco-Prussian War. In 1882

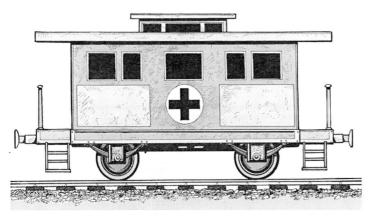

German ambulance railcar (1870).

a company of the Royal Engineers was created and specialized for developing military trains, particularly in the overseas colonies.

RUSSO-TURKISH WAR (1877–1878)

Historical Background

The short but extremely bloody Russo-Turkish War originated in a rise in nationalism in the Balkans. It was partly a legacy of the Russian defeat in the Crimea a quarter of a century before, since the Russians wanted to recover the territorial losses they had then suffered. The Tsar also wanted to re-establish a Russian presence in the Black Sea, and for this purpose he supported the political movement attempting to free Balkan nations from the decaying Ottoman Empire. The bad treatment of Christian minorities in the Ottoman Empire provided a pretext. The vicissitudes of this war are extremely complex, spreading from the Balkans as far as Crete, Lebanon, and the Caucasus, involving not only Russia and the Ottoman Empire, but also several other people, nations, nationalities and minorities, who at the time were supported by the great Western European powers (notably Britain, which send a fleet to put pressure on Russia). It would be pointless to tell here in detail all the complicated moves, tortuous diplomatic maneuvering, battles and events, and the numerous atrocities committed by all sides behind the screen of religion. Suffice to say here that as a result of Russia's victory in the war, the Ottoman Empire was greatly weakened. The principalities of Romania, Serbia and Montenegro formally proclaimed their independence. After almost five centuries of Ottoman domination (1396–1878), the Bulgarian state was re-established, with Sofia becoming the new state's capital. The Congress of Berlin also allowed Austria-Hungary to occupy Bosnia and Herzegovina and the United Kingdom to take over Cyprus, while the Russian Empire annexed Southern Bessarabia and the Kars region.

Russian Railroads

Russia expected a victorious battle and a triumphal march into Constantinople, but the logistics proved a real problem. Under a convention that had been agreed to with Romania in April 1877, Russia was allowed a free passage for her troops through that country. She was also to have the use of the Romanian railroads and of all their transport facilities. But the Romanian rail network was a primitive affair, limited in extent. The tracks had been indifferently constructed and badly maintained, and the rail system had inadequate personnel, together with an insufficiency both of rolling stock and of terminal facilities. Besides, the Russian railroads had a broader gauge (5 feet) than those of Romania (4 feet 8 and a half inches). This caused great delay in the transfer at the frontier from the one system to the other, not only of 200,000 men, but of the 850 field and 400 siege guns, of the ammunition, and of much other matériel the troops required to take with them. As for the road system, it was poor, difficult to use in rainy weather conditions, and impassable in winter. The war also lasted longer than expected, and Russia set about the construction of a series of new lines of military railroads. First, a line in Russia, from Bender on the Dniester to Galatz, establishing direct communication between the Odessa railroad and the Romanian frontier, and affording improved facilities for the sending of reinforcements to the battlefront. Second, a track from Fratesti, on the Bucharest-Giurgevo rail line, to Simnitza, a point on the north bank of the Danube. Third, a line from Sistova, on the south side of the Danube, to Tirnova (Bulgaria), situated about thirty miles southeast of Plevna, and about twenty-five miles north of the Shipka Pass. The construction of these three lines allowed other nations' military experts to gain a fresh lesson as to the importance of the role played by railroads in war. Also, it offered a striking example of what could be achieved in the way of rapidly providing military transport in a time of emergency.

NARROW-GAUGE RAILROADS

From the start, the difference in gauge (the distance between the two rails on a track) was a useful asset as a defensive measure against invaders. But it could also be a hindrance when one sought to use the railroad to supply an offensive into conquered neighboring lands. Conversion consisted of adding another rail just inside an existing one, provided the gap allowed for enough space. If this was not the case, changing the gauge involved dismantling and refixing a rail, which took time and involved significant manpower. Narrow gauge rolling stock could relatively easily have axles extended to permit running on a wider gauge, but the reverse procedure was not possible. Besides, structures such as tunnels, bridges and station platforms were often designed for matching only one gauge system. So in many cases it was required to create a totally new railroad network with cheap narrow gauge, an important step in the development of military railroad. Pioneered by the French engineer and businessman Paul Decauville (1846–1922), this major innovation presented many advantages. It made use of ready-made prefab standard sections of light and narrow tracks fastened to steel sleepers. This track unit was portable and could be assembled and disassembled very easily by unskilled laborers and soldiers. It cost much less to build because it was lighter in construction, using smaller cars and locomotives as well as smaller bridges and tunnels, simpler ballasts and tighter curves. Therefore prefab narrow-gauge track was (and still is) often used in mountainous terrain, where the savings in civil engineering work can be substantial, and it can be quickly and cheaply laid and removed by military engineering corps for a temporary campaign. As just pointed out, the main disadvantage was that narrow-gauge railroads could not freely interchange equipment such as locomotives

and cars with the standard-gauge or broad-gauge railroads they linked with. That meant that there was always a delay caused by trans-shipping freight from one system to the other.

Starting in 1875, Decauville's company produced engines and cars as well as track elements using 400 mm gauge. Decauville later refined his invention and switched to 500 mm and 600 mm gauge, and the latter dimension became the standard. Narrow-gauge railroads were exported to many countries, in particular to the colonial possessions of European powers. The French military became interested in the Decauville system as early as 1888 and chose the 600 mm gauge track to equip strongholds and to carry artillery pieces and ammunition during military campaigns.

Narrow and standard gauge were widely used to supply fortifications, particularly in the 1870s, 1880s and 1890s, as many important cities were defended by rings of forts and detached batteries. For example, Bucharest, the capital of Romania, was defended by a ring of 36 forts and batteries built between 1884 and 1895. Placed at about 12 or 13 km from the city, the detached forts were supplied by a circular railroad that was built within 100 m behind the line of forts, with connections with the civilian railroad network. At Paris, the Chemin de fer de Petite Ceinture (little belt railroad), built between 1852 and 1900, was a 32-km railroad that connected Paris's main railroad stations and was also used to supply the fortified walls of the city. The Grande Ceinture (large belt) was a 157-km (98-mile) circular railroad line built between 1875 and 1886 intended to interconnect railroad lines around the capital of France, but also to supply forts and batteries outside Paris. At Verdun a 45-km-wide belt of forts was built before 1914. Placed at about 7 km from the center of the city, it included 43 major forts and 135 artillery batteries, numerous infantry positions and shelters, as well as protected supply and ammunition stores and an airfield. All were connected by permanent 60-cm narrow-gauge railroads with a total length of 185 km. The fortress of Verdun was armed with a total of one thousand artillery pieces and mortars of all calibers. It was planned to have a garrison of 66,000 men.

Similar military railroads were installed to build and supply forts around many other European cities and capitals. In Britain, for example, convicts were used to build Fort Borstal (located at Chatham in Kent) between 1875 and 1885, and it was first proposed to house them at Fort Clarence, Rochester, which had previously been used as a military prison. However, Rochester Corporation objected against this, so a new prison was built at Borstal. A light railroad was constructed to carry building materials and convicts to the fort. The railroad started at the Borstal Manor Cement Works, next to the River Medway, and building materials could then be transported up the hill to Fort Borstal. The railroad had a spur that ran to the prison, and the line continued to Fort Bridgewoods, Fort Horsted, and then to Fort Luton, where the railroad line ended.

Decauville tracks were widely used during colonial military expeditions by the end of the 19th century, and in numerous campaigns in

Top: *Laying narrow-gauge track.*
Above: *Narrow-gauge track.*
Left: *Decauville locomotive.*

Above: *Narrow-gauge diesel locomotive and tip wagons.*

Bottom: *Navvies. Derived from the term "navigator," the word navvy was originally used to describe the workers who excavated the earth for canals in the development of the British canal network during the late 18th and 19th centuries. Later the term designated any laborer working on a major engineering project. Note the use of skips on narrow gauge tracks used to transport excavated material away.*

both world wars of the 20th century. Light railroads experienced their biggest upswing in and after World War I (1914–18). Their second and last heyday was after World War II (1939–1945), when the light railroads were used in the removal of debris and ruins. In the late 1950s the use of light railroads on narrow gauge declined rapidly as more and more heavy trucks and vans took their tasks over.

BOER WARS
(1880–1881 AND 1899–1902)

Historical Background

Two Boer Wars were fought between the British Empire and the two independent Boer republics, the Orange Free State and the South African Republic (aka Transvaal Republic), founded by Dutch settlers known as *Boers* (peasants in Dutch) or *Afrikaners* (Africans in Dutch).

In fact, Britain had always wanted to strip the Dutch settlers of their independence, and to unify rich South Africa under the Union Jack. The longstanding hostility between the two colonizing forces had been bubbling away for many years. The immediate casus belli was the British demand for voting rights for their citizens living in the Transvaal—a demand the Transvaal President Paul Kuger (1825–1904) was reluctant to accept. As a result, the bellicose Sir Alfred Milner (1854–1925), the British High Commissioner in South Africa, sabotaged the negotiations and decided to use force. The First Boer War, also known as the Transvaal War, was a brief conflict (during the winter of 1880–1881) in which the Dutch Afrikaners successfully resisted a British attempt to annex the Transvaal, and re-established their independent republic. In the following years, the discovery of vast mineral wealth, particularly diamonds and gold in 1886 in the Transvaal, further exacerbated greed and increased hostility between British mining companies and the Boers. Inevitably, insatiable longing for wealth, clashing with conservative intransigence, caused rising tensions and led to another armed conflict.

The Second Boer War (1899–1902), by contrast, was a terrible and bloody conflict involving large numbers of troops from many British possessions, which ended with the conversion of the Boer republics into British colonies (with a promise of limited self-government). These colonies later formed part of the Union of South Africa.

The war started in October 1899. In the first phase, the Boers (discreetly supported by Germany) captured large areas in the British colonies, including a long railroad line, and besieged three British settlements at Ladysmith, Kimberley and Mafeking. After several humiliating setbacks, these places were relieved in early 1900. In the second phase of the conflict, the British used the railroad to advance north, re-establishing their control in the lost territories and starting the invasion of the Boers' lands. The Boers retreated, using guerrilla tactics for the protracted harassment of British troops, and sabotaging lines of communication in order to deprive them of essential supplies. In the third phase, in order to

Boer raider. The Boers were on the whole good marksmen and experienced cavalrymen. Armed with modern German-made Mauser rifles, they had above all inherited an innate stubbornness and tenacious courage from their Dutch ancestors. They were also deeply racist and religiously intransigent, and saw themselves as a white Calvinist elite chosen by God to rule the black continent. Militarily, their main asset was mobility and speed, which caught the British off balance during the early days of the war. They proved an elusive enemy for the British regulars.

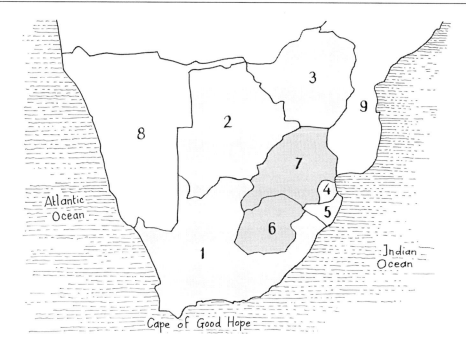

Top: *Map of South Africa. The British colonies included the Cape Colony (1, today South Africa), the Protectorate of Bechuanaland (2, today Botswana), Rhodesia (3, Zimbabwe), and Swaziland (4). Zululand (5) and the Boers' lands, including Orange Free State (6, a part of which since October 1966 is the independent kingdom of Lesotho), and Transvaal (7) are now part of South Africa. On the Atlantic Ocean side there was German Southwest Africa (8, today Namibia), and on the side of the Indian Ocean was Portuguese East Africa (9, today Mozambique).*

Bottom: *Train in South Africa. The second Boer War gave much scope for developments both in operating and in maintaining railroads under war conditions.*

deny the Boer forces adequate supplies, the British resorted to astonishing cruelty. A ruthless scorched-earth strategy was practiced, along with harsh "pacification" and barbaric anti-insurgency tactics, resulting in inhumane treatment of elusive South Africans. The British initiated the usage of a new system: concentration camps. This policy consisted of burning farms, killing cattle, and destroying crops, as well as rounding up, herding by train, and isolating the Boer civilian population into camps, in fact holding hostage a whole civilian community estimated at 107,000 people. The wives and children of Boer guerrillas were sent to overcrowded camps with poor hygiene and little food. The mortality in the camps was appalling—a quarter of those deported did not survive, a ghastly prefiguration of Nazi World War II concentration camp system. The death and suffering of innocent civilians caused a scandal in Britain, notably when the barbaric methods used by the British army were decried by the Liberal leader Sir Henry Campbell-Bannerman. But in the end, ruthlessness and scorched-earth policy broke the guerrillas' will. The Boers were forced into accepting British peace terms, and their territories were incorporated into the British colonial empire. After lengthy negotiations, the bloodiest and most costly of Britain's wars between 1815 and 1914 came to an end in May 1902. In all, the war had cost around 75,000 lives, including 22,000 British soldiers (7,792 battle casualties, the rest through disease), 6,000–7,000 Boer combatants, 20,000–28,000 Boer civilians, mostly women and children, and an estimated 20,000 native black Africans.

British Military Railroads in the Boer War

The Boer War proved to be a testing ground for the British use of railroads in time of war. The British army had already used improvised armored trains during the conquest of Egypt in 1879–1882, the campaigns in Sudan in 1885 and in India in 1886. The Royal Navy led the

British infantryman (c. 1900). The depicted man wears a colonial pith helmet (often replaced with a slouch hat), a khaki serge tunic with matching trousers, and puttees (leather leggings). He is armed with a Lee Enfield rifle.

way by fitting railcars with guns, iron plates and sandbags, as well as placing an expendable railcar at the front of the train to protect the main body in the event of a mine or a deliberately loosened rail. These early experiments set the stage for the use of armored and military trains in the Boer War. The South African campaigns indeed afforded the greatest, most instructive, and also their most anxious experiences. Military trains began to reach maturity in the hands of British armies during this conflict. The campaigns brought out, on their own scale, the familiar difficulties: how to deal with a friendly but highly independent civil railroad administration within one's own territories; how to organize a railroad service in captured hostile land; whether to carry out reconstruction with army troops or civilian personnel; and how to impress on military commanders a proper regard for the functioning of the railroad. The campaign also saw the development of all facets of operations linked with the railroad, such as wholesale destruction of railroads and bridges by retreating troops and their consequent reconstruction; aggressive guerrilla warfare against vulnerable lines of communication; and effective use of armored trains and of heavy rail-borne artillery. Inevitably all major battles and key operations took place in railroad towns and cities or in countryside directly accessible from the railroad lines. The British brought control of the railroad to a fine art. Owing to an efficient and highly disciplined organization, the Second Boer War definitely established the usefulness of both armored and transport trains as efficient instruments of war. In 1899 and 1900 some 6,160 officers, 229,097 men, 29,500 horses, and 1,085 wheeled vehicles were carried by the London and South Western Companies to Southampton, where they embarked for South Africa. The conveyance of this traffic, which was conducted with great smoothness, involved the running of 1,154 special trains, in addition to a large number of others carrying weapons, baggage, supplies and stores.

Once in South Africa, the British military had to operate their own railroads, and also the network they took possession of in the enemy's country. When the Boers declared war in October 1899, the various railroad systems working in direct communication with one another in South Africa had a total length of 4,628 miles, including the following: British South Africa, 3,267; the Transvaal, 918; the Orange Free State, 388; and in Portuguese territory, 55. The railroads in South Africa were rather primitive and basic. They consisted of single tracks with narrow-gauge lines (3 feet 6 inches), never designed for such heavy traffic as the transport of an army and all its equipment and stores would involve. It was, however, obvious from the start that railroads would play a role of first importance, given the limited and poor state of the road network, and the huge size of the theater of operation. From Cape Town, the principal base of British forces, to Pretoria, their eventual objective, the distance was 1,040 miles. From Port Elizabeth it was 740 miles, and from Durban 511 miles.

The British government created a Department of Military Railroads, and appointed at its head the Canadian-born engineer Percy Cranwill Girouard (1867–1932), a man of great experience who had rendered valuable services in connection with military railroads in the Sudan, and who was then president of the Egyptian Railroad Administration. Put in charge as director of railroads for the South African Field Force (composed of railroad companies, Royal Engineers and fortress companies), Girouard gathered a team of assistants, engineers and officers who had skills and experience in railroad technics, and who brought into existence an elaborate organization responsible for the conduct of military transport. In November 1899, considerable portions of the lines both in Cape Colony and in Natal were in the possession of the Boers. Thus the British must fight for every mile of railroad before they could make use of it. After regaining possession of the lines in British territory controlled by the Boers, they had to repair the damage the retreating enemy had inflicted on the tracks. The occupation of Bloemfontein led to that place's becoming the base of supplies for an army of 35,000 men, soon to increase to 100,000. Many of the employees of the Netherlands Railroad Company refused to serve the British and left their jobs. They were replaced with soldiers and railroad men from the Cape Colony, and also by local black workers. In September 1900, the staff employed on the Imperial Military Railroads comprised close to 18,000 officers and men. By that time trains had carried 177,000 passengers, 86,000 animals, and 520,000 tons of goods. This was done under circumstances of exceptional difficulty.

Indeed, since the American Civil War, the art of railroad demolition had made considerable advance owing to the use of dynamite (patented in 1867), which caused enormous destruction. Owing to their good organization, the British were able to quickly repair the damage done, but amid continuous guerrilla attacks by the Boer raiders, protecting the supply line became the key strategy for the British. The construction of fortified blockhouses began towards the end of 1900, at a time when the war was reaching a stalemate and Boer military strategy was shifting from the battlefield to the redeployment of troops into highly mobile detachments of mounted guerrilla commandos. By then the Boers withdrew and fought defensively, displaying their greatest destructive and sabotage activity. Tracks, stations, water tanks, bridges and telegraph lines were the principal targets. To guard against the attacks made on the railroad lines, entrenched posts were placed at every bridge exceeding a 30-foot span, and constant patrolling was maintained between these fortified positions.

Gradually, protective chains of blockhouses designed by General Elliot Wood of the Engineering Corps were erected along all the railroad lines. The distance between blockhouses, about 1,000 yards (910 m), was calculated to enable overlapping fire and mutual defense. Each blockhouse was garrisoned by about eight to ten men, and they were connected to each other by telephone and telegdefensehe fortlets consisted of a watchtower with quarters for the garrison topped with a corrugated iron plate. Access to the first floor was by means of a two-piece, bulletproof steel door located high above the ground floor. This could only be reached by means of a retractable ladder, which was hoisted upwards by means of steel tackle. Often the post featured a small defensive perimeter enclosed with a bank of earth, a low brick wall, or a breastwork made of sandbags with barbed wire entanglements, and possibly a ditch or trenches. In order to prevent the Boers from passing unnoticed between them, the gaps between blockhouses were filled with barbed wire fences. The fences often featured bells or metal cans containing stones or other devices that could alert the troops to movement or activity somewhere along the length of the fence. In 1901 a cheaper circular model designed by Major R.C. Rice was adopted. About 8,000 of these fortlets were constructed in the period from 1900 to 1902 by the British Royal Engineers. They demanded the service of 50,000 British troops and 16,000 African auxiliaries to supply them—about twice the total number of Boer combatants in the last phase of the war. Even though relatively few blockhouses saw action, they nonetheless played an important deterrent role in thwarting the Boers' mobility.

Another method adopted for the safeguarding of railroad lines was the use of armored trains. For the first time, armored trains were especially designed, and extensively and successfully used at war. For the purposes of scouting expeditions, patrol, escort of ordinary traffic trains, track protection and support in attack on the enemy, six armored trains were constructed. They became sophisticated weapon systems, often consisting of a locomotive in the middle, pushing heavily armored cars protecting soldiers armed with rifles and machine guns. The trains also included gun-trucks at each end to allow cross-fires. To obviate the danger of mines, each train pushed a flat control car with low sides and ends. They did not obstruct the view or arc of fire from the train, and they performed the double purpose of exploding contact mines and carrying the railroad and telegraph repair materials. Locomotives, too, were armored, and heavy armor plates were placed on each side of the driver's cab. Sometimes improvised and unusual materials were used. For example, in 1899 there was a locomotive covered with thick layers of ropes in order to resist small arms projectiles; this engine was nicknamed Hairy Mary. On the occupation of Bloemfontein by the British, more armored trains, virtually gun batteries on wheels, were built, and eventually the number available was increased to a fleet of twenty, so invaluable was the service they rendered.

The crew of an armored train generally consisted of an infantry escort and Royal Artillery and Royal Engineer detachments. Armored trains performed the following tasks: accompanying, supporting, and protecting flanks of infantry columns; reinforcing camps, posts, blockhouses and stations; escorting supply trains; reconnoitering; patrolling day and night; and protecting the track.

Artillery cars were also developed by the British in support of offensive operations. Since the American Civil War, heavy artillery placed on tracks had made significant advances. For better aiming and extended line of fire, artillery cars incorporated turntables and recoil systems. However, they were seldom used, as it was difficult to bring these unwieldy armored railguns within range of a battle site on a single track already heavily used by other army transport trains.

Military trains were formidable weapons that proved useful. The Boers feared and disliked them. The presence of such a steaming monster had a great impact on morale, but they were not invulnerable, and often had to be escorted by cavalrymen.

A very well-known incident occurred on November 15, 1899. Winston Churchill (1874–1965), then a young war correspondent for the Morning Post, was traveling onboard an armored train in southern Natal. Ambushed by Boer commandos, Churchill and many of the train's crew were captured. Just a month later, Churchill managed to escape captivity by climbing over the wall of the State Model School in Pretoria whilst his compatriots distracted the guards. He walked to the nearest railroad line, hid on a train, and managed to reach the port of Lourenço Marques in the then Portuguese colony of Mozambique. This attack highlighted the vulnerability of armored trains facing a determined enemy and made it clear that they could not operate independently without a scouting party ahead.

For the purpose of reconnaissance, the British experimented and introduced railroad bicycles with flanged wheels involving two men sitting and pedaling side by side, with a cruising speed of 10 mph. Interestingly, the Royal Engineers also used tethered balloons for observing the open, rough grassland terrain of the veldt.

At the same time, sanitary trains were also developed. Seven hospital trains, all adapted from existing rolling stock in Cape Colony or Natal, were made available for the transport of sick and wounded. The hospital train Princess Christian, for example, was specially constructed for and financed by the British Central Red Cross Committee. Sent out to South Africa early in 1900, it consisted of seven carriages—in effect, rolling wards—each about 36 feet in length and 8 feet in width, including beds formed of boards laid on shock-absorbing springs. There were also a kitchen, a pantry, and a compartment for the guards and medical personnel. The train carried everything that was necessary for a squad of guards, 100 patients, and a staff composed of nurses and doctors. Between May 1900 and September 1901, *Princess Christian* made many journeys, mainly on the Natal side and on the Pretoria-Koomati Poort line. It ran a total of 42,000 miles, and carried a total of 7,529 sick and wounded, of whom only a few died en route. As for showing the extent of the work done by the other hospital trains during the course of the war, it may be added that train No. 2 ran 114,539 miles in 226 trips between November 1898 and the end of August 1902, conveying a total of 10,796 sick and wounded.

The British use of military railroads in the Boer War confirmed their usefulness under especially difficult conditions. The political and strategic importance of railroads was becoming better understood. The Boer War had proved that even when a line of rail communication was attacked and sabotaged by a determined enemy, the final result of the campaign was not affected. This demanded a strong and well-organized force of railroad

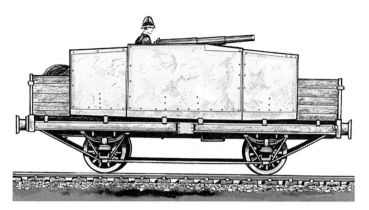

Top: *One-pounder gun truck. This early model was simply a freight car strengthened with metal side plating. All cars could be fitted with a folding canvas tent for protection against rain and sun.*

Middle: *4.7 cm gun on a railroad truck mounting, 1900.*

Bottom: *British armored train. Fitted with loopholes for riflemen's fire and carrying Maxim machine guns, armored trains were used to patrol and protect lines of communication, and to rescue beleaguered stations or posts. By 1902 the British had no fewer than 20 armored trains. Late models generally consisted of a locomotive in the middle pulling or pushing armored cars containing crew quarters, a searchlight, generators and telegraph equipment, a water tank, one or several cars mounting 6- or 12-pounder guns, and armored trucks carrying infantrymen and machine guns. In front of the train there was often a flatcar with a cowcatcher intended to sweep obstructions and to explode contact mines.*

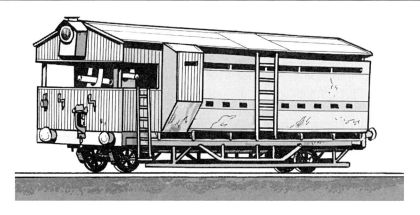

Top: *British armored rail car in the Boer War. This standard pattern armored roofed car could carry a section of infantry, and was armed with two or three Maxim machine guns or one light quick-firing one-pounder cannon. Such an armored train was dangerous to attack, so Boer guerrillas preferred to halt them by demolishing bridges or sabotaging the track.*

Middle: *British armored locomotive in the Boer War.*

Bottom: *British 6-in. railgun. The car was fitted with pivoting wooden girders at each side, which could be quickly swung out as stabilizers when firing.*

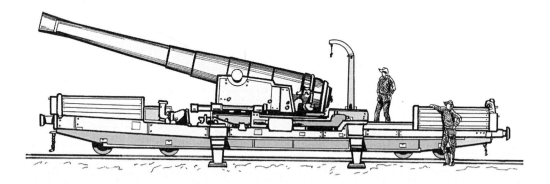

Top: *Pompom gun. The 37-mm Nordenfelt-Maxim or "QF [quick-firing] 1-pounder," introduced during the Second Boer War, fired a shell one pound in weight accurately over a distance of 3,000 yd (2,700 m). The barrel was water-cooled, and the shells were fed from a 25-round fabric belt. The Boers used them against the British, who, seeing their utility, had the design copied by Vickers, who were already producing Maxim guns.*

Middle: *12-pounder railgun. Based on a standard bogie car underframe, this railgun included a central rotating turret armed with one 12-pounder having all-round field of fire.*

Bottom: *British 9.2-inch gun on rail mount. The car was fitted with an ammunition lifting hoist, and screw jacks to stabilize the car when firing.*

Top: *British blockhouse. For the most part, the design of blockhouses was standard, consisting of a substantial rectangular masonry building three stories high, with rifle holes and two small flanking turrets placed at opposite corners. Designed by General Wood, these stone blockhouses were quite expensive and time-consuming to build, so another model was designed by Major Rice in 1901. All of the 8,000 blockhouses built during the South African War were intended to do the same job: keeping the ever-mobile Boers from accessing British supply lines. Therefore, most of the blockhouses were erected near essential railroad routes to protect vital supply lines.*

Bottom: *Circular corrugated blockhouse. Designed by Major Rice, this model consisted of a mass-produced circular drum made of corrugated iron with a sloped roof, and a base reinforced with stones or sandbags. Blockhouses designed by Wood and Rice were standard models, but other designs were used. Some resembled large granaries, others modern-day electricity substations, while others appear as fanciful little castles. Sometimes blockhouses where built using existing structures along the tracks. Although most blockhouses were eventually dismantled, a number still remain in silent testimony of the bitter and foolish Boer War.*

troops following close on the advancing army. These units carried out repairs and reconstruction with such speed that comparatively little material delay was caused.

SPANISH-AMERICAN WAR (1898)

The Spanish-American War was a conflict in 1898 between Spain and the United States. The war was the result of American intervention in the ongoing Cuban War of Independence. American attacks on Spain's Pacific possessions led to involvement in the Philippine Revolution and ultimately to the Philippine-American War. The Spanish-American War lasted for ten weeks, and was fought in both the Caribbean and the Pacific. American naval power proved decisive, allowing U.S. expeditionary forces to win the war. The result was the 1898 Treaty of Paris, negotiated on terms favorable to the U.S. It allowed temporary American control of Cuba and ceded indefinite colonial authority over Puerto Rico and Guam Island. The treaty also allowed the U.S. to purchase the Philippine Islands from Spain.

During that conflict, the task of mobilizing and deploying a largely volunteer force to Cuba and the Philippines emphasized the need for a separate transportation service within the quartermaster department. Army transporters worked with both the civilian railroads and the maritime industry to pull together a successful intermodal operation.

COLONIAL RAILROADS

Colonialism

The Industrial Revolution of the second half of the 19th century gave the Europeans weapons, machines, tools and instruments, as well as a belief in their technical and intellectual superiority, giving rise to an aggressive and racist spirit that assured them world dominance. The consequence of this spirit was a scramble to conquer and establish permanent colonies overseas in underdeveloped regions of the world. The aims were to obtain cheap raw materials, create economic markets, and incidentally "civilize" native populations regarded as backward, savage, and ignorant, and therefore inferior, to be treated as no more than exploitable forced labor and slaves. Imperialism was not new, of course; it had existed since antiquity, and had been revived at the time of the great discoveries in the Renaissance. But in the second half of the 19th century it dramatically developed, particularly in Africa and Asia, at the same time creating new tensions between rival powers. By 1900 large parts of Africa and Asia had been explored, mapped, measured, conquered, divided and exploited by European powers. This had been made possible by technologically superior military powers, the combination of a monopoly on modern firearms, and professional qualities of drill and discipline. Steamships and railroads opened up the interior of the African and Asian continents, giving European invading armies a mobility that compensated for their small size.

There is little point here in describing all European colonial empires, such as the French in Africa and Indochina, the Dutch in Indonesia, the Belgians in the Congo, and the Portuguese in Angola. The following sections are examples of British and German expansionism and an illustration of how railroads helped in the making of colonial empires. As the greatest colonial power in the world, Britain was involved in the largest number of conflicts with non–Europeans.

Abyssinian Campaigns, 1867–68

The war against the unstable King Tewodros (Theodore) of Abyssinia (today's Ethiopia) was caused by the imprisonment of several British subjects by Theodore. In January 1868 a punitive expedition under Sir Robert Napier (afterwards Lord Napier of Magdala) began the long march of 300 miles to Magdala, the Abyssinian capital. Magdala is 300 miles from Annesley Bay, the base of operations on the Red Sea. After an arduous approach, the city was stormed in April 1868, Theodore committed suicide, and the force was withdrawn. A railroad was specially constructed for the purpose of assisting the military expedition on the occasion of that campaign.

In January 1868 the construction of the railroad line was started. It was twelve miles in length, from the landing place to Koomayleh, at the entrance of the Soroo Pass, the route to be taken by the expedition on its journey to the Abyssinian highlands. The details of this melancholy story are almost comic. The line had a gauge of 5 feet 6 inches, and was to be operated with great difficulty by four old and worn out locomotives (not well adapted to the one-in-sixty gradient) and sixty primitive wagons (with no springs, no proper buffers, and plain cast-iron axles-boxes without grease) rolling on bad quality rails (with fishplates, bolts and boltholes that did not fit each other) and traveling through a hot, sandy, timberless, practically waterless country. The Indian laborers sent to lay the line proved unsuitable and recourse had to be made to work gangs of Chinese picked up in Bombay. Given all these circumstances, one cannot be surprised that the construction went at a slow rate.

At the end of April 1868, news arrived that the object of the expedition had been attained, and that Magdala had fallen. It was then decided not to complete the unnecessary line, but to devote all efforts to preparing for the heavy traffic to be dealt with in the conveyance of troops, baggage and supplies on the return journey. In the end, the Abyssinian railroad was not a success. It was a quite unimportant affair that only helped the men of the expedition to quickly re-embark for home. The Abyssinian experience taught no fresh lessons. It only demonstrated what was already known, namely that the construction of military railroads was not possible without an organization created in advance, and that defective material, unsatisfactory labor, and administrative mismanagement were absolutely to be avoided.

Egypt 1882

The expedition of 1882 opposed the Egyptian army, led by Ahmed Urabi, against the British military forces. After discontented Egyptian officers under Urabi rebelled in 1882, Great Britain reacted to protect its financial and expansionist interests in the country, and in particular the Suez Canal, opened in 1869. Lord Kitchener, the British commander in chief, arranged for the construction of a standard-gauge railroad line to provide a supply route from his base on the Nile, and armored trains were used in that campaign.

One put together to assist in the defensive works at Alexandria had two of the trucks fitted with iron plating and sandbags as a protective cover. It carried one Nordenfelt and two Gatling guns. A 9-pounder gun was also placed on one of the trucks, together with a crane by means of which it could be lowered out immediately. Other trucks, rendered bulletproof by sandbags, carried a force of 200 soldiers. In July 1882, the train participated in a reconnaissance mission and shots were fired at it by the enemy, but without damage. The mission was a complete success insofar as it enabled such repairs to be done to the railroad as gave the use of a second line between Ramleh and Alexandria.

So useful had the train been found that it was soon further improved by the addition of one 40-pounder cannon placed on a truck shielded by an iron plate. The locomotive was put in the middle of the train and protected by sandbags and iron plates. The strengthened train went into another reconnaissance-in-force mission carried out from Alexandria in August. One month later, the armored train, consisting of five cars, and having on this occasion one Krupp gun and one Gatling machine gun in addition to the 40-pounder, took part in the attack on Tel-el-Kebir. It was followed by another train loaded with materials, tools and appliances for the prompt carrying out of any repairs that might be necessary.

British railgun. Egypt, 1882.

the linking up of Egypt and the Sudan by means of a single line of railroad from Cairo to Khartoum, with a branch to Massowa, on the Red Sea. However, the cost was regarded as prohibitive, and the scheme was abandoned.

The project was eventually revived, however, in a modified form. It was then proposed that the line should start at Wadi Halfa and be continued to Matemmeh (Shendy), situated about 100 miles north of Khartoum, a total distance of 558 miles. In 1875, work started with the building of this railroad, which was to consist of a single line, with a gauge of 3 feet 6 inches. In 1877, after an expenditure of about £400,000, construction had been carried out no farther than Sarras, only thirty-three and a half miles from the starting-point, and work was stopped for lack of funds. In the autumn of 1884, when the British expedition to Khartoum was resolved upon, it was then decided to extend the Sudan Railroad beyond the point already reached, at Sarras, in order to facilitate still further the journey of the troops along the Valley of the Nile. Following the fall of Khartoum in January 1885 came the decision to extend the line to Firket (103 miles) in view of a then projected further campaign in the autumn of that year. The extension was sanctioned towards the end of February 1885, and fifty-two miles of permanent way were ordered from England. In August 1885 the extension was completed as far as Akasha (87 miles).

What had thus far been successfully achieved in the Nile Valley ended in failure on the Red Sea, due to constant Dervish attacks both on the line under construction and on the workers. Several actions were fought, and at Tofrik, near Suakin, the British suffered a serious defeat. Posts were erected as the work

In the futile attempt made in 1885 to construct a railroad from Suakin to Berber, in support of the Nile Expedition of 1884–85, another armored train carrying a 20-pound cannon was engaged for the purpose of protecting the line from the constant ambushes to which it was subjected by the enemy.

The aftermath of the 1882 expedition was a great success for Britain. The rebellious Urabi was captured and sentenced to death, the British but feared sparking an uprising, and so later exiled him to Ceylon (now Sri Lanka). The Khedive Tawfiq was formally reinstated twelve days later. The guarantees and concessions he made marked the start of the British military occupation of Egypt, which was to last until 1954.

The Sudan 1896

The vast tracts of the Sudan (formerly a part of the Turkish Empire), one of Africa's largest countries, was a thorn in the side of the Victorian British Empire. At the turn of the 19th and 20th centuries, the Sudan was the scene of some of the bitterest fighting in Britain's imperial history as generals like Kitchener battled the followers of the Islamic leader known as the Mahdi. One of the decisive weapons that were used was the Sudan Military Railroad. Already during the time that Saïd Pasha was Viceroy of Egypt (1854–63), an ambitious scheme was envisaged for slowly progressed, and a bulletproof armored train was used for patrolling the line at night. But in face of all the difficulties encountered, the construction was permanently abandoned when only twenty miles of the intended track had been completed. The British troops were recalled in June 1885.

Reverting to the Sudan-Nile Valley Railroad, it provides an example of a military railroad that rendered great services in facilitating the conquest of a vast area. Although designed for the purposes of war, and constructed partly during the progress of the campaign, it eventually developed into a successful system of government railroads operated, in turn, for the purposes of peace and commercial development.

The Egypt-Sudan railroad could have been a section of a yet more ambitious Cape-to-Cairo railroad linking British South Africa to Egypt, from end to end of the African continent, as the Russians were doing in Siberia. Conceived by Cecil John Rhodes (1853–1902; businessman, mining magnate, and politician in South Africa) at the high water mark of later 19th century British imperialism, the project of the transcontinental Cape-to-Cairo railroad remained a dream.

At the turn of the 19th and 20th centuries, military railroad was taken so seriously that Britain built in 1903 a large base ground and camp in Hampshire designated Woolmer Instructional Military Railroad (in 1935 renamed Longmoor Military Railroad, LMR). There, Royal Engineers could train on railroad construction and operations. At its peak, LMR ran to over 70 miles (110 km) of operational laid track, loop lines and sidings. After World War II, with a declining military role for railroads both in Britain and the rest of the world, it was inevitable that the significance of the facilities offered by LMR would be reduced in later years, and LMR was closed down in December 1969.

German African Colonies

Germany came late to the business of imperial acquisition. As prime minister of a relatively new united Empire (1871), Chancellor Bismarck was reluctant to join the fray. However, Kaiser Wilhelm II, was eager to plant the German flag on distant shores, and soon his nation joined the "Scramble for Africa." In the 1880s Germany began to build a colonial empire in Africa, and once started, they did the job of colonization with their usual thoroughness. Now a strong, wealthy and powerful unified industrial nation, Germany demanded colonial markets to relieve the economic pressure caused by the speedily growing industrialization. In 1884, German commercial establish-

British train in the Sudan, 1896.

ments on the west coast of Africa were proclaimed protectorates, soon followed by a colony known as German South-West Africa (present-day Namibia).

In the same year, Togo and Cameroon were obtained by forced annexation. A year later, East Africa (present-day Rwanda, Burundi and Tanzania), as well as part of New Guinea and the Marshall Islands, were added to their possessions. In 1889 the Caroline, Marianne and Palau Islands in the Pacific were purchased from Spain. By the end of the 19th century the German colonial empire included an aggregate area of over one million square miles with a native population of about twelve million.

In order that Germany might economically develop her African possessions (and also be prepared to take action against the British in South Africa at a moment's notice), it was essential to have railroads and troops on the spot. Railroads were indispensable on account of the considerable distances to be covered in forest, bush, savanna and stretches of desert. In the 1890s the Northern Railroad was built to as a means of communication between Swakopmund and the capital of the colony. Its original purpose was to provide an outlet for the copper obtained from the mines in the district of Otavi, but it was also designed to serve military strategic purposes. The line was extended in 1908 to Keetmanshoop, a distance inland of 230 miles from Lüderitzbucht.

In fact, the Germans' ambitious and secret long-term plan was for the smashing up of France and Great Britain. The conquest of their colonies thus would lead to the whole continent of Africa's becoming a German possession. The system of railroads in German South-West Africa, combined with river and road transport, was developed in accordance with secret plans for eventual attacks on British territory in three separate directions: Cape Province; Bechuanaland; and Rhodesia. Also, the rich Portuguese possession of Angola was a tempting target, and a track was built in that direction, openly as a means of peaceful commercial exchange. Another essential part of the general scheme of conquest was an ambitious railroad line that stretched right across German East Africa from Dar-es-Salaam, the capital of the protectorate, to Kigoma on Lake Tanganyika, and north of Ujiji for a total length of 1,439 miles. A southeastern section of track was also developed with the Belgian Congo, whose coal, gold and iron mines, as well as great tin

Map of German colonies in Africa.

German soldier in Africa.

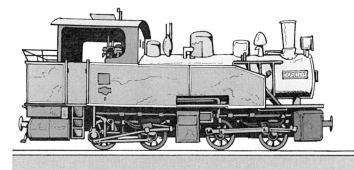

Right, top: *German Feld-bahn 0-8-0. Because of the long distance between usable water supplies, locomotives in colonial areas were often equipped with auxiliary water tenders. The 0-8-0 was a successful engine fitted with the Klien-Lindner method of wheelbase articulation, enabling the 60 cm locomotives to traverse sharp curves.*

Right, middle: *Motor trolley. The Germans in Africa were among the first to realize the value of an internal combustion–engined trolley (for example, for inspection of the track or personnel transport) on light field railroad.*

Right, bottom: *German locomotive Orenstein & Koppel 1905. This locomotive had a gauge of one meter, and was used in Togo in West Africa. Togo was a German colony from 1884 to 1918.*

and copper belts and furnaces in the Katanga district, could not fail to appeal strongly to the Germans.

German troops deployed in these territories consisted of mounted infantry, field artillery, machine gun battalions, intelligence service, an engineer and railroad corps, field railroad divisions, a camel-mounted corps, a police force and a reserve force. This represented altogether (apart from native auxiliaries) a trained European army of approximately 10,000 men, whose duties and location in the event of war had all been assigned to them in advance. The Germans assembled their first armored train in 1904 during the Herero revolt in their colony of South-West Africa. When the First World War broke out in August 1914, the German African Schutztruppen (protection troops), headed by General Paul von Lettow-Vorbeck, were immediately engaged and fought a forgotten war far away from the muddy trenches of northern France. Although these colonial troops were undefeated, Germany's dream of an African empire vanished with the defeat of 1918. The Treaty of Versailles of 1919 stripped Germany of all her colonies. They were nominally placed under the administration of the League of Nations, but actually were added as "mandates" to the colonial empires of the Allied powers, mainly Great Britain, the USA, and France.

Baghdad Railroad

Just as avowedly strategic lines in Africa were to lead the way to the creation of a German African empire, so in turn was that system of economic-political-strategic lines encompassed within the scheme of what was known as the Baghdad Railroad. With funding and engineering provided by German banks and companies, this was designed to ensure the establishment of a German middle-Asian empire. The whole Baghdad Railroad affair was intended to bring under German control the entire region from the Mediterranean to the Persian Gulf, and to provide convenient stepping-off places from which an advance might be made on Egypt in the one direction and India in the other.

In Europe it was proposed to link Berlin and Dresden (Germany) down to Vienna, Presburg, Budapest (Austrian-Hungary), Belgrade and Nish (Serbia), Sofia (Bulgaria) and Constantinople. From there, the first section of the Baghdad Railroad proper, a length of about seventy miles, extending from Haidar Pacha (situated on the northeastern coast of the Sea of Marmara, and opposite Constantinople) to Ismidt, was built in 1875 by German engineers to the order of the Turkish government. An extension on the east to Angora in 1892, and another on the south to Konia in 1896, were built, increasing the total length of line to 633 miles. The building work was carried out mainly by the Frankfurt firm of Philipp Holzmann, and the railroad line played a significant role in cementing relations between Germany and Ottoman Turkey.

Despite the difficult terrain, work progressed quickly. Then in 1911 the German-controlled Baghdad Railroad Company acquired the right to build a new port at Alexandretta (Iskenderun), with quays, docks, bonded warehouses, and other facilities, and to construct thence a short line of railroad connecting with the Baghdad main line at Osmanieh, east of Adana. By these means the Germans acquired control over, if not an actual monopoly on, the traffic to and from one of the most important ports on the eastern seaboard of the Mediterranean. From Muslimiyeh, a little town to the north of Aleppo, there was a short branch connecting the Baghdad Railroad with the Hedjaz line from Damascus to Medina, which eventually was to be continued on to Mecca. From Rayak, north of Damascus, a branch built in a southwest direction was to be carried to within a short distance of the Egyptian frontier. From the junction for the Aleppo branch, the main line was to continue across the Mesopotamian plain to

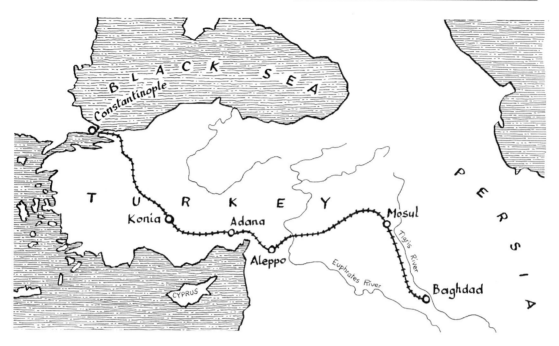

Map of the Baghdad Railroad.

Baghdad (whence a branch to Khanikin, on the Persian frontier, was projected) and so on to Basra, for the Persian Gulf.

The program of Weltpolitik comprised in the German scheme embraced not only countries but continents. In addition to the aspirations cherished as regards Europe, that program aimed at the eventual annexation to the German Empire of three other Empires: the Turkish, the Indian, and a new one to be known as the German-African. If it was to terminate at Baghdad, the railroad might possibly have been regarded as an internal Turkish affair; but since it was planned to run to Basra, it was getting too close to the Persian Gulf, which the British in India regarded as a special preserve of their own. The Germans conceived that part of the railroad line as a way of giving them access to a port on the Persian Gulf, allowing them to trade with the Middle East, India and the Asian Far East without having to go through the British-controlled Suez Canal. When it was suggested that the line should run to Kuwait, well down the Gulf, then there was very great anxiety indeed.

So the Baghdad Railroad was a manifestation of a dramatic and alarming growth of German economic power. It poisoned the international atmosphere and became a source of instability and disputes during the years immediately preceding World War I. Although it has been argued that these disputes were resolved in 1914 before the war began, it has also been argued that the Baghdad Railroad was a leading cause of the First World War. Technical difficulties in the remote Taurus Mountains and diplomatic delays meant that by 1915 the railroad was still 480 kilometers (300 miles) short of completion, severely limiting its use during the war, in which Baghdad was occupied by the British. By then the already completed Hejaz railroad in the south was attacked by Arabian guerrilla forces led by the legendary Thomas E. Lawrence "of Arabia" (1888–1935). War and the collapse of the Ottoman Empire brought the building work to a halt in 1918. Construction of the Baghdad Railroad was resumed in the 1930s and completed in 1940, but then things had changed so much that only people of an older generation could remember what all the fuss over it had been about.

RUSSO-JAPANESE WAR (1904–1905)

Historical Background

Japan entered the modern age in 1868, with a new young emperor determined to make his archipelago a world power. After decades of steady progress, Japan began its own practice of colonialism, defeating China in 1894. As the Japanese began to develop "spheres of influence" in Manchuria and Korea, they ran into the Russians, who were doing the same.

The Russo-Japanese War was in many respects a railroad war. Railroads allowed the delivery of huge armies and supplies, but not only did the railroad play a central role in the way the war was conducted, but the construction of a line actually triggered the conflict itself. As expressed by the historians Felix Patrikeef and Harold Shukman in their book *Railroads and the Russo-Japanese War* (2007): "The Russo-Japanese War of 1904–1905 would not have been fought on the scale it was, had the railroad not been built, and indeed could not have been fought at all in the absence of railroad." The war opposed Russia to Japan, but it was fought entirely in territories (Manchuria and Korea) of other nations—a feature that was made possible by the efficiency of railroad lines of communication. Indeed, the cause of that war was the rivalry between Russia and Japan for dominance in Korea and Manchuria. In 1898, Russia had pressured China into granting it a lease for the strategically important port of Port Arthur (now Lu-shun), at the end of the Liao-Tung Peninsula, in southern Manchuria. Russia thereby entered into occupation of the peninsula, even though, in concert with other European powers, it had forced Japan to relinquish just such a right after the latter's decisive victory over China in the Sino-Japanese War of 1894–95. Moreover, in 1896, Russia had

concluded an alliance with China against Japan, and in the process had won rights to extend the Trans-Siberian Railroad across Chinese-held Manchuria to the Russian seaport of Vladivostok, thus gaining control of an important strip of Manchurian territory.

However, though Russia had built the Trans-Siberian Railroad, it still lacked the transportation facilities necessary to reinforce its limited armed forces in Manchuria with sufficient men and supplies. Japan, by contrast, had steadily expanded its army since its war with China in 1894, and by 1904 had gained a marked superiority over Russia in the number of ground troops in the Far East. Of the non-western civilizations, only the Japanese displayed the ability to adopt the weapons and methods of the West, and turn them with success against their developers. Few would have predicted it.

After Russia reneged in 1903 on an agreement to withdraw its troops from Manchuria, Japan decided to strike. The war began on February 8, 1904, when the main Japanese fleet launched a surprise attack and siege on the Russian naval squadron at Port Arthur. In March the Japanese landed an army in Korea that quickly overran the country. In May another Japanese army landed on the Liao-Tung Peninsula, and on May 26 it cut off the Port Arthur garrison from the main body of Russian forces in Manchuria. The Japanese then pushed northward, and the Russian army fell back to Mukden (now Shen-Yang) after losing battles at Fuhsien (June 14) and Liao-Yang (August 25), south of Mukden. In October the Russians went back on the offensive with the help of reinforcements received via the Trans-Siberian Railroad, but their attacks proved indecisive owing to poor military leadership. The Japanese had also settled down to a long siege of Port Arthur after several very costly general assaults on it had failed. The garrison's military leadership proved divided, however, and on January 2, 1905, in a gross act of incompetence and corruption, Port

Arthur's Russian commander surrendered the port to the Japanese without consulting his officers, and with three months' provisions and adequate supplies of ammunition still in the fortress.

The final battle of the land war was fought at Mukden in late February and early March 1905, between Russian forces totaling 330,000 men and Japanese totaling 270,000. After long and stubborn fighting and heavy casualties on both sides, the Russian commander, General A.N. Kuropatkin, broke off the fighting and withdrew his forces northward from Mukden, which fell into the hands of the Japanese. Casualties in this clash were exceptionally high, comprising about 89,000 Russian and 71,000 Japanese.

The naval Battle of Tsushima ultimately gave the Japanese the upper hand in the war. The Japanese had been unable to secure the complete command of the sea on which their land campaign depended, and the Russian squadrons at Port Arthur and Vladivostok had remained moderately active. But on May 27–29, 1905, in a battle in the Tsushima Straits, Admiral Togo Heihachiro's main Japanese fleet destroyed the Russian Baltic fleet, which, commanded by Admiral Z.P. Rozhestvensky, had sailed in October 1904 all the way from the Baltic port of Liepaja, across the Atlantic and the Indian Oceans in order to relieve the forces at Port Arthur, and at the time of the battle was trying to reach Vladivostok. Japan was by this time financially exhausted, but its decisive naval victory at Tsushima, together with increasing internal political unrest throughout Russia, where the war had never been popular, forced the Russian government to negotiate.

President Theodore Roosevelt of the United States served as mediator at the peace conference, which was held at Portsmouth, New Hampshire, from August 9 to September 5, 1905. In the resulting Treaty of Portsmouth, Japan gained control of the Liao-Tung Peninsula (and Port Arthur) and the South Man-churian railroad (which led to Port Arthur), as well as half of Sakhalin Island. Russia agreed to evacuate southern Manchuria, which was restored to China, and Japan's control of Korea was recognized. Within two months of the treaty's signing, a revolution compelled the Russian tsar Nicholas II to issue the October Manifesto, which was the equivalent of a constitutional charter.

The unexpected Japanese victory dramatically transformed the distribution of power in Asia. It introduced Japan as a modern, incontestable, and leading power into international affairs. It was also the first defeat of a major European imperialist power by an Asian country. It clearly showed that the western white men could be defeated by a native Asian nation.

Trans-Siberian Railroad

By 1850 there were some 370 miles of railroad in Russia, but between 1854 and 1884 construction went rapidly ahead. In 1880 the mileage was about 15,000, and 31,000 in 1900. The 1904–5 war was as much a test of the military strength of the two belligerents as of their ability to keep open their respective means of communication. Japan was able to rely on her fleet and her considerably developed mercantile marine; and as soon as she had paralyzed the Russian fleet and established her own command of the sea—as she did within two days of the outbreak of hostilities—she could land her forces whenever she chose at almost any convenient point on the seaboard of the theater of war. From Moscow to Port Arthur the distance is 5,300 miles, and save for the sea journey via the Baltic, the North Sea, the Atlantic and the Indian Ocean, the Russians were dependent for the transport of their troops and supplies to Manchuria on trains.

The Trans-Siberian Railroad (TSR) was a great strategic line stretching across Central North Asia, facilitating the development of a vast territory, uniting the remote provinces of the largest nation in the world, imposing the rule of the Tsar on the distant Asian lands, but it was also intended to serve military purposes. Its construction was discussed in the 1860s, but it was not before 1891 that work on it began. By 1896 the western section had been carried through Irkutsk to Lake Baikal, and from the eastern shores thereof to Strietensk. In the meantime the eastern section (known as the Usuri Railroad) had been made through Russia's maritime province from Vladivostok to Khabarovsk. Towards the end of 1896, Russia obtained from China the concession for a railroad which, starting from Chita, Trans-Baikalia, about 200 miles west of Strietensk, would pass through Manchuria to Vladivostok, avoiding the great bend of the Amur River. This part was to be operated by a newly created Chinese Eastern Railroad Company. Russia's occupation of Port Arthur in March 1898 led in the spring of the following year to the further construction of a southern branch of the Chinese Eastern Railroad from Harbin, a station on the Chita-Vladivostok line, to the extremity of the Liao-Tung peninsula. These two railroad lines, the Trans-Siberian and the Chinese Eastern, terminating at Vladivostok in the one direction and at Port Arthur in the other, played a central role in the war of 1904–5.

When completed, the Trans-Siberian was an amazing undertaking, running for 4,627 miles from Chelyabinsk in the Urals to Vladivostok on the Pacific Ocean.

During the first period of exploitation the Trans-Siberian railroad proved its efficiency and importance to the economy's development, and encouraged rapid growth of shipment of goods. But its traffic capacity happened to be insufficient. When the Trans-Siberian was first built, the desire to avoid undue expenditure led to the adoption of draconian measures of economy. For example, the width of the earth bed in such places as mounds and excavations was decreased, ballast layer was made thinner, lighter rails were used, the number of sleepers per kilometer was decreased, major construction works were planned only for the big bridges, and smaller bridges were built of timber. This greatly hampered the quality of the design, making the tracks inadequate to cope with heavy traffic. Furthermore, the single track of the Trans-Siberian stopped on each side of Lake Baikal, where everything had to be unloaded, ferried across the water, and then reloaded again. In the winter, rails were laid across the lake's frozen waters. When the war with Japan broke out in 1904, the line was extended around the south of the lake.

In spite of what has just been said, passenger service grew rapidly. In 1897, 609,000 people were transported; in 1900, 1.25 million passengers; and in 1905, 1.85 million. When war broke out in February 1904, the number of trains that could be run was, however, rather limited. The capacity of the line of communication as a whole was fixed by that of the Eastern Chinese Railroad between Chita and Harbin. After three months of war it was still possible to run from west to east no more than three military trains in each twenty-four hours, one light mail train, and, when necessary, one ambulance train. The speed at which the trains ran, allowing for necessary stops in stations or at crossing places on the line, ranged from five to eleven miles an hour, with seven miles an hour as a good average. For the journey from Moscow to Mukden, the military trains took forty days. The Russian reinforcements arrived in driblets, and during the hostilities from May to October 1904, only 21,000 men were brought to replace 100,000 killed, wounded or sick. Under these conditions the Japanese, free to send their own armies by sea to the theater of war, and able to concentrate them with far greater speed, had all the initial advantage. As long as the Russian army was comparatively small, it could depend mainly on local resources, but when it increased in size it became more and more dependent on supplies from faraway

Map of the Trans-Siberian Railroad. Built between 1891 and 1916, the TSR, with a length of 9,289 km (5,772 miles), is the longest railroad line in the world.

European Russia. Obviously the improvement of the essential railroad communication between Russia and Siberia became top priority.

Soon enormous works were undertaken in difficult climatic conditions and adverse, thinly populated country, with huge forests, many strong rivers and lakes, swamps and permafrost tundra. Peasants and townspeople from Siberia, and also peasants and lower-middle-class people from the European part of Russia, were involved in the improvement of the track. At the beginning of construction in 1891 the total number of workers on the line was 9,600. In 1895–1896 it went up to 89,000. The improvements made in the traffic facilities included, for example, the provision of coal, water and store dumps at regular intervals, as well as sixty-nine additional loop lines for the passing of trains. These betterments were such that by the time peace was concluded in September 1905, the Russians had ten or even twelve pairs of full-length trains running every twenty-four hours. The capacity of the lines had been increased practically fourfold, but in spite of the efforts made to improve the track, the connection of the Russian forces in East Asia with their home country was and remained an unreliable and uncertain factor in the calculations of Army Headquarters. After all, the Trans-Siberian had not been built to sustain a war, but to provide a stimulus to colonization in Siberia—a job it eventually certainly did.

What the poorly constructed single-line railroad did, however, was an impressive task, enabling the Russians to bring over such a great distance an army of 1,000,000 men, together with enormous quantities of weapons, ammunition, and supplies of all kinds. In terms of construction speed (12 years), length (7500 km), volume of work completed, and difficult building conditions, the Trans-Siberian railroad construction was the largest in the world. The necessity of destroying the enemy's rail system, which would seem so ob-

Trans-Siberian Railroad. The TSR was an impressive achievement, but during the Russo-Japanese War (1904–1905), the single track could not move from the West enough supplies, men and ammunition as were necessary. This caused significant strategic and logistical difficulties for the Russians.

vious as not to require comment, was not always taken for granted. The Japanese took no real advantage of the fact that the Russians were entirely dependent upon the Trans-Siberian.

Another remarkable feat was the construction of 350 miles of military narrow-gauge tracks during the siege of Port Arthur. During the course of the war, the traffic carried on these strategic lines (although frequently destroyed by the Japanese) included over 58,000 tons of stores, ammunition and other supplies, 75,132 sick and wounded, and 24,786 other troops.

The Russian achievement in keeping their one single-track Trans-Siberian line open was remarkable, but ultimately inadequate. The build-up of troops had come too late.

Impressive as the Trans-Siberian was, Russia was, in fact, distinctly behind Western nations in many respects in the war of 1904–

1905. The need for placing her military transport system on a sounder basis was among the many lessons she learned and acted upon as the result of her experience in the ill-fated war with Japan.

Because of its remote location, the Russo-Japanese War of 1904–05 has often been seen as a conflict of limited importance. Yet it was, to that time, the largest, most technologically advanced and complex war the world had ever witnessed. It was a prelude to the sort of war that broke out a decade later in Western Europe. It featured modern weapons like the machine gun, trench warfare, barbed wire, naval mines and torpedoes, heavy artillery, armored steam battleships, electric communications by telegraph and telephone, and of course the railroad that changed the nature and scale of warfare. The Russo-Japanese War brought recognition to Japan as a major world power. Russia's defeat in the war increased the Russian public's dissatisfaction with the Tsarist government and precipitated substantial social upheavals in 1905–and ultimately led to the collapse of the Tsarist regime in 1917.

The Boer and Russo-Japanese Wars clearly displayed the important role of railroad—a crucial function confirmed during the First World War, which started in 1914.

PART 2

Railroads in World War I

HISTORICAL BACKGROUND

Developed in the 19th century, the concept of a nation-in-arms came to full fruition with the fusion of manpower, technical, managerial and political components during the First World War (1914–1918). Technically World War I demonstrated that the early 20th century had put into the hands of the major industrialized nations war machines of far greater power than any known before. The world in which war broke out in 1914 was much different from the mid–Victorian era of the 1870s. Northern and central Europe largely industrialized in that period with a remarkable growth of railroad. It was a clash of modern 20th-century technology with old-fashioned 19th-century tactics and ways of thinking, resulting in appalling casualties. Metallurgists and ballistics experts made machine guns and artillery weapons ever more accurate and powerful. Communications, which then included the telephone and wireless radio, were swifter. Logistics became ever more voluminous and therefore more complicated than before. Railroad lines were more numerous and more efficient, while gasoline-powered vehicles started to appear in great number. Decisive World War I lethal innovations included the airplane, the tank, poison gas, the flame thrower, and the oceangoing submarine armed with torpedoes. To make matter worse, the technical advances were accompanied by a near-collapse of the forces previously serving to limit war, including that of common prudence. Indeed, the development of new weapons and the growth of the railroad in the period 1870–1915 convinced many military and political leaders that attack was the best means of defense. As a result, despite previous evidence clearly demonstrating the contrary, most European powers adopted a military strategy characterized by offensive operations based on a quick and massive mobilization of their forces, immediately followed by a smashing rush resulting in a decisive and fast victory—at least in theory. World War I was indeed a barbaric and purposeless war which no one seemed to know how to prevent, and which, once started, no one seemed able to stop, as all belligerents were convinced that they had to hurtle headlong into offensive action in order to gain the initiative. Actually, that was a huge mistake. Another tragic error was the belief that artillery would smash a way through to victory. The Western Front in France was particularly noteworthy for the mass of artillery employed by all sides.

The hasty end of hostilities in November 1918 left German soldiers still on French ground.

This was the source of the myth called *Dolchstoss* ("stab in the back"), later exploited by Hitler, that Germany had not really lost the war but had been betrayed by enemies of the German people at home: the Jews, democrats, communists, pacifists and profiteers.

Transport by Rail

The populations of all World War I belligerent nations were deeply involved in the conflict. Coal mines worked at full strength, ammunition plants rose from the ground as mushrooms, and weapon factories and shipyards worked around the clock to make good losses suffered at land and at sea. The burden thrown on transport (horse and rail, and later in the war motor vehicles) was considerably larger than that borne by the supply trains during the wars of the late 19th century. The heavy industry of the mass-production age produced locomotives, cars and trucks by which transportation was revolutionized. At the same time it spewed out an enormous quantity of weapons and ammunition that massive armies devoured in short time as rates of consumption increased exponentially.

The railroad system became essential and crucial and, to start with, an integral part of the mobilization procedure. Because mobility had been increased, it became imperative to reach the front before the enemy. This brought immense dangers. Without a breathing space between the call to arms and the opening of hostilities, there was no time for second thoughts or last-minute diplomatic efforts to avert war. Railroad movement to the front was rigid and complicated; once started, the program could hardly be halted, and mobilization became a virtual declaration of war. All World War I belligerents were concerned with the need for careful preparation, which went along with mass production. The mobilization plan was the principal peacetime tenet to each general staff. It was a complicated set of secret documents to regulate the movement of millions of men, hundreds of thousands of horses, and millions of tons of supplies. It was in fact a vast detailed railroad timetable, and the plan's limits were fixed by the railroads' capacities. About military railroad organization, the First World War threw up again the same basic questions of control and administration.

On the whole these issues were resolved after the manner that experience had demonstrated to be right. That was first by making the railroad service in the military zone a military service, but independent of the army's other activities on the technical side. And secondly by ensuring that the traffic put on rail was controlled throughout by a specialized staff, which was ultimately responsible directly to the commander-in-chief and was independent of the authority of local commanders.

The mobilization of 1914 justified all the efforts the European general staffs had put into the perfecting of railroad organization in the preceding years of peace. Enormous armies were picked up from their peacetime garrison and mobilization places, and swiftly conveyed to the battlefields within a month after the declaration of war. This included, for example, 62 French infantry divisions (each with 15,000 men), 87 German, 49 Austrian, and 114 Russian. Of course, crowding and discomfort in troop transports were common, but on the whole, soldiers did not complain, as all sides expected a short and victorious conflict. Once they had arrived, however, soldiers found that the almost miraculous mobility conferred by rail movement evaporated. Indeed, trains were very vulnerable at the front itself when within range of enemy artillery. Face to face with each other, belligerents were no better able to move their heavy weapons and supplies than Napoleonic troops and ancient Roman legions had been. Forward of railheads, soldiers had to walk, and the only means of provisioning them, and transporting their heavy equipment and field artillery, was by horse-drawn vehicles. Even when the conflict developed into a deadlock in trenches in the West, the cult of the offensive preceded by tremendous artillery bombardments still had many followers, so it took some time before a coherent system of supplying entrenched armies was established.

In November 1914, with the ending of the war of movement, and the establishment of a static front line with trenches that stretched 200 miles from the English Channel through eastern France to (neutral) Switzerland, a different task emerged for the railroad. Neither side had anticipated a stalemate. All had planned a quick, decisive and victorious campaign. Neither side had prepared for a static war of attrition. The railroad networks were highly developed, but motor transport was still in its infancy. In the first two years of the war, there were indeed very few motor vehicles, and these were reserved for generals and senior staff officers. Besides, the location of the fighting lines was determined by topography rather than accessibility. So troops and supplies were brought to large railheads behind the front, and then goods and artillery were dispatched by horse-drawn carts and wagons while the men slogged along to reach their combat trenches. Railroads lacked the flexibility of motor transport, and this disadvantage had repercussion on the conduct of the war. Later in the war, transport trucks became an integral part of the logistics in all belligerent armies. But in 1914, motor vehicles were few and primitive, suffering accidents and breakdowns on bad roads that were dry dust trails in the summer and became impassable quagmires when it was raining.

As the war went on, logistics activities behind the static front line of trenches became increasingly mechanized. Reserves, ammunition and supplies were moved on a large scale by conventional railroads to dumps and railheads, and then conveyed by trucks and by means of another type of railroad running on tracks, as we shall see below. Full tracked artillery tractors appeared, capable of crossing rough and muddy terrain. However, moving artillery on the front line remained largely a horse-drawn affair, and horse-drawn wagons remained important means of supplying the entrenched armies until the end of hostilities. During the war, in all armies forage for pack animals took more space than ammunition for

the weapons or food for the men. Fodder was indeed the largest cargo at French ports for the British army on the Western Front until 1918.

Despite its disadvantage in the close vicinity of the combat zones, the railroad once again allowed for mass troop movement, increasing the slaughter to gigantic proportions. Without doubt the train, the machine gun and heavy artillery brought about the butchery of the First World War. The Western Front in France, opposing Germany to the Franco-British allies, was the most important battlefield. Inevitably the magnitude of the carnage there overshadowed events and operations elsewhere. It should not be forgotten, though, that the war was fought on many other fronts where new or existing railroads played an important role, such as in South Tyrol, northern Italy, the Balkans, Russia, Palestine, Greece, Mesopotamia, and a number of forgotten campaigns in Africa.

With motor transport and aerial bombardment both still in infancy, World War I undoubtedly marks the high point of mass use of the railroad at war—in particular the specialized military system. Without the railroad it would have been difficult, if not impossible, to deploy and supply millions of combatants.

The war placed a considerable strain on the civilian rail networks, and had a decisive impact on the development of railroad equipment—particularly the rapid improvement of gasoline- and diesel-engine machines, as well as narrow-gauge networks. It was also during World War I that there appeared the first gasoline-powered vehicles intended for use both on road and on track by replacing rubber tires with metallic flanged wheels.

Since operable locomotives were at a premium during war or even in peacetime, it was not always economical to use them on missions for which a smaller and cheaper vehicle would suffice. Therefore, for the purpose of inspecting tracks, delivering small amounts of supply to isolated posts, and performing scout and reconnoiter missions, the concept of the *draisine* (self-propelled armored lightly armed trolley) was developed. The term draisine comes from the German Baron Karl Christian Ludwig Drais von Sauerbronn, who in 1817 invented the first successful, two-wheeled, steerable human-propelled bicycle, called a draisine or velocipede. Later the term designated a small human-powered railroad vehicle (also called speeder or handcar), until it designated a light armored self-propelled rail-car—a sort of mobile tank purposely designed for use on rail.

Another military use of train was mobile headquarters, and most World War I senior commanders had special trains with rather comfortable coaches serving as living quarters with bathrooms, lavatories and bedrooms, as well as kitchens, pantries, restaurants and dining rooms for VIPs and their assistants, aides, clerks, staff personnel, and guests. Such a train, of course, included supply and service cars and coaches serving as map and staff meeting rooms, telephone exchange, power plant, a car for bodyguards, etc. In 1918 the English King George V (reigned 1910–1936) made an inspection tour in France. For the occasion, engineers of the 2nd Army constructed a special railcar with a hut at one end and an observation verandah at the other,

Top: *Railroad handcar. Also called a pump trolley, pump car, jigger, velocipede, kalamazoo, or draisine, the handcar was a railroad car powered by its passengers. The illustration shows a typical hand-operated design consisting of an arm, called the walking beam, that pivots seesaw-like on a base, which the passengers alternately push down and pull up to move the car's wheels.*
Bottom: *Powered draisine. Developed in the late 1890s in the USA, the powered draisine (also known as a speeder, railroad motor car, putt-putt, crew car, jigger, trike, quad, or trolley) is a small rail personnel vehicle generally powered by a gasoline or electric engine. It was mostly used for inspection and maintenance of the track, or for moving work crews quickly to and from work sites on the line. Today vintage speeders are often used for tourist recreation.*

both covered with corrugated-iron plates. It was inside Marshal Ferdinand Foch's personal railroad coach that the Armistice, putting an end to hostilities on the Western Front, was signed at Rethondes in the forest of Compiègne, France, on November 11, 1918. Twenty-two years later, by order of a vengeful Adolf Hitler, the very same coach was used at the very same location for the signing of France's surrender on June 22, 1940. The Rethondes railcoach was subsequently taken to Germany, displayed in Berlin, and put up during the Second World War at the stations of Ruhla, Ohrdruf and Crawinkel. Finally the coach was destroyed by fire in April 1945 by order of Hitler.

So railroads played a crucial role in World War I, and everywhere railroad men performed the best they could. However, due to intensive use, maintenance neglect and overwork, there was a dangerous decline of safety. All belligerent nations put an enormous stress on maintenances, and inevitably there was a dramatic increase in incidents such as derailments, collisions and deadly accidents.

Ambulance Trains

By the end of the 19th and beginning of the 20th centuries, impressive advances in medicine were of considerable account in preventing disease and epidemics. Owing to significant medical and surgical development, soldiers in the First World War had more chance to survive wounds than any of their predecessors on countless battlefields in the past—provided they could be evacuated and treated in time, which of course was not always possible. As with many aspects of the military use of the railroads, the lessons on the provision of medical evacuation trains had to be relearned, despite the experience and progress made in previous wars. The Boer and Russo-Japanese Wars had attracted much public interest on the subject of the evacuation of the wounded, but quite astonishingly none of the belligerents entering World War I had de-

signed a worked-out program to cope with casualties. Ambulance trains made improvements between 1914 and 1918, but developments were slow and haphazard. Although medical evacuation of casualties to the rear with as little further harm as possible in specially adapted cars became more common, in the early months of World War I, evacuation of wounded was made up mainly of freight boxcars fitted with racks to support stretchers, and supplemented by straw-strewn vans for the lightly wounded. These trains were easy to load and unload, since the doors were wide. But the carriages could not easily be heated or ventilated; they offered no conveniences for administrative work, and it was very difficult for the medical personnel to attend to their patients once the train was running. Moreover, unless the vans were drawn from passenger trains (and this was comparatively rare), they were mounted on four wheels only, had very ineffective springs, and practically no brakes. These primitive trains were gradually replaced with trains built up of ordinary passenger coaches supplemented by a saloon or restaurant car for administrative purposes. The compartments were so arranged that they had a capacity of four stretcher cases lying at right angles to the line of travel. Most of the coaches used had six or eight wheels, were much better sprung, and had better brakes than simple freight cars. They were also much better lighted, ventilated and heated, but loading and unloading was not easy, since the doors were narrow. Also only rarely was it possible to arrange for intercommunication between all the carriages, so that some of them could be visited only by doctors walking along the foot-board or by stopping the train. There was much discussion about the best way of installing beds in an ambulance car. The American favored rubber loops into which the stretcher handles could be inserted. The Germans chose a hammock-like system. The Russians developed a system of suspended springs. Gradually better types of ambulance cars were introduced, often partly of corridor car coaches for patients able to sit up, partly of specially constructed ward carriages intercommunicating cars with tiers of berths down each side and a middle passageway between them. These berths were open at the ends, and had both wire and ordinary mattresses and blankets and sheets, and the patients were habitually put to bed in them, unless for some reason, such as the existence of an injury to the spinal column, it was desired to avoid moving a patient off his stretcher. In such cases the stretcher was laid on the top of the berth. Various types existed, for example, with tiers of beds arranged parallel to the line of travel, and capacities were also various depending on the size of the cars. The ward carriages had wide external as well as internal doors, so that they were easy to load and unload, and the train was electrically lighted, and heated by steam from end to end. The wide doors of communication between the carriages allowed doctors and nurses to attend to the patients, as they afforded a passage from one end of the train to the other. All ward carriages were mounted on well-sprung eight-wheeled chassis often with compressed-air automatic or hydraulic brakes. There was, of course, not only one arrangement possible for a medical evacuation train, and obviously a great variety existed. There could be, for example, working from the engine and tender backwards: a coach with its compartments arranged as sleeping quarters for the medical staff and nursing personnel; a kitchen coach; several ward carriages; an administrative carriage, providing an office, a room for the performance of operations, and a dispensary; four or five coaches for sitting-up patients; a carriage for general cooking purposes; a coach to serve as sleeping quarters for the subordinate personnel; a van for stores; and a guard's van. Information as to the hour of the probable arrival of the ambulance train was telegraphed or telephoned at its destination to an officer who met the train with a sufficient number of stretcher-bearers and horse-drawn or motor ambulance cars to distribute the patients promptly among various hospitals. As soon as the patients had been unloaded, the whole train was cleaned, bed linen changed, dirty linen dispatched to the laundry, and fresh supplies of stores loaded. Then the train could start another journey.

Narrow-Gauge Railroad

The First World War saw a great development of the narrow-gauge rail, a technology intended to solve the problem of keeping soldiers supplied during the long static trench warfare phase. The large concentrations of soldiers and artillery at the front lines required delivery of enormous quantities of food, fresh water, and ammunition as well as fortification construction materials (e.g., tools, planks, corrugated plates, beams and

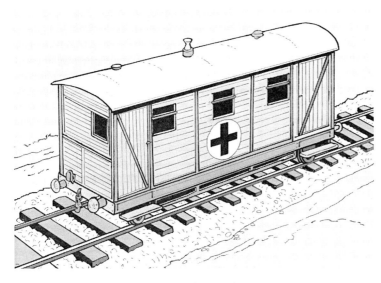

Ambulance car.

barbed wire) in areas where peacetime civilian transportation facilities had been damaged or destroyed. Reconstruction of conventional roads and railroads was too slow, and fixed facilities were attractive targets for enemy artillery. So narrow-gauge railroads were widely employed.

As already said, a narrow-gauge track was provided in prefabricated sections and could be laid quickly even by unskilled labor. Teams of laborers and squads of soldiers could quickly assemble, repair, or extend prefabricated 5-meter sections of track weighing about 100 kilograms along roads or over smooth terrain. To support the weight on marshy, uneven or devastated ground so often encountered near the front lines, an improvised roadbed could first be laid. It consisted of saplings and branches running parallel with the track. This was overlaid with perpendicular logs at less than one-yard intervals, then two lines of square timbers were laid end-to-end the same width as the track. Finally the track sections were laid atop the timbers and secured by spikes. The track distributed heavy loads to minimize development of muddy ruts through unpaved surfaces. These quickly laid trench railroads linked the front lines with standard-gauge railroad facilities beyond the range of enemy artillery. Small locomotives (and often manpower or mules) moved short trains of ten-ton capacity cars through areas of minimum clearance and small-radius curves. This was naturally not without danger, as the small trains operated near the front within enemy sight and fire. So transport generally took place at night. Derailments were common, but the light rolling stock was relatively easy to re-rail. On the way back, empty cars were often used to carry litters for returning wounded from the front to the rear. Steam locomotives typically carried a short length of flexible pipe (called a water-lifter) to refill water tanks from flooded shell holes. Steam locomotives produced a lot of smoke, which revealed their location to enemy artillery.

They often required fog or darkness to operate within visual range of the front, and therefore daylight transport usually used animal power or soldiers pushing. A great improvement to this vulnerable and primitive system was the introduction of smokeless diesel or gasoline-engined rail tractors. However, large quantities of hay and grain were carried to the front as horses and mules remained an essential part of military logistics. In many cases the grounds right at the rear of the static front line was so shell-torn that even installing light narrow-gauge railroad networks proved impossible, the more so when the rain turned wide zones into impassable morasses. There supplies had to be laboriously brought up on foot or on animals.

Germany and France were rather well prepared and equipped with 60-cm light railroad, but Britain was not. Indeed, British commanders thought that a war of movement could break out at any moment and narrow-gauge railroads were not needed. Only in 1915, when it dawned on them that static warfare was to last longer than expected, did they conform and develop excellent light trains on narrow-gauge tracks.

At their peak by the end of the war in 1918 on the Western Front there were more than 1,000 miles of narrow-gauge railroads on the Allied side of the front. They connected to dumps, marshaling yards and numerous stations where supplies could be transferred from standard-width gauge to front line narrow-gauge trains. As for the Germans, they had installed even more mileage and installations both on the Western and Eastern Fronts.

Railroad Artillery

The First World War was an artillery war par excellence, witnessing the dramatic development of indirect fire and artillery fire control. Although artillery mounted on railroad had already been used since at least the 1860s, it was not until World War I that rail guns reached their true potential. Indeed, the war brought the heavy railroad gun into prominence. It was primarily a weapon of continental powers that, with numerous borders to defend or attack, required their heavy reserve artillery to be highly mobile. By the end of the 19th century, new heavy rail artillery pieces had been designed, but there had been little opportunity to use them except in a few occasions in the Franco-Prussian War and the Boer War in South Africa. World War I was to prove the testing ground and railroad artillery came into full flower.

When trench warfare developed in 1915, it seemed to many generals that the only solution to win the war was the use of more powerful projectiles fired by bigger and heavier guns, in order to tear holes in the opposition, wreck barbed wire, demolish trenches, and finally steamroll a breach through enemy lines. As the war progressed, field and railroad heavy guns became increasingly larger and numerous. The naval guns of the day were the largest guns, and often weighed hundreds of tons apiece. Thus, a method for transporting these guns was essential, and railroads became the favored means. As each belligerent nation increased the firepower and range of its heavy artillery, the other nations responded likewise in order to prevent the technological superiority of any given military power. The largest U.S., British, and French rail guns were, however, severely outranged by the German Krupp, Max E., and Paris guns. Particularly on the Western Front, monster guns mounted on railcars did have a definite value in long-range harassment of enemy rear area. Although they had not a great rate of fire and although they had a limited traverse (often requiring a special siding—called a firing curve—pointing in the appropriate direction), they had a considerable demoralizing effect when firing on villages and towns miles behind the front. Besides, they had a great mobility and could rapidly move from one position to another owing to the dense railroad network in northern France, western Germany, and Belgium. In order to thwart air observation from airplanes, railroad guns were very often painted in a brown/green motley pattern, placed under camouflage nets, or whenever available, concealed in forests or hidden inside tunnels. Many railroad guns had their own locomotive and service cars for their numerous crews. Shells were stored and transported in an ammunition car placed at the rear of the gun and brought up to the breech for loading by a hoisting device.

The attrition trench warfare of the Western Front was dominated by artillery, requiring a vast manufacture of guns and ammunition, which were brought by rail. Despite their sophistication, range and enormous power, field

World War I landscape. As a result of endless artillery bombardments, the front line and no man's land were torn up into impassable quagmires. Indeed, battlefields were often shattered, churned up, and deformed by shell craters full of rainwater, with trees smashed to stumps. Roads, woods, forests, fields, meadows, farms, villages and any other signs of peacetime civilian country life were no longer recognizable.

guns, mortars, howitzers and heavy rail-mounted artillery pieces did little to break the stalemate that settled on the Western Front. Intended to batter the enemy into submission, artillery achieved much less than expected. Because of intensive and prolonged artillery bombardments, battlefields were churned up into wasteland so characteristic of World War I. As a result, mobile warfare was paralyzed by the devastation that the intensive use of heavy artillery could bring within impressive range. It was the massive intervention of the USA in 1918, and the introduction of the tracked armored fighting vehicle (known as the tank), with its promise of a new method of beating down barbed wire and neutralizing machine guns without having to shell them for days beforehand, which finally helped to break the entrenched stalemate and brought back mobile warfare and victory to the Allies.

Armored Trains

Although armored trains were one of the growing forms of armored vehicles that took their place alongside early armored cars and primitive tanks, they played only a limited role during World War I—at least on the static Western front. In spite of the success they had enjoyed in the Boer War, none of the major belligerents had considered the use of armored trains in their attack plans. At the beginning of the war, the British War Office had commissioned two armored trains, deploying one on the coast of Norfolk and the other near Edinburgh, for an eventual German invasion that never came. On the Continent, the Belgian Army had four armored trains in 1914, and the German forces had some armored trains operating in the region of Belfort. All those trains briefly saw action in the opening (mobile) phase of World War I. When the front congealed into static attrition trench/siege warfare in late 1914, they became useless and were withdrawn.

By and large, the Western Front in northern France, with its wide and complicated static trench systems, offered indeed no opportunity for armored trains. But on the Eastern Front, Germany and Austria fought a rambling war of movement against Russia. On the Eastern Front and in the Middle East, the areas to be covered were so vast, and the distances from the supply bases so great, that trench warfare in the European style could not occur. On those fronts, military authorities regarded them with interest. All belligerents developed armored trains, principally to protect their supply lines through the long expanses of Poland and steppes of Russia. At a time when airplanes were in their infancy, and provided there was a continuous and unbroken stretch of railroad track, as well as reserves of coal and water available at regular intervals, advantages of armored trains were many. In vast lands like Russia with only a few roads, its towns and urban centers separated by huge distances, trains offered an innovative way to quickly move troops and firepower into position. They could travel from one locale to another in a rapid fashion practically in all sorts of weather. They played an important support role by accompanying infantry or cavalry. They combined armed units with impressive lethal firepower, offering the combat commander extraordinary flexibility. The First World War also saw the appearance of the rail cruiser and armored draisine, a sort of tank on rail armed with artillery and machine guns often placed in rotating turrets. However, the great potentiality and qualities of armored vehicles on rail were not yet fully understood and exploited by the military authorities in general.

FRANCE

Transport

The Franco-Prussian War of 1870–71 was considered in France as unfinished business. The French wanted both provinces of Alsace and Lorraine back. An added source of tension was the colonial expansion, notably Morocco, where German and French interests and prestiges clashed. When war broke out in 1914, the French were determined to take their revenge in a quick and victorious campaign that would bring them to Berlin. The tragic lessons of 1870 were not forgotten, and the mobilization of troops and transport by train were carried out rather smoothly.

Right before World War I, France made

provision for military control of the civilian private railroad companies in time of war, especially in the case of the Nord (North) and Est (East) Companies, the enemy obviously being Germany. When World War I broke out, the French, with the war being fought on their own soil, mobilized their railroad staff at their posts. There were a few French railroad troops in the field, in different numbers as required from time to time, but the main force remained with the private railroad companies, which came under military control exercised by a Commission du Réseau (Network Committee) for each system.

However, the French railroad and France's military plans had been largely disrupted by the speed and magnitude of the German advance in the autumn of 1914. They had lost a considerable amount of stock, and many important engineering works near the front lines were destroyed before the fronts stabilized. The French had to rely upon rapid improvisation before effective procedures were adopted and before standard war locomotives and rolling stock appeared in quantity. One the most spectacular improvisations took place during the Battle of the Marne (September 5–12, 1914) when some 6,000 French reserve troops were transported by Parisian taxicabs to the front. In the aftermath of this battle, both sides dug in, and four years of gruesome stalemate ensued.

Top: *French Crochat type 22 LN2 Locomotive. The Henri Crochat Company from Paris built about 320 of these gas/electric engine locomotives between 1908 and 1918.*

Bottom: *Chemin de Fer Meusien. Built in 1878, the private local railroad was the only one left when the Germans started their offensive against Verdun. Placed under control of the 10th Section of French Military Field Railroad, it played an important logistical role during the battle of Verdun. The line survived World War I and was closed only in 1936.*

At the Battle of Verdun—a pointless carnage, which between February and December 1916 accounted for many thousands of both French and German casualties—the Germans had expected their better logistics be decisive and victorious. But in due course they underestimated the resilience and flexibility of the French. The best-known French transport system was the notorious meandering, narrow, unpaved, 75-km-long *Voie Sacrée* (Sacred Road), linking the railhead and dumps at Bar le Duc at the rear to the site of the battle. About 50,000 solid-tired trucks were collected from all over France to supply besieged Verdun with men and ammunition. The traffic frequency on that road was about one truck every twenty seconds, so any vehicle that broke down was simply pushed off the road. Without the automobile, Verdun would probably not have withstood the siege, but the railroad also played a role.

Much less known and unsung was the windy *Chemin de Fer Meusien* (Meuse River Railroad) that ran quite parallel to the road. At the time, this local 1-meter-gauge railroad line had 800 freight cars and 75 locomotives that operated up to 35 trains a day, and carried a substantial proportion of supplies—about one-third of the garrison's need. Later in the war, improvements, both technical and operational, allowed for running about 150 daily trains.

The French railroads also had to cope with the deployment of thousands of troops and supplies for the British Expeditionary Forces stationed in northern France. Amazingly, the British accepted without demur that a part of their logistics system be manned and controlled by the French.

Narrow-Gauge Railroads

With the coming of static trench warfare, the roads leading to the front suffered severely from the constant traffic of motor vehicles and horse-drawn wagons, as well as marching troops, especially in bad weather. As a result, quickly built, easily repaired and flexible narrow-gauge railroads proved extremely useful and even indispensable. France had developed portable Decauville railroads for agricultural areas, mining, and temporary construction projects. The French standardized 60-centimenter-gauge military Decauville equipment (adopted by Germany, the British War Department Light Railroads, and later by the United States Army Transportation Corps) was considerably developed and encouraged by the army.

Although the doctrine of the offensive at all cost permeated the French staff, and although it was confidently expected before the war that combat would be fought on enemy (German) soil, extensive permanent networks of narrow-gauge railroads were established behind the front. These improvised narrow lines were crude; they had no lights and no signals. The trains ran on unstable ballast hastily placed on mud, and they were rather slow (about six to eight miles per hour), but despite their small size, narrow-gauge trains had a remarkably heavy workload. Hauling on these small single-track lines was by animals or by manpower, or using small gasoline or diesel locomotives. Captain Péchot of the French Artillery designed a 10-ton Fairlie articulated 0-4-4 locomotive. The French military had 62 Péchot-Bourdon types built between 1888 and 1914. But French industry was put under such pressure that locomotives had to be imported from abroad. The U.S. Pennsylvanian Baldwin Locomotive Works Company built 280 more during the war. Two hundred fifty 8-ton 0-6-0T of Decauville's Progrès design were built for military service. Thirty-two 0-6-0T of American design and six hundred 55 kW gasoline mechanical locomotives were purchased from Baldwin Locomotive Works. Gasoline-driven tractors and electric locomotives were also used, since they made much less noise and did not produce a cloud of smoke. In many areas, however, the ground was so churned up that supplies had to be carried by men or mules—an operation that required extraordinary amount of effort and manpower. It was also a dangerous affair, as the front line was within range of enemy artillery.

Baldwin 0-6-0. Some hundred U.S. designed Baldwin 0-6-0ST were produced for the French Artillery Railroad in 1916. The simple although rather low-slung locomotive was fitted with a water lifter to enable it to take water anywhere, and a chimney was equipped with a large spark arrester since the machine often pulled ammunition trains.

French Rail Artillery

France was possibly the most prolific nation in the production of railroad artillery. The outbreak of the First World War saw the French army with a shortage of heavy field artillery. In compensation, large numbers of heavy static fortress coastal defense guns and naval guns were moved to the front, but these were typically unsuitable for field use and required some kind of mounting. So existing naval or coastal fortress guns and mortars converted to railroad mounts provided the obvious solution. The French pioneered the use of curved offshoot tracks for field of fire. Given the static front conditions in the period 1915–18, and the proliferation of rail feeder lines, which sprang into being behind the Western Front, the railroad gun was in its element and France built a large and innovative arsenal of railroad artillery. The Artillerie Lourde sur Voie Ferrée (ALVF; heavy railroad artillery) included several types designed by the Saint Chamond, Schneider and Batignolles companies. These rail guns were very heavy with impressive long range, like the St. Chamond 240 mm, the Schneider 320 mm, or the Batignolle 320 mm rail-mounted gun, which could fire shells weighing 454 kg (1,000 lb). The 370 mm (15-in) railroad gun could fire a 500 kg projectile to a maximum range of 16 km (ten miles). The St. Chamond 400 mm gun mounted on tracks was capable of firing 680 kg (1,500 lb) shells. The French also had a 370 mm mortar, firing 113 kg (250 lb) shells over 5 miles with a quick rate of fire. On the whole, the French had a high proportion of heavy caliber weapons and used a greater number of guns than the British in the bombardment, with devastating results. Most World War I French ALVF were moved by locomotive type 140 produced by the British Company Vulcan Foundry. Seventy units were purchased between 1915 and 1920 and designated ALVF 1 to 70. In 1920 these locomotives were declassed and sold to the civilian Compagnie des Chemins de Fer de l'Est (Eastern Railroad Company) and to the Compagnie des Chemins de Fer de Paris à Lyon et à la Méditerranée (PLM Southern Railroad Company). The French guns served their purpose, and as World War I went on, better and stronger pieces were developed and produced. By the time the war ended, the French possessed a formidable collection of ALVF, of which many remained in service until the Second Word War.

GREAT BRITAIN

Transport

The story of the work and growth of military transportation in World War I bears the normal imprint of early British campaigns. Begun on too small a scale with limited

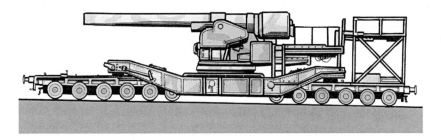

St. Chamond 240 Mle 93/96. The Saint Chamond 240 mm (9.45 in) Model 93/96 was a gun extracted from the coastal defenses of various French colonies, returned to France and mounted on a railroad carriage by the Saint Chamond Company. The gun was emplaced on its coastal pedestal, allowing it to traverse the full circle and fire in any direction. To support the gun when firing across the track, outriggers were provided for the rear side and rail clips for the muzzle side. If firing over the ends of the carriage, elevation was limited to 29 degrees; otherwise the recoiling breech would strike the raised end of the carriage. The gun was provided with an ammunition car, which coupled to the rear and had an overhead crane system enabling the crew to deliver projectiles to the loading platform behind the breech. The carriage had an overall length of 19.5 m (64 ft), and weighed in action 140,000 kg (137.75 tons). The gun had a muzzle velocity of 840 m/sec (2755 ft/sec), its high-explosive shell weighed 162 kg (357 lb), and had a maximum range of 23 km (25,159 yards).

Schneider 320 mm. The Schneider 320 mm (12.55 in) Model 1870/93 was another of many naval or fortress guns pressed into service on the Western Front. No recoil system was provided, so recoil was absorbed by the entire mounting and wheels, which slid backwards along the track. The gun was rigidly installed on its mount, so there was no traverse; the gun was pushed around a curved siding track until the barrel pointed in the required position. After firing several rounds, the whole carriage had to be brought back to its original position. The carriage had a length of 25.9 m (85 ft), and weighed in action 162,000 kg (159.3 tons). The gun had a muzzle velocity of 675 m/sec (2215 ft/sec), it fired a 388 kg (854.5 lb) shell to a maximum range of 24,800 km (27,120 yards).

resources and with no provision made for expansion, British military railroad was improvised against time at immense expense. The Railroad Executive Committee had been created as early as 1912 in order to coordinate the railroad companies and the military, but on the whole, the outbreak of World War I found Britain rather unprepared. However, military railroads soon became a very large branch of the British forces in France, working closely with the French.

Britain also organized an effective cross-Channel ferry service involving a complete new port at Richborough just north of Sandwich on the coast of Kent. Indeed, Great Britain had the problem of having first to ship all troops, supplies and equipment across the Channel before they could join in the war. By the end of 1917, Richborough—at the same time a training base, shipyard and ferry terminal—had expanded to 2,200 acres of sidings, berths, barracks and workshops. Operating day and night, the base was connected to the South Eastern & Chatham Railroad. War matériel, including military railroad equipment, was shipped over to French harbors in freight ships and seagoing barges with a capacity of 1,000 tons. In 1916, shipping became a dangerous affair owing to Germany's aggressive naval attacks using submarines and torpedoes to sink any Allied ship in the Channel and the North Sea.

Once in France, the key to success of logistics was the appointment of French-speaking railroad transport officers and clerks in the principal depots and stations (notably at Amiens) in good liaison with the French military and railroad authorities. The Railroad Operation Division on the Western Front created new stations, extra sections of lines and a series of important cross-country links. Its personnel numbered 18,400, organized in 67 companies. At its peak at the time of the Armistice (November 1918), there were in all 76,000 transportation troops; in addition, 48,000 labor servicemen engaged on work for the railroad department.

Britain alone produced more than 25,000 artillery pieces between 1914 and 1918 and expended more than 170,000,000 shells of all calibers. However, the smooth machinery sometimes jammed; for example, in May 1915 before the British attack in the Battle of Frezenberg Ridge near Ypres. There was a continuous four-day bombardment by 433 guns and howitzers, but this used up so much of the stock of ammunition that there was not enough left to give adequate support to the attack, resulting in a bloody failure. The nineteen-day bombardment at the Third Battle of Ypres in 1917 used 321 trainloads of shell, a year's production for 55,000 war workers. In September 1918, during the final offensive against the German positions, nearly one million projectiles were fired by British artillery in one twenty-four-hour period. These impressive tonnages were of course transported by rail.

The Somme offensive (launched by the British army between July 1 and November 18, 1916) was notable for the importance of air power, the first use of the tank, and the incredible casualties: no fewer than 794,238 British and 537,918 Germans. In their sectors in the Somme, the British engineers laid some 1,000 km of narrow-gauge railroad (60 cm was used in order to fit the French system) with about 700 steam locomotives and over a thousand gasoline- and electric-engined tractors. Close to the front, in the zone exposed to enemy fire, they established improvised but valuable light railroads, small trench tramways, rail trolleys, and even monorail and suspended ropeways. These were often blown up and damaged, but were directly repaired or rebuilt. After having brought stores, food, water, supplies and ammunition, they were used to evacuate wounded to dressing stations, and so saving them a painful journey plodding through shell-torn mud. Other light railroad lines were installed in order to interconnect all networks. After the war, some former British trench railroad equipment was put to civilian use—for example, rebuilding the village of Vis-en-Artois between Arras and Cambrai. The 60-cm railroad also proved invaluable in mid–1917 during the Passchendaele offensive, aka the Battle of Ypres in Flanders, another pointless carnage that cost 300,000 lives for an advance of only seven miles.

As the war dragged on, however, Britain's industry started to deteriorate. It could not build enough locomotives, and U.S. engines had to be imported. World War I locomotives used by the British included Hunslet Engine Company 4-6-0T designs; 15-ton 4-6-0 Baldwin locomotives; American Hudswell Clarke and Andrew Barclay Sons & Company 0-6-0T locomotives; 15-ton 2-6-2T of the American standard military designs were later purchased from ALCO's Cooke Locomotive Works for British use. Britain pioneered the use of gasoline and electric powered locomotives, called tractors, for daylight use within visual range of the front. Total production was 102 7-kW Ernest E. Baguley tractors, 580 15-kW Motor Rail tractors, and 220 30-kW Motor Rail tractors. An additional two hundred 30 kW gasoline-electric tractors were produced by British Westinghouse and Kerr Stuart. Twenty Hudswell-Clarke and Barclay 0-6-0T, seven ALCO 2-6-2T, and 26 Baldwin 4-6-0T remained in French service until 1957.

The British were among the first to convert gas-driven vehicles for use on both road and track. These improvised and primitive convertible hybrids included Ford Model T cars and Crewe tractors.

Between 1914 and 1918 more than 2.6 million British wounded soldiers were transported by ambulance trains. At first trains were not numerous, not comfortable, lacking supplies, and with a capacity of only 300 stretchers. Gradually the situation was improved, and by the end of the war the British had a fleet of thirty trains, most of them able to accommodate some 1,000 lying-down casualties.

Other Fronts

Britain was also fighting on other fronts, and there were military transportation units in Greece, Palestine and Mesopotamia. For example, at Saloniki, Greece, the joint Franco-British forces started with horse-drawn carts and soon established military railroad facilities to supply their static positions on the Struma and Dvina fronts. A large network of 60-cm railroad was constructed by a force of 4,000 Turkish prisoners of war. The Salonika front came into being in November 1915 as a belated and rather desultory attempt to help Serbia against Austria and Bulgaria. Beset from the start by indecision and lack of heavy equipment, this front too stagnated in a bloody static entrenched stalemate for most of World War I.

Great Britain was also militarily involved in the Middle East. The British officer Thomas Edward Lawrence (1888–1935), the legendary "Lawrence of Arabia" managed to rally Arab tribes in 1916. Lawrence and the rebellious Arabs waged a sort of guerilla warfare against the Ottoman Turks by repeatedly ambushing and blowing up sections of the important Hejaz Railroad lines thereby greatly thwarting Turkish lines of communication. In May 1917, British bombers attacked the Line at the station of Al-Ula. The Hejaz Railroad was a narrow gauge railroad (1,050 mm or 3 ft 5) built on the order of Ottoman ruler Sultan Abdulhameed II. Originally the Hejaz line was intended for transporting pilgrims heading to the Muslim sanctuary of Mecca in Saudi Arabia. The holy pilgrimage to Mecca is one of the five pillars of Islam. The railway line had a length of 1,300 kilometers (810 mi) but did not reach further than Medina, 400 kilometers (250 mi) short of Mecca, because its completion was opposed by the local Harb tribe claiming the loss of financial costs of transporting pilgrims on camel backs, the Sultan then proclaimed that the railway shall not go beyond Medina. The railway line started at

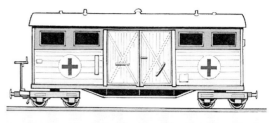

Right, top: *British World War I ambulance wagon.*

Right, above: *British Crewe tractor. Designed by engineer Crewe of the London & North Western Railroad Work, this convertible light vehicle used the chassis of a standard Ford Model T, and flanged railroad wheels fixed on a movable plate frame. About 132 of these strange railcars were used, but proved a failure as a tractor because their light weight produced only a poor adhesion on the rails.*

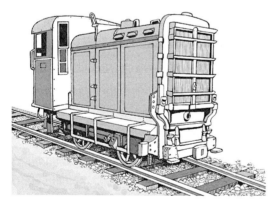

Left, top: *British Andrew Barclay Ltd. 0-4-0 switch locomotive. One of a motley collection of small steam locomotives, the Barclay 0-4-0 had a 14 in. by 21 in. cylinders, a boiler pressure of 160 lb/square inch, a wheelbase of 5 ft 6 in. and a coupled wheel diameter of 3 feet.*

Left, middle: *Locomotive S5 Kerr Stuart (1916). This locomotive, built in Stoke by the Kerr Stuart Company, was similar to engines produced by the French company Decauville.*

Left, bottom: *British Westinghouse gasoline-electric locomotive. Steam locomotives were too conspicuous for operating within range of enemy artillery, so smokeless electric or diesel machines were developed. The 4-wheel Westinghouse weighed 8 tons, and was powered by one 55-h.p. 4-cylinder water-cooled gasoline engine driving two 22.5-h.p. electric motors via a 30-kW generator set at 500 V.*

Top: *British Simplex armored locomotive. This four-wheeled gasoline tractor was totally armored for service near the front line. It had only narrow vision slits for the driver and was reputedly appallingly hot and noisy to operate. Only 27 were produced and put into service.*

Bottom: *Hejaz Railroad map.*

Damascus in Syria, had a secondary branch line to the port of Haifa on the Mediterranean Sea, and ran to Constantinople -the capital of the Ottoman Empire. Therefore the Hejaz Railway played an important religious, economic, political and military role.

British Rail Artillery

Following their experience in the Boer War, the British found that they could use numbers of naval gun barrels produced for reserve stocks, and proceeded to turn out rail mounting to suit. They developed and introduced notably three 12-inch (305 mm) railroad howitzers, and four 14-inch (356 mm) guns, which were engaged in France. A number of coastal heavy artillery 9.2-inch guns were placed on railroad mountings and sent to France too. Old Mark V and VI pieces, dating from 1888, were sent out first, soon followed by the new Mark XIV of 1916, which could fire a 380-in. shell to a range of 26,000 yards.

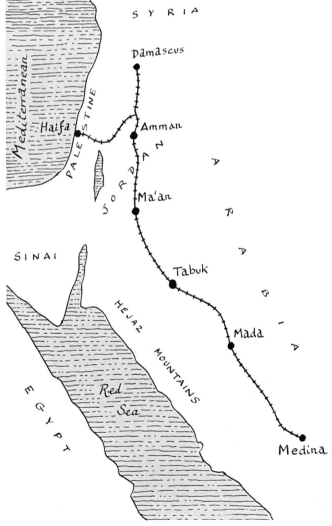

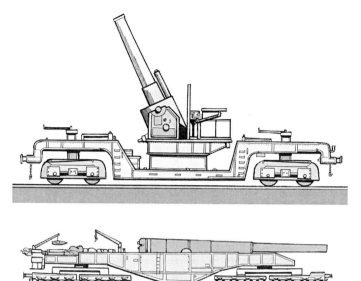

Top: *British 12 in. Howitzer Mark V. Designed by the Vickers Company, the Mark V had an all-round 360-degree traverse and was stabilized by jacks and outriggers when firing. The car had an overall length of 12.19 m (40 feet), weighed 77,168 kg (75.95 tons), and could fire a 340 kg (750 lb) shell to a maximum range of 12.121 m (14,350 yards). The long-lived Mark V was refurbished in 1939 and took service again as anti-invasion coastal gun during World War II.*

Bottom: *British 13.5 in. railroad gun. The carriage had an overall length of 26.62 m (87 ft 4 in), weighed 243,892 kg (240 tons), and could fire a 576 kg (1250 lb) shell to a distance of 36,575 m (22.72 miles). During World War II, the four guns designated Scene Shifter, Peacemaker, Gladiator and Boche-Buster were deployed at Dover as defense against a German invasion that in the end never came.*

UNITED STATES

In the early 1910s the United States of America wanted to observe strict neutrality and maintain national unity in a country where one in four people was born abroad or had parents born in the two European antagonistic blocs of alliance. But President Woodrow Wilson (1856–1924; presidency, 1913–1921) also warned Germany that submarine attacks against American ships supplying goods to Allied nations would mean war. Germany decided to take the risk, and tried to win the war by cutting off supplies to Britain, thereby sinking several American ships. The fact that the United States had huge economic investments with the British and French was another reason to go to war. If they were to lose, then they would not be able to pay the U.S. debt back. Then came the revelation of the Zimmermann Telegram, in which Germany attempted to enlist Mexico as an ally, promising Mexico that if Germany was victorious, she would support Mexico in winning back the states of Texas, New Mexico and Arizona from the U.S. Although there were large German communities living in the USA, a moral sense had developed in the United States that democratic Britain and the French Republic were fighting for the good cause and for freedom against dictatorship, aggression and evil. As a result, the United States Congress voted to declare war on Germany in April 1917.

American money, food, supplies and ammunition soon arrived, but it took some time to gather an army, which first had to be constituted, equipped, trained and transported across the Atlantic Ocean. In the summer of 1918, American soldiers under General John J. Pershing arrived at the rate of 10,000 a day. They were particularly welcomed by the French and the British, as they came at the right time to stop large-scale German offensives. After the Bolshevik Revolution of 1917, the new Russian regime had made peace with Germany, and as a result, German troops that until then had been deployed on the Russian Front were now transferred on the Western Front for new vigorous attacks in the spring of 1918. Thanks to the decisive American help in both men and supplies, the Franco-British Allies could win the war, while Germany was unable to replace its losses.

Transport

When the United States formally entered World War I in 1917, railroads were essential to the war effort. In the USA, matériel, supplies and weapons had to be moved from production plants to Atlantic ports from where they were shipped to France. Soldiers too were transported by train from home to training camps and to the same ports for the same destination. In 1917 the 700 American railroad companies were in a poor state, reluctant to work with each other, and not prepared to take the huge traffic the U.S. Army needed. By Christmas 1917 the predicament had reached a crisis point, forcing the government to intervene. The federal government assumed control of American railroads as a wartime measure, and President Wilson appointed his son-in-law, William McAdoo, to take the general direction and coordination of what became the National Railroad Administration. Then improvements occurred and soldiers and freight arrived in U.S. ports, whence they were shipped to Europe in time.

The American Expeditionary Force that deployed to France during World War I emphasized the need for a single transportation manager. William W. Atterbury, a former railroad executive, was appointed director-general of transportation, and a separate motor transport corps of the national army was established in August 1918.

In July 1917, the first U.S. soldiers from the 15th Engineering Regiment arrived in France. Their headquarters was installed at Tours, and they established the General Intermediate Supply Depot at Gièvres in the department of Loir-et-Cher in central France. They participated in the construction and operation of railroads between the Atlantic ports of Saint-Nazaire and Nantes and the front in the east, allowing the transport of 59 U.S. divisions.

Soon, because the existing French ports could not take the strain and amplitude of the U.S. traffic, other landing facilities were established at Brest (Pontanézen) and around Bordeaux (Bassens, Paulliac, La Rochelle-La Pallice, and Le Verdon-sur-Mer). From the French Atlantic harbors, the American Expeditionary Force troops were transported across France using two main railroad lines. The north line ran from Saint-Nazaire and Nantes to Tours, Vierzon, Bourges, Cosnes, Clamency, Auxerre and Saint-Dizier near the front. The south line ran from Bordeaux via Périgueux, Issoudin, Bourges, Nevers, Chagny, and Is-sur-Tille to Nancy, Lunéville, Saint-Dié and Belfort. The cities of Gièvres, Vierzon and Is-sur-Tille (with their marshaling yards) became huge troop camps, immense store dumps, and main dispatching points, being about halfway between Atlantic ports and the front. The Americans brought a lot of railroad equipment with them, including heavy steam locomotives, and small electric and gasoline rail tractors. Davenport Locomotive Works built one hundred 15-ton 2-6-2T, and Vulcan Iron Works built thirty more. Whitcomb built seventy-four 7-ton 4-wheel gasoline mechanical locomotives. The American troops used French rolling stock (notably the famous 40/8 boxcars), but the U.S. Army also brought their own railcars. Some 1,695 cars were built by Magor Car Corporation, American Car and Foundry, and Ralston Steel Car Company. Most were flatcars, but some had gondola sides, others had roofs (either with open sides or like conventional boxcars), and others carried shallow rectangular tanks with a capacity of ten thousand liters of fuel or drinking water. The boxcars and tank cars were regarded as top-heavy and prone to derailment; so most loads were carried on flatcars and gondolas. Approximately 1,600 four-wheel side dump cars were produced in several versions for construction and earth-moving purposes.

By the end of hostilities in November 1918, there were 1,981,704 U.S. troops in France. Of

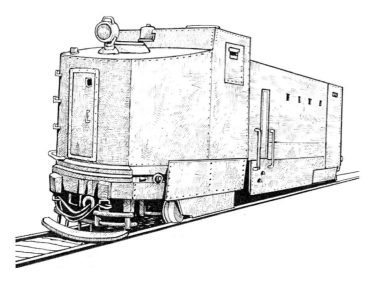

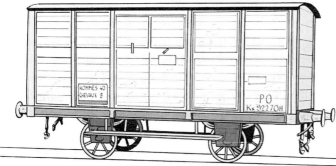

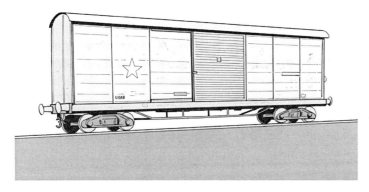

Top: *American armored locomotive. Locomotives were initially painted gray with black smoke boxes. White lettering was applied to early production, but black lettering was used in France. For service close to the front line, the U.S. military railroad made several projects of totally armored electric and gasoline locomotives.*

Middle: *Forty & Eight car. The "Forty and Eight" railcar draws its origin from World War I, when the United States troops were transported to and from the front in French boxcars. Each boxcar was stenciled 40/8, meaning that it could carry either 40 hommes ou 8 chevaux (40 men or 8 horses). The rather primitive and uncomfortable cars were cramped, only 20.5 feet long and 8.5 feet wide. Memories of riding in them were not always pleasant, so the cars became a symbol of misery, deep service, sacrifice and suffering. In 1920, the symbol 40/8 was used by a fraternity, formed within the American Legion. Later the fraternity became a veteran's charitable association (with secret ritual) named* La Société des Quarante Hommes et Huit Chevaux, *with national headquarters located at Indianapolis, Indiana.*

Bottom: *American freight car. The standard American military railroad car was 170 centimeters wide and 7 meters long, riding on two 4-wheel archbar bogies.*

these some 644,540 were in the Service of Supply (SOS) with the addition of 23,772 local civilians. By then the U.S. Army railroad personnel totaled some 30,400 soldiers operating 14,000 cars and 1,380 locomotives. There was also a huge fleet of cars, trucks, ambulances, and motorcycles, as well as many pack animals. Rail, wheels and hooves transported the American Expeditionary Forces into battle and victory. The arrival of American troops with their own matériel placed further strain on the already overloaded French railroad network, and caused tensions between the U.S. and French railroad workers. Nevertheless these difficulties should not mask the prodigious efficiency of Allied and American logistics that managed to bring enormous amounts of equipment, and huge numbers of men.

U.S. Rail Artillery

U.S. 14-in. railroad gun, 1918. Manufactured by Baldwin Locomotive Works in Philadelphia, Pennsylvania, this gun had a range of 38 km (42,000 yards). In 1918, it served to support General Pershing's army offensive in the Argonne sector and fired from the forest of Compiègne at the German railroad center of Tergnier in support of an Allied offensive. It remained in active service until the 1920s as U.S. coastal defense.

When the United States entered World War I in 1917 it was severely underequipped. The young country had fought several wars for its 140-odd years of existence, but its military had never fought a war in Europe. A scramble was underway to get the American Expeditionary Force (AEF) organized, armed and sent to France. One of the areas that needed the most attention was artillery. The U.S. Army was enthusiastic for railroad guns, and quickly adopted several French designs including the 75mm field gun and 155mm howitzer, but was still lacking in heavy artillery. As for the U.S. Navy, the possibility of using railroad guns as a mobile coast artillery reserve was appealing. Rear Admiral Ralph Earle of the U.S. Navy Ordnance Bureau recommended to the Chief of Naval Operations in November 1917 mounting naval 14-inch guns on trains to give the AEF long-range firepower. Two weeks later the Navy Department approved the construction of five guns as well as a command train. In May 1918 the Navy offered to turn the trains over to the Army, along with naval crews.

In August 1918 the guns arrived at Saint-Nazaire, France, and by September they were deployed to the front, where they fired their first shots. It was originally envisioned that the guns would attack targets deep in the enemy's rear, such as railroad yards, army headquarters, airfields, ammunition dumps, and bridges. They were also given the mission to destroy the infamous "Paris Guns" that were firing on the capital of France. But before the American guns could be brought into action, the Germans had withdrawn their super-heavy guns. The American gun #4 fired the last railroad battery round of the war on November 11, 1918, just before the armistice commenced. In the course of their short time in combat, the American guns were taken under counterbattery fire by German long-range guns on several occasions; one sailor and eight attached army engineers were killed. After the war, the guns were shipped back to the United States and kept in reserve for use as mobile coastal artillery. Accounts vary, but it is known that at least two guns continued in this service through World War II, although they never fired again after 1918.

The rise of the airplane effectively ended the usefulness of the railroad gun. Like the battleship, they were massive, expensive, and rather easily immobilized or destroyed from the air. Of the five guns that went to France in 1918, the only 14-inch Navy railroad gun still existing today is on display in front of the U.S. Navy Museum, Washington, D.C., Navy Yard.

Russia

The First World War also took place on Russia's western doorstep and in eastern central Europe, opposing Russia to the German Empire, the Austro-Hungarian Empire, and their allies. Unprepared militarily and industrially, Russia suffered demoralizing defeats (notably the Battle of Tannenberg, August 26–30, 1914). On the Eastern Front a very different kind of war took place. Unlike the Western Front, where a stalemate soon emerged, on the Russian front it was the absence of dense railroad networks that resulted in a relatively mobile conflict. Although Russia could mobilize reasonably quickly in August 1914, logistics and transport by train were hampered by the same kind of confusion and chaos that had characterized France's management during the 1870 war against Prussia. The Russians' misuse of telegraph and railroad (which had a different gauge) impeded them from profiting from their huge superiority in number of troops. The main Russian offensives were stopped, but their threat pinned down numerous German divisions, and tied up vast resources which otherwise could have been used against the French and the British on the Western Front.

The Eastern Front was also radically different in size. It was an immense theater of operation that stretched from the Baltic Sea through to Moscow, about 750 miles, and down to the Black Sea, another 1,000 miles. These huge distances and too few troops thwarted the establishment of any Western front-like static trench warfare. Instead a series of bloody battles were fought in these vast regions, particularly near key strong positions and along the axis of the few main railroad lines and important junctions. Taking over the enemy's rail lines was a characteristic of the war, as well as repairing the damage inflicted to the networks. There was also the issue of regauging long stretches of 5-ft line used by the Russians to the standard 4 ft 8-and-a-half

in. The Germans converted some 5,000 miles of track in Poland, Belarus and Lithuania. They had the advantage of superior railroads on their side, but they were overstretched by having to fight on two fronts, therefore lacking weapons and troops in sufficient number to bring about a decisive attack. As for the Russians, they had the manpower but no efficient logistic organization, and never enough trains to supply them, so their offensives often petered out.

It should be noted that during World War I the Murmansk Railroad was constructed. This 1,450-km-long line connects Saint Petersburg (in the south) and Murmansk (in the north). It has always been of vital military importance because Murmansk is an ice-free port on the Arctic Sea. The northern part of the line, between Petrozavodsk and Kola—with a length of 1,054 km—was built between 1915 and 1917, using a large number of German prisoners of war.

In every theater of operations where railroads played an important role, all belligerents obviously developed armored trains. As early as 1912 the Russians had built armored trains, similar in structure to those employed by Britain during the Boer War. Four of them took part in successfully combating Poland in the first months of the war. The fleet was greatly expanded, reaching a total of fifteen, seeing considerable combat actions until the end of Russia's involvement in the war in 1917.

The war on the Eastern Front came to an unexpected end when severe food shortages, inflation, economic collapse, bad management of the army and poor direction of the war caused internal unrest and a social revolution in Russia. By February of 1917, Russian workers, soldiers, and the general population had had enough of the despotic tsarist regime. Garrisons mutinied, riots broke out in St. Petersburg, and workers' soviets (revolutionary councils) were set up, triggering the October Revolution. The Bolshevik faction took over power, and the leader Vladimir Lenin (1870–

1924) sued for peace. Interestingly, the Germans, keen to sow disorder in Russia, had allowed Lenin and his retinue (then in exile in Switzerland) to travel with a special train across Europe and across the front to spark off the revolution. The Bolsheviks seemed able to free Russia from the unsolvable problems caused by the war. By the harsh and costly Treaty of Brest-Litovsk (March 1918), Russia lost many territories to Finland, Estonia, Lithuania, Poland,

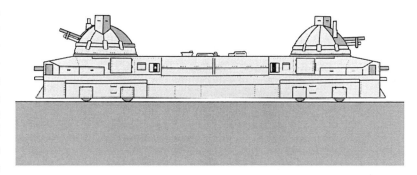

Zaamurets. The Russian tsarist army used several armored trains and vehicles during World War I. One of them was the famous Zaamurets (meaning "from the Amur Region"). This self-propelled rail-cruiser was built in the Odessa railyard and introduced in 1916. It had a weight of 130 tons, and was powered by two 60 hp gasoline engines with a maximum speed of 45 km/h. It was protected by armored plates 12 mm to 16 mm thick, and its main armament (placed inside fully rotating turrets) included two 57 mm guns, upgraded in 1917 to 76 mm guns, plus four additional machine guns. Until 1917, the Russian Army used this train on the southwestern front. After Russia's withdrawal from World War I, Zaamurets was used during the Russian Civil War, and this was not the end of its career, as we shall see in Part 3.

and the Ottoman Empire, but the burden of the war was over. With peace made in the East, the Germans could withdraw their troops, and deployed them in France on the Western Front for offensives in spring 1918.

The Bolshevik grip on power, however, was by no means secure, and a lengthy struggle broke out between the new "Red" regime and its "White" opponents, as we shall further discuss in Part 3 about the Russian Civil War.

GERMANY

Transport

Of the major European powers involved in World War I, Germany was without doubt the most thoroughly prepared and experienced. There were over 38,000 miles of railroad in the German Empire by 1914. The German military railroads on the Western Front, which meant all the main lines west of the old Belgian and French frontiers, employed 220,000 railroad men by April 1918, of which 58,000 were troops. Another 50,000 railroad troops

were on the Eastern Front and Southeastern Front. Railroad was indeed very important, as General Ludendorff declared: "There will come a time when locomotives are more important than guns," while General von Molke added: "Construct no longer fortifications, build railroad." In this positive context, German railroad equipment made significant progress.

In Germany the civilian railroad system was under military control with a staff officer assigned to every line. The civilian personnel, especially the Prussians, were organized largely on military lines, and their equipment and rolling stock were easily convertible to military use. No track could be laid or changed without permission of the General Staff. Before 1914, annual mobilization war games kept railroad officials in constant practice and tested their ability to improvise and divert traffic by telegrams reporting lines cut and bridges destroyed. The Germans were rather well prepared, even anticipating a war on two fronts. The 1870 war and the colonial African railroad in Namibia had brought fruitful experiences. When World War I broke out in August 1914, mobilization went as smoothly as planned. However, the German advance was thwarted when using another country's railroad network, notably in Belgium, where they met unexpected resistance and sabotage of the railroad system. The Germans were also surprised by the rapid arrival of the British Expeditionary Forces in northern France by train. Further, the invasion of France was stopped by a decisive counterattack, the Battle of the Marne, that forced the invaders to retreat and dig themselves in along the Aisne River, where they were to remain until 1918.

Several months later, when the conflict settled down to a stalemate with the opposing armies facing each other across static lines of trenches, it was the Germans who were quickest off the mark. By mid–1915 a complete network of military railroads spread out behind their front line, run on proper principles. To move one German army corps (about 2.5 percent of the German Army), it took 140 trains comprising the following numbers of railroad cars: officers, 170 cars; infantrymen, 965 cars; cavalry, 2,960 cars; artillery, 1,915 cars; and it took the same number of cars, about 6,000, to transport all of their supplies.

Until the end of the war the Germans never stopped improving their railroad lines. The famous World War II Remagen Bridge, which was captured by soldiers of the U.S. 9th Armored Division on March 7, 1945, was originally built during World War I as a means of connecting the Right Rhine Railroad, the Left Rhine Railroad, and the Ahr Valley Railroad (Ahrtalbahn) for the purpose of moving troops and logistics west over the Rhine to reinforce the Western Front in France. The bridge, called Ludendorff Brücke, was designed by Karl Wiener, an architect from Mannheim. Built between 1916 and 1919, it was 325 meters (1,066 ft) long, had a clearance of 14.8 meters (49 ft) above the normal water level of the Rhine, and its highest point measured 29.25 meters (96.0 ft). The bridge carried two railroad tracks and a pedestrian walkway. Since the bridge was a major military construction project, it included defensive elements like a small fortress. Both abutments of the bridge were provided with fortified foundations, as well as armed defensive towers and pillboxes equipped with loopholes for the bridge garrison, storage, and accommodations for troops. The Ludendorff Bridge was one of three bridges built to improve railroad traffic between Germany and France during World War I. The other two were the Hindenburg Bridge at Bingen-am-Rhein and the Urmitz Bridge on the Neuwied–Koblenz railroad near Coblence.

Narrow-Gauge Railroads

As a result of colonial experience and the foresight of the General Staff in preparing for war, a large quantity of 60-cm-gauge Feldbahn (field railroad) equipment had been stockpiled, and procedures

Belgian locomotive captured and used by the German occupiers.

worked out for deployment of narrow-gauge railroad. The German *Feldeinsenbahn Abteilung* (Field Railroad Section) developed efficient links between railheads and narrow-gauge line supplying the front lines. The Orenstein and Koppel GmbH Companies manufactured portable track, and the Krauss Company designed 0-6-0T Zwillinge (twin) locomotives intended to be operated in pairs with the cabs together. The Zwillinge offered Mallet locomotive performance through tight curves, but damage to one unit would not disable the second. One hundred and eighty-two Zwillinge were manufactured from 1890 through 1903, and shortcomings were evaluated in German South-West Africa and China's Boxer Rebellion.

An 11-ton 0-8-0T Brigadelok design with Klein-Linder articulation of the front and rear axles was adopted as the new military standard in 1901. Approximately 250 were available by 1914, and over two thousand were produced during the war. A Brigadelok typically handled six loaded cars up a 2 percent grade. Germany also had approximately five hundred 0-4-0T, three hundred 0-6-0T, and forty 0-10-0T locomotives of other designs in military service. The Deutz

Top: *German Deutz tractor. The standard 20-hp gasoline tractor was powered by a 2-cylinder water-cooled engine.*

Bottom: *German Feldbahn locomotive, World War I.*

Company from Cologne produced two hundred 4-wheel internal combustion locomotives with an evaporative cooling water jacket surrounding the single-cylinder oil engine. Approximately 20 percent of the Brigadeloks saw postwar use.

After the war, the good German railroad materials and rolling stock were confiscated by the victors. Yugoslavia, Macedonia, Serbia and Poland made extensive use of captured German military locomotives. Significant numbers were used in Hungary, France, Latvia, Bulgaria, and Romania, while smaller numbers went overseas to Africa, Indonesia, Japan, and even North America.

Armored Trains

During World War I the Germans had several armored trains that were used on the Russian front, where the nature of the war greatly differed from the static trench warfare in the West. In a context of mobility in a large country, armored trains proved notably effective for securing the long communication lines in a land where roads were in poor condition and totally impracticable for months in winter. For this reason, Germany constantly increased the number of armored trains, but they rarely participated in battle, as the German army had only a limited experience of how to use them in offensive combat. Questions of tactics and operational doctrines for their use were not yet developed, while foreign experience was not collected and analyzed. As a result the German staff did not clearly understand the purpose, features, and advantages (and limitations) of armored vehicles in general and armored trains in particular. In contrast to the Russian and Austro-Hungarian armored trains, the German trains were improvised and simply protected designs rather than refined industrial vehicles. One had to wait until the Russian Civil War of 1918–1921 to see the complete understanding and

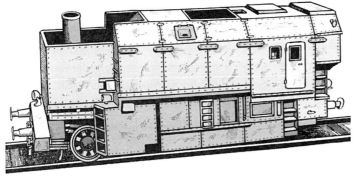

Top: *German World War I armored locomotive type T 9-3.*
Bottom: *P8 Locomotive. A famous and long-lived German locomotive was the rugged, simple and effective Prussian P8 two-cylinder class 4-6-0. Designed in 1906 by engineer Robert Garbe, it had a total weight of 17.7 tons, and a maximum speed of 100 km/h. The Königlich Preussiche Eisenbahn Verwaltung (KPEV, Royal Prussian Railroad Administration) built some 3,800 of these machines. In 1968 approximately 300 P8s were still in stock, mainly with the East German Deutsche Reichsbahn.*

full development of the
military armored train.

German Railroad Artillery

If Germany was not so
enthusiastic about ar-
mored trains during
World War I, it however
led the field in the domain
of heavy Eisenbahnar-
tillerie (railroad artillery),
mainly through the ex-
pertise of the Krupp Com-
pany. The Germans, as be-
fitted a country with a
dense rail network and

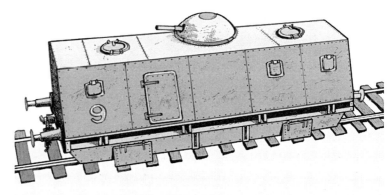

German World War I armored rail car. This 1914 armored artillery car featured a light gun placed in a turret installed on top of the car. It was a part of a Bavarian train comprising an armored locomotive, an infantry car, a machine gun car, and a command car.

many frontiers, took up railroad gun design, and produced long-range artillery that was quite effective during World War I. German cannons reduced the forts around Liege, attacked allied coastal ports, and even bombarded Paris itself. The Germans, with a wide railroad gauge able to take heavy loads, put the railroad to use to transport and fire superheavy artillery. Some of these guns were permanently fixed to a bed set on railroad wheels; others were brought in as parts by rail and reassembled at the front, like the 420 mm howitzer, popularly known as Big Bertha. Designed in 1906 by the Krupp Company, it weighed nearly 70 tons and fired one 820 kg (1807 lb) round every seven minutes to a range of 9,375m (10,252 yards). It had been presented before the war as a naval piece, so the Allies were much surprised when the monster gun appeared on dry land, and was employed to smash Belgian forts at Liege in August 1914. Later it was used on the Russian front at Przemysl and Brest-Litovsk, and was also deployed at the Battle of Verdun in 1916.

Other German designs included the 17cm K(E) Samuel, a wartime expedient, basically a standard field gun bolted to a railroad gondola car. Samuel fired a 138-pound shell to a maximum range of 26,270 yards. The 21 cm

SKL/40 aka Peter Adalbert and the 38 cm SKL/45 Max entered service in 1916. Max was a very successful rail gun, firing an 882-lb shell up to 51,950 yards. Another innovation was the 30-cm long-barreled rail gun. On the whole, German rail guns had the same general appearance as the British and French railroad pieces. They displayed similar bogie mounting, shell hoisting devices, and deep heavy girder framing, but often had shrapnel-proof armored plating protecting the loading crew, where Allied rail guns generally used thick removable canvas awnings.

A summit in super heavy artillery was achieved by the Germans by the end of World War I. In the spring of 1916, the German army had ordered from the Krupp Company extraordinary guns with a range of 75 miles, with the intention to launch a terror bombardment on Paris and break the morale of the French.

In late 1917 the big *Kaiser Wilhelm Geschütz*, known as the Paris Gun or erroneously Grosse Bertha, was ready. A battery of three monster cannons was set up in great secret, carefully camouflaged in the forest of Crépy-en-Laonnais near Laon 120 km (70 miles) from the heart of Paris. Each cannon was transported by rail, assembled with cranes, and placed on a firing platform consisting of a circular casing, mounted on a turntable fitted with ball bearings on which the gun could traverse; the whole rested on a solid concrete foundation. Indeed, the huge Paris Guns dwarfed all other designs. Each gun barrel had a total length of 37 meters (121.4 feet), and in order to keep it straight, a series of struts along the barrel held it braced. Each of the guns had an overall weight of 750,000 kg (738 tons). Their shells of caliber 21 cm (8.3 in) were propelled by a charge of 250 kg (550 lbs). They left the barrel at a speed of 2000m/sec (6560 feet per second), a velocity allowing them to pass into the stratosphere. Allowance had to be made for the rotation of the earth. After a curving flight of 92 miles in 179 seconds, the shells fell down and exploded in Paris. During firing, gunners and engineers got out of sight, seeking cover in large concrete shelters. Such was the formidable arrangement designed to demoralize the French. Over 20 projectiles fell on Paris on each of the first two days of the bombardment that began on March 23, 1918.

One of the Paris Guns exploded accidentally, killing most of its crew, and there was a lull for three days, until firing resumed on Good Friday, March 29, producing the greatest slaughter so far. At 4:30 p.m. a shell struck the Saint-Gervais Church in the Rue Miron, near the Hôtel de Ville (City Hall) in the 4th Arrondissement. The roof fell down on the congregation, killing 90 people and injuring 70. The firing continued with more or less intensity in April, May, June and July. On Friday, August 9, 1918, the last shell fell in the suburb of Aubervilliers. In all, 367 shells were fired on Paris, being directly responsible for 250 deaths and a further 620 wounded. In the balance of effort, time and money expended versus damage done, the Paris Guns were a waste, but as propaganda weapons they had immense value. They surprised the world, and the shelling had a corrosive effect on the morale of the Parisians who experienced the terror of being struck in the heart of their city from behind an enemy line supposed to be a safe 70 miles (112 km) away. In September 1918, the advancing Allied troops found no trace of the guns, which had been removed by train as carefully as they had been assembled months before in preparation for the attack. After the war, no Allied Armistice Commission was ever able to find the secret monster guns in defeated Germany. They had

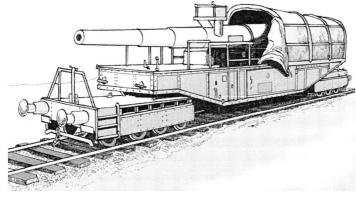

Top: German 28 cm long-barreled rail gun.
    Bottom: German 15 cm SK Nathan Geschütz. Designed by Krupp in 1926, the German Nathan rail gun weighed 55.5 tons, and had a maximum range of 22,675 m (24,798 yards).

World War I German Eisenbahngeschütz (rail gun).

70/76 cm narrow-gauge railroad with tunnels and bridges from railheads up to the craggy valleys and high plateaus. They had special military railroad construction companies that could erect standard prefab bridging equipment, notably the Kohn-Brückengerät that could take a maximum axle-load of 15 tons and a maximum span of 45 m. Among other spectacular realizations was the Fleimstalbahn from Auer in South Tyrol to Predazzo in Trentino. Other military railroads included the Dolomitenbahn from Tolbach, and the Grödnertal (Val Gardena) lines. The Val Gardena Railroad or Klausen-Plan was a 760 mm (2 feet 5⅞ inches) narrow-gauge railroad operating in the Val Gardena in the Dolomites of northern Italy. The railroad was constructed in 1915 when the region was part of the Austrian Empire. It was 32.5 km (19.5 miles) long, and operated 0-8-0T Kraus steam locomotives. The line closed in 1960.

The Austrians also innovated by establishing ropeway and cable suspension systems, which overpassed valleys and climbed at very steep angles.

The Austrians also put convertible road vehicles on rails, allowing rapid transport over lightly laid lines in difficult terrain. Conversion involved replacing the road tires with steel flanged rail-wheels, but with only a hand brake and with no synchromesh on the gearbox, this must have resulted in some dangerous situations on steep mountainous lines. The Germans did the same in East Africa in 1917 with converted American Ford T 1-ton trucks.

On the Eastern Front, the Austro-Hungarians built several Feldbahnen (military railroad) lines to supply their troops in southern Cen-

been demolished and their parts scattered, so mystery still surrounds the precise details of the infamous "Paris Guns."

AUSTRIA

Germany's main ally, the Austro-Hungarian Empire, had a long and experienced history with railroad, as the first military railroad troops had been constituted way back in 1873. In 1914 Austria-Hungary was less prepared than Germany, but had for some time been using military railroads in Bosnia and Herzegovina, and had stockpiled equipment for military use. The Austrians calculated that the new military lines might be long and would pass through difficult mountain terrain, so that reasonable load-carrying capacity would be needed.

Italy joined the war late in May 1915 on the Allied side. The war between Italy and Austria in 1915–1918 was fought under difficult natural conditions in the mountains separating the two countries, notably in South Tyrol along the Dolomite Alps. During much of that time the front, after a series of indecisive battles, remained fairly static. As a result, military railroad lines ranging from standard to 60 cm narrow-gauge were laid down to supply the belligerents. Austria constructed lengthy

tral Europe. One of these lines, for example, was the twenty-one-mile Benzino railroad between Bargaului and Dornisoara in northern Romania, a windy and slow line that ran along the side of a mountain pass and proved important in keeping a section of the front supplied. The Austro-Hungarian Empire developed armored trains, and by 1916, ten of them—built by the Magyar Allamvasutag (MAV, Hungarian Railroads)—were deployed on the Russian, Romanian and Italian fronts. They also developed the concept of *Motorkanonwagen*—scouting draisine and self-propelled armored rail-cruiser.

On the Eastern Front the Austro-Hungarians deployed several rail guns. On the Italian Front they had 380 mm M-16 rail-mounted howitzers, built by the Czech Skoda Company in 1916. The M-16 weighed some 81.7 tons in firing position. Although it was no small affair moving about these monsters, the heavy howitzer was surprisingly mobile, considering its weight. The M-16 was transported in a disassembled state in a convoy of

Top: *Autro-Hungarian armored train.*
   Middle: *Autro-Hungarian Panzerzug, World War I.*
   Bottom: *Fleimstalbahn. The Fleimstalbahn running from Auer in South Tyrol to Predazzo in Trentino, about 50 km in length, took two years to build and included fourteen major bridges and six tunnels.*

four loads (barrel; carriage; right side of platform; and left side of platform). It took some 6 to 8 hours to reassemble and deploy the piece, which also required the digging down and siting of the big base box. The M-16 could fire a 740 kg heavy shell to a distance of 15,000 meters. The maximum rate of fire was 12 rounds per hour. The two first guns (nicknamed "Gudrun" and "Barbara") were used in support of the Austro-Hungarian offensive in 1917 at the hotly contested Isonzo River Front in Slovenia (where Ernest Hemingway's novel *A Farewell to Arms* is set). During the series of battles that lasted from May 1915 to October 1917, with enormous casualties resulting only in a standoff, the Austro-Hungarian High Command ordered other M-16 guns. They were used on all fronts, and at the end of the war, the Austro-Hungarian Army had ten of these monsters in service. One M-16 was captured by Romanian forces, and its four-car convoy is still exhibited today at the Military Museum in Bucharest. Another rail gun used by Austria was the 38 cm "Lulo," which could fire a 1,874-lb shell to a maximum range of 41,557 yards.

Top: *Austro-Hungarian Motorkanonwagen (motorized gun car) was a self-propelled rail car featuring a fully rotating turret armed with a 70 mm Skoda cannon. The rail-cruiser saw action in 1916 and was destroyed on the Romanian front.*

Bottom: *Austrian 38 cm M-16 Haubitz (howitzer) railgun. The 38cm M-16 was one of the famous big guns manufactured by the Czech Skoda Company during World War I.*

PART 3

Railroads in the Period 1918–1939

GENERALITIES

The end of World War I saw the collapse and disappearance of four great empires (Prussian Germany, Austria-Hungary, Russia, and Ottoman Turkey). This gigantic upheaval led to a series of crises, conflicts and civil wars as nations attempted to regain independence and increase their territories.

After the war came the reckoning. Between 1914 and 1918, civilian railroads had been put under enormous pressure, and in many places near the front seriously damaged or totally destroyed. Railroads played an important role in repairing the destruction caused by four years of war. Locomotives and rolling stock of the defeated were requisitioned as reparations by the victors. In all countries involved in the conflict, military railroads were removed, but many miles of the well-engineered ones were partially regauged, restored, and turned into proper secondary lines for some years for civilian passenger and freight transport. Long after the end of the war, many railroads stayed on in seasonal use as agriculture lines, and indeed some World War I lines were still in use in the mid–1960s. A few lines have even survived and have been preserved to these days. The Froissy-Dompierre light railroad, for example, is a narrow-gauge light railroad near Amiens in the northern Upper Somme region of France. It is now 7 km long, and run as a historical tourist attraction by the *Association Picarde pour la Préservation et l'Entretien des Véhicules Anciens* (APPEVA, Picardy Association for the Preservation and Maintenance of Ancient Vehicles). It is the last survivor of one of the 60 cm gauge lines of the World War I battlefield. Between 1916 and 1918 this railroad was near the front line and transported some 1,500 tons of materials daily.

In the period 1918–1939, World War I was known as the Great War. It was supposed to be the "war to end all wars," but that did not prevent the military from keeping a very lively interest in warfare in all its forms, notably the armored combat vehicle, the airplane, artillery and railroads.

In France the heavy rail artillery continued to be developed, and 60 cm narrow-gauge railroads were essential parts supplying the Maginot Line with ammunition and materials. In England the training base of Longmoor was retained and became a focus for experimentation with military trains. All colonial powers continued to develop railroads with the dual purpose of economic exploitation and of supplying their armies in the case of war, such as the French in Indochina and North Africa, and the Italians in Eritrea and Somaliland. In Germany, particularly after the seizure of power by the Nazis in 1933, everything connected with railroad was controlled by the state and the military, and designed as much as possible with an eye on a hypothetical future war.

Armored trains were very much a Central European and Russian specialty, since their principal utility was firstly as a mobile reserve to move quickly to a threatened area on a long and empty border, and secondly to protect lines of communication through regions devoid of settlements but possibly infested with guerrillas, partisans and civilian saboteurs. In the period right after World War I, the aircraft was not much developed yet, and thus did not represent a serious threat to the military railroad in general and to the armored train in particular.

The period 1918–1939 indeed represents something of a "golden age" for military combat trains. The Russians made good use of armored trains during their civil war in 1918–1921, and this weapon system reached its technical pinnacle in the 1920s and early 1930s. The Russian Civil War had shown what the armored train really could achieve. During the period 1919–1939, many nations developed armored trains, notably Finland, Poland, Czechoslovakia, Japan, and China, just to name a few. In that period the form of armored train had developed that was to remain in use into World War II. This included the combination of artillery (mostly 7.5 to 10.5 caliber placed in armored rotating turrets); infantry (armed with light weapons, machine guns and light mortars); and shock or assault troops (cavalry, later tanks) that could rapidly disembark and operate outside the train. These components soon became standard features and were often decisive.

All the cars and locomotives were armored, usually only against small-caliber guns and shrapnel to keep the weight down. The trains, of course, were assembled in various configurations, but usually the cars were arranged as symmetrically as possible around the locomotive running in the middle with the infantry and command cars closest in, then the artillery cars, whose guns would point inward and outward. Finally at the head and tail of the train were the so-called controllers or pusher cars, intended to push away obstacles and explode mines. These pushers were also loaded with track-laying material, allowing for rapid repair of the line. The armored train was very often a self-complete unit that could operate independently.

In the two decades between World War I and World War II, the role and function of the armored train were clearly understood and exploited, namely: reconnaissance, invasion of enemy territory, offensive action in battle, and pursuit of retreating enemy forces; blocking enemy advances, launching surprise counterattack; rear-guard protection in case of withdrawal; mobile coastal defense; supporting infantry attack; patrolling and guarding communication lines, troop concentration and supply dumps. Armored trains also had the advantage of a tough and often astonishing survivability. Much damage could be done to it, but usually only part of it was damaged, and even a badly mauled train could practically always be withdrawn and repaired—provided, of course, that the track was intact. In the worst cases, many spare parts could be obtained from cannibalized trains.

However, the use of military trains was not without disadvantages. Armored trains and rail artillery were bound to the network of railroad; they offered a relatively large target, and were expensive to build, man, operate, and maintain. In the 1930s, rivals appeared in the form of more mobile armored fighting wheeled and tracked vehicles (armored cars and tanks). There was also the increasing efficiency of antitank weapons, which could penetrate armor plates. And above all there was the increasing threat of air attack. Airplane technology made enormous advances in the 1930s, notably the bomber and the dive-bomber, which could attack and destroy not only the train, but also tracks, bridges, switches, and all other railroad facilities, rendering rail guns and armored trains useless and motionless monsters.

The period between 1918 and 1939 marked the true beginning of the motorized age. Before World War I, automobiles were rare and owned by a few wealthy people, while the railroad carried the bulk of freight even over short distances. In the 1930s this had changed completely as cars, trucks, vans, and autobuses were commonplace.

RUSSIA

The Russian Civil War

Between 1918 and 1921, Russia was torn apart by a civil war, one the most important conflicts of the 20th century. The war changed and cost the lives of millions of people and dramatically shaped the geography of Eastern Europe, the Far East and Northern Asia. After the October 1917 Revolution, many groups of Russian society (monarchists, militarists, landowners, devout members of the Russian Orthodox Church, and other conservatives, known as Whites) took arms against Lenin's Bolsheviks, known as Reds. The White Army initially had success in Ukraine, where the Bolsheviks were unpopular, but gradually pro–Bolsheviks armed supporters took control of Ukraine. By early 1918, the Whites held no major areas in Russia, and the main threat to the Bolsheviks was the German Army that was advancing towards Petrograd (former name of Saint Petersburg and Leningrad).

In March 1918, Vladimir Lenin, who thought the Bolsheviks had nothing to gain by fighting in a capitalist-Tsarist war, ordered his team of negotiators to sign the Brest-Litovsk Treaty, getting Russia out of World War I. This resulted in the Russians' having to surrender territories in Ukraine, Finland, the Baltic provinces, the Caucasus and Poland. This disastrous peace increased the hostility inside Russia towards the Bolsheviks. The White Army then regained strength, and won battles at Simbirsk and Kazan. Lenin appointed Leon Trotsky (1879–1940) as Commissar of War and sent him to rally the Red Army in the

Bolshevik. The Bolsheviks (Russian for "Those of the Majority") were members of the radical wing of the Russian Social-Democratic Workers' Party. Led by Vladimir Lenin (1870–1924), they seized control of the government in Russia in October 1917, and became the dominant political power. The group originated at the party's second congress (1903) when Lenin's followers, insisting that party membership be restricted to professional revolutionaries, won a temporary majority on the party's central committee. They assumed the name Bolsheviks and dubbed their opponents the Mensheviks ("Those of the Minority"). The depicted soldier of the Bolshevik Red Army wears the typical budenovka (a pointed woolen soft hat with a red star at the front; a sheepskin or fur cap was an alternative) and a long and thick brown greatcoat. He is armed with an M1891 7.62 mm Mosin Nagant rifle.

Volga. Trotsky proved an outstanding military commander as Kazan and Simbirsk were recaptured in September 1918.

After the armistice of November 1918, which marked the end of World War I on the Western Front, the White Army benefited from support from Britain, France, Japan and the United States. By December 1918, some 200,000 foreign soldiers fought at the side of the anti–Bolshevik coalition. The White armies represented many factions and ideals, and therefore they were never a really united force, which may be one of the reasons why they were ultimately defeated. In the meantime, the Red Army continued to grow, and had over 500,000 soldiers in its ranks. The hostilities took place as far as Turkestan, Crimea, and Siberia. With the end of Allied support and evacuation of foreign troops, the Red Army was able to inflict defeats on the remaining White government forces, leading to their eventual collapse. The Allied intervention and the presence of foreign troops were effectively used by the Bolsheviks to argue that Western capitalists backed the enemies of the Russian people. In the end, the Red Army won the war, resulting in the foundation of the Union of Soviet Socialist Republics (USSR) in December 1922. About 800,000 soldiers were killed during the Russian Civil War. It has been estimated that 8 million civilians died from starvation and disease as direct result of the war.

Armored Trains in the Civil War

In sheer contrast with the static trench lines of World War I in France, where battles were fought in densely populated areas and massed armies faced each other, the Russian Civil War was a war of movement capitalizing on mobility and shock. In the immense and bare landscapes of Russia, advances were counted not in yards but in hundreds of miles. Armies of the Russian Civil War became entrenched only on a few occasions. On the whole there were no fixed and defined fronts between

Reds and Whites. Rear areas were frequently insecure, with partisans of other factions and brigands ravaging towns and countryside. With air power still extremely limited and few roads or cars, mobile tactics combining cavalry and armored trains proved to be the decisive weapon system, particularly well suited to the ill-defined conditions of the Russian Civil War. By all kinds of weather, trains could indeed carry large loads of supply, weapons and manpower over long stretches of empty lands. In 1917 Russia had 60,000 km (37,000 miles) of railroad track. Therefore the railroad lines were the main arteries of advance for all combatant forces and control of railroad installations and facilities were central to the planning of most offensives. Control of railroad lines with junctions and facilities enabled the rapid deployment of supplies and troops.

As said before, the Tsarist Russian Army had already fielded seven official armored trains during the First World War. The first trains were improvised and poorly armored, but as the Civil War proceeded, designs were improved, and firepower increased with warship configuration featuring guns placed in "dog-houses" and rotating turrets. Together with armored cars designed for carrying infantry, armored trains were used as mobile artillery fortresses. When the Tsarist regime was overthrown, and when the Bolsheviks made peace with Germany, many Russian armored trains were taken over and re-used by the Germans, and a few came into Bolshevik hands.

The more fluid situation of the Civil War, in which the armies were much smaller and there were often no fixed front lines, brought forth greater use of armored trains. These armored trains were used, for example, to spearhead an advance or to cover a withdrawal. With their long-range guns and heavy armor plates, they were like land-based battleships. Such a rolling fortress typically included one or more armored locomotives, and a various number of armored cars bristling with guns and machine guns. A single train could easily bring a battalion's worth of firepower to bear on its target. Armored train tactics reached their full maturity during the Russian Civil War.

Red Army

Armored trains played an important role in the Red Army in keeping the supply and reinforcement routes open and supporting offensive operations as much against the White forces as against the Polish Army. Russia did not possess an advanced automotive industry capable of turning out tanks and armored cars (few nations did in 1919), but the Russian factories at Petrograd, Moscow, Nizhny Novgorod, Kolumna and Bryansk (held by the Reds) that produced locomotives and rolling stock could easily turn their hands to making military armored trains. In early 1918, the Red Army had 43 armored trains. By October 1919 the number was 73. In July 1920 they had 110 trains, of which 88 were engaged in action. By the end of the war the Red Army had 122 official armored trains, and about 100 locally made trains and improvised semi-armored units.

Of course, at the beginning of the war there was no such thing as a standardized Bolshevik armored train, and soon the confusing variety of trains prompted a Red Army directive in the autumn of 1918 stipulating that armored trains should conform to the regular 1915 Russian Tsarist Army pattern. The Red Army's armored trains ran the gamut from crude improvisations through sophisticated multi-turreted moving fortresses. The first armored trains had been hastily manufactured using whatever means available. Although total standardization was never achieved, gradually a typical Red Army train would be constituted of: two armored wagons carrying weapons and men; one armored locomotive and tender; and a crew of 95, of which 24 would operate the train itself, and 71 would serve the weapons. Trains were often given ferocious or revolutionaries' names like Red Hurricane,

Death or Victory, Communards, Avenger, In Honor of Rosa Luxemburg, or Comrad Nazarov. They would have a length of about 30 m, and because of the tremendous weight of weapons and armor, they had a rather slow speed with a maximum of 45 km/h. Stocks of coal had become depleted by 1918 and many trains had to use wood as fuel. Weapons were usually standardized because the Bolsheviks had inherited the stockpiles of Imperial Russian arsenals. The heavy artillery carried by many of the trains were naval guns ranging from 3-inch to 6-inch caliber. The corps usually drew their personnel from the highly motivated pro–Bolshevik crews of the former Tsarist Baltic and Black Sea fleets. The sailors also had a much higher literacy rate than regular army soldiers, and often had technical training and skills as well.

As the Russian Civil War proceeded, tactical configuration changed, and trains generally included one armored steam engine and tender in the center; two armored cars with guns and machine guns; and control cars at the front and rear loaded with engineering materials and supplies. Standardized patterns emerged (allowing trains to negotiate all bridges and tracks), and armor was improved (often consisting of two sheets of metal 16–20 mm thick with concrete filling in between). Designs became more sophisticated, notably the arrangement of weapons (machine guns) to ensure that the train could not be approached through blind spots. On several occasions, observation balloons tethered to a special car were used for artillery spotting and fire control. Crews were larger and their technical and military training had been greatly improved. Also political Bolshevik commissars ensured that they had good morale, strict discipline and strong communist faith, and patriotic motivation to fight. Soon armored train troops were classed as elite; they wore distinctive black leather coats, created their own glorious tradition, and developed their own harsh mystique of steadiness and relentlessness.

Their esprit de corps was illustrated by the idealistic character of train commander Pavel Strelnikov in Boris Pasternak's 1957 novel *Doctor Zhivago*. The novel was made into a highly popular epic drama-romance film directed by David Lean in 1965.

The Bolsheviks were quick to learn and exploit to the full the potentialities of armored trains. They turned them into coherent units combining men and machines, mixing artillery, infantry and raiding cavalry parties, although a kind of specialization also appeared. Red Army armored trains were divided into three main sorts. First, the Bronyedpoyezd or BEPO were armored trains carrying shock troops into the field. Second, the Bonyobatoreyo or BP carried heavy guns for mobile artillery support. Finally, there were supply trains bringing men, railroad materials, ammunition, water and fuel from rear base depots. The Red Army practice often teamed these trains in groups supporting each other. According to strategic need or to match the requirement of a specific mission, light armored BEPO trains armed with machine guns would carry infantry troops, and sometimes even a group of cavalrymen, for reconnaissance or a raiding team (generally an infantry company tasked with security purposes, but also with offensive actions), while heavy armored BP trains provided fire support. Finally, maintenance trains would be ready to bring forth what was needed to deal with the armored train's greatest weakness: damaged tracks.

Although the purpose of armored trains was not to fight other armored trains, there were inevitably clashes and battles opposing Red armored trains to those belonging to the White faction or to the Polish army. For example, in the summer of 1920 during the Russo-Polish War of 1919–1921, a Polish armored train fought an artillery duel with a Bolshevik armored train, and destroyed it when a round hit the Soviet train's ammunition store car, resulting in a spectacular and devastating explosion.

By 1920 the Red Army was using rail-cruisers (see below) and armored trains in even larger groups, sometimes six or more of them at a time. In August 1920, the Bolshevik armored railroad force was reorganized into standardized Types A (basic field assault), B (heavy armored artillery), V (special purpose artillery), and M (with various configurations, armament and number of crews for different tasks and various purposes).

Trains operated by the Reds were painted gray or olive green, sometimes with camouflaged shades of various green, gray and brown. In winter, trains were commonly camouflaged and painted white. Revolutionary slogans, emblems and names of trains could be occasionally painted in red or white on the sides of locomotives, tenders and cars. Red flags and painted red stars were in general use.

Self-propelled independent rail-cruisers had already been used by the Austro-Hungarian and Tsarist regimes in the First World War. The inspiration came from the prewar Automotrice, a self-propelled passenger rail car developed in France. The powerful and rapid rail-cruiser reappeared during the Russian Civil War with 360-degree traverse revolving armored turrets for machine guns, mortars, cannons, and later antiaircraft weapons. Rail-cruisers could be incorporated into armored trains as additional artillery or be operated independently as scouting and reconnaissance patrolling cars. The finest Russian World War I rail-cruiser was certainly *Zaamurets*, which was later captured by the Czech Legion.

It should also be noted that on several occasions and following the outcome of an operation, it could happen that armored trains, rail-cruisers, cars and other rolling stocks were captured by the enemies. Even if the trains were badly damaged, there were steel plates, weapons and other spare parts that could always be recycled and reused. Intact armored rolling stocks were extremely valuable, and when changing hands they also changed designation and names.

The Russian Civil War also saw the continuation of the use of VIP and command trains. Leon Trotsky made many tours of inspection in the period 1918–1921 and travelled with his own command train simply referred to as *The Train*. Formed in August 1918, Trotsky's train was composed of two armored locomotives and a few cars. Eventually it included armored guns and machine-gun cars, supply cars, a printing press, a telegraph station, a secretariat car, a power plant, a kitchen/restaurant car, and special cars for a musical band, a library, two airplanes and five automobiles—one of which was Trotsky's personal armored command Rolls-Royce, armed with machine guns. In all, the train had about 250 personnel, and in addition there was a force of 300 cavalrymen scouting the tracks ahead. For security the train never traveled faster than 70 km/h.

Armored trains were widely used every-

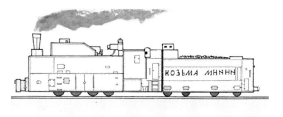

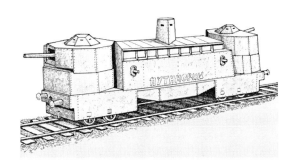

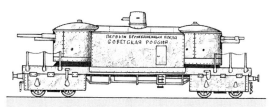

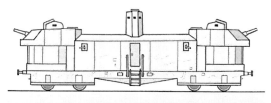

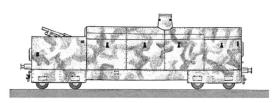

Left, top: *Armored locomotive train "Kozma Minin."*

Left, middle: *Artillery wagon in Red Russian armored train No. 6 Comrad Lenin. Train No. 6 included one armored locomotive and two such cars armed with 76.2 mm guns and machine guns on the sides.*

Left, bottom: *Profile artillery wagon in Red Russian armored train No. 6 Comrad Lenin.*
Right, top: *Armored locomotive Train No. 6 Lenin.*

Right, middle: *Train No. 98 "Soviet Russia." This train included a locomotive and two identical armored artillery cars armed with a 107 mm gun (left) and one 76.2 mm Model 1902 (right) both placed in rotating turrets, and one machine gun housed in the top turret on the roof. The inscription reads: "First Armor-Turreted Train, Soviet Russia."*

Right, bottom: *Red Hurricane Train. Train No. 96 "Red Hurricane" was built at Novgorod in 1918. In 1920 it comprised one armored locomotive with tender, one four-axle car with one 76.2 mm gun, and two "tankette" gun cars.*

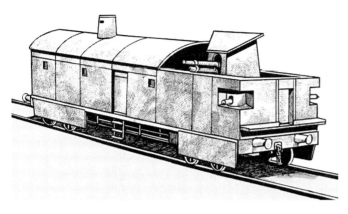

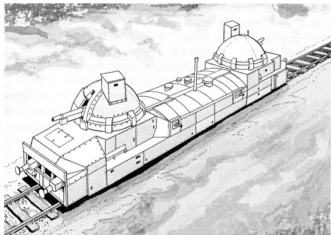

where in Russia where key battles were fought, and also on the Trans-Siberian Railroad—the mighty line barely twenty years old and arguably the greatest engineering achievement of the 19th century. There an awful war was waged in appalling conditions when the withdrawing, defeated White forces were pursued by Trotsky's Red armored trains.

White Forces

The White forces were led by Admiral Alexander Kolchak (1874–1920), who established an anti-communist government in southwestern Siberia known as the Provisional All-Russian Government, based in Omsk.

For a year and a half, Kolchak was the internationally recognized leader of Russia. He tried to defeat Bolshevism by ruling

Top: *Soviet Red Train No. 63 "Destruction to the Counter-Revolution," 1920. Train No. 63 was composed of one armored locomotive with tender, and two different armored artillery cars armed with 76.2 mm guns. One car included two turrets and the other one turret with machine gun posts at the front.*

Bottom: *Rail-cruiser Zaamurets, 1919–20. The huge size and poor infrastructure of Russia made it an excellent area for armored train operations, during World War I and during the chaos of the Civil War. Zaamurets (meaning "from the Amur Region") was a self-propelled rail car sporting four machine guns and two 57 mm Nordenfelt quick-firing cannons, with a rate of fire of 60 rounds per minute, placed in armored rotating turrets allowing a traverse of 360 degrees. The car was fitted with searchlights, periscopes and lookouts for observation and scanning targets. Dubbed a "rail cruiser," it fulfilled many of the duties of a seaborne cruiser, moving relatively fast, being comparatively well armored, and packing a decent punch. As can be imagined, the interior of the machine was quite noisy and cramped, but it seems to have been relatively well appointed, at least by Russian military standards, with a heating system provided by the twin gasoline engines' exhausts. Railcruiser Zaamurets used a large flatcar with two Pullman-pattern two-axle railroad trucks. It was powered by two Italian Fiat 60 hp gas engines allowing a maximum speed of 28 miles per hour. It had a famous and remarkable career, and though it went through a number of changes throughout its life, it retained the same basic twin turret configuration. It was built in early 1916 in the Odessa railyard, and saw some fighting in 1916–1917 in Tsarist service. It then made its way through the hands of the Bolsheviks under the name Lenin. It was captured by the Czech Legion and incorporated into the Orlik armored train. Later it passed to the Chinese Nationalist Army, and eventually to the Imperial Japanese forces, having traveled the whole length of the Trans-Siberian Railroad line.*

as a dictator, but his government proved weak and ineffective. He also failed to unite the numerous but disparate and sometimes mutually antagonistic anti–Bolshevik factions. Kolchak refused to consider autonomy for ethnic minorities and refused to cooperate with non–Bolshevik leftists.

He also relied too heavily on outside aid. The leading Western powers, France, Britain, the United States and (westernized) Japan, supported the anti–Communist Whites. However, exhausted after World War I, these war-weary nations could not mobilize and send substantial armies. The Western Allies' contribution consisted of supplies and weapons (e.g., artillery pieces, which were installed on improvised armored trains), and token intervention forces. These included a small British detachment under Lieutenant-General Sir Brian Horrocks, an 8,000-man American Expeditionary Force, and a battalion of 600 volunteers from the First Regiment of the French Foreign Legion headed by Major Monnot. There were also two Greek infantry divisions (23,500 men) that were withdrawn after three months, some 2,300 Chinese and 15,000 Japanese soldiers deployed in the Eastern region, an Italian mountain unit of 2,500 men called Legione Redenta, and the Czech Legion, described below. The Western Allies' support was only halfhearted; in October 1919 these units were withdrawn, and as a result Kolchak's government collapsed. As the White military forces fell apart, Kolchak was betrayed and captured by independent units. They handed him over to local Bolsheviks, who executed him.

As far as armored trains are concerned, the White forces started with nothing, as all Tsarist railroad military materials and heavy weapons had been seized by the Germans after the peace of Brest-Litovsk, and by the Bolsheviks. Armored trains had to be built from scratch in the few factories they controlled, or else captured from the Reds. In spite of the handicap, the Whites had about 80 armored trains by the end of the war.

In East Russia in May 1919, the White forces had only four trains operating west of the Ural Mountains. The White warlord Ataman Semenov had 14 armored trains in action between Lake Baikal, Manchuria and Vladivostok. Some 300 American engineering personnel (forming the Russian Railroad Service Corps under the overall Inter-Allied Railroad Committee) built several light armored trains for the Whites. The British constructed three trains with naval 12- and 6-pounders from HMS *Suffolk*, anchored off Vladivostok, in 1919.

The Czechs living outside the Austro-Hungarian Empire, as well as deserters and Czech prisoners-of-war stranded in Russia, joined the Allied war effort—in the hope of the establishment of a Czech-Slovak state by the Allies, should they be victorious. They made an important contribution with a legion of 50,000 highly motivated and steadfast volunteers manning 32 armored trains. The Czechs captured some 5,000 miles in the eastern section of the Trans-Siberian Railroad. They transported goods, produced daily newspapers and carried mail. They also played an active military role, capturing and defending cities along the Volga River and industrial cities in the Ural Mountains. After the defeat of the White Russians in the summer of 1919, the Czechs continued to fight defensive actions on the Trans-Siberian line from Omsk to Vladivostok. In one of the most colorful and extraordinary episodes of the war, they captured the Russian national gold reserve in Kazan and used it as a bargaining chip to force the Bolsheviks to allow them to return home. After their withdrawal and departure from Vladivostok in April 1920, some leaders of the legion (e.g., Stefanyk, Masaryk, and Benes) played a central role in the foundation of the new Czechoslovakian state.

On the North Russian front, on the railroad lines between Murmansk to Petrograd and Archangel to Vologda in 1918–1919, the British had two armored trains, the French one, the Americans one, and the Russian Whites two (called Admiral Kolchak and Admiral Nepenin), and two more were under construction. On the northwest front between the Estonian border and Petrograd, the White army had four armored trains, but these failed to cut the tracks south of Petrograd, a failure that enabled the Reds to capture the city. In the south, the Don Cossacks had several armored trains in August 1918. The anti–Bolshevik General Anton Denikin (1872–1947) and his volunteer Armed Forces of South Russia (AFSR) had five armored trains, all cap-

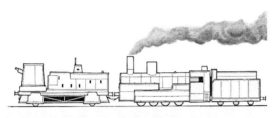

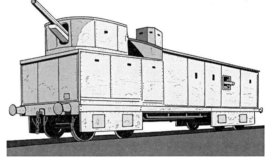

Left, top: *Czech armored train, Orlik, 1919–1920.*

Left, middle: *British 18-pounder in revolving turret, north Russia, 1919, in White Russian service.*

Left, bottom: *French light armored car. The light car carried a 75 mm field gun rudimentarily protected by wooden logs and sandbags. It belonged to a small French military formation operating against the Red Army in the region of Archangel in 1919 in north Russia.*

Right, top: *White armored car, probably of train General Drozdovsky at Rostov-on-Don in 1919.*

Right, middle: *Artillery car with 107 mm gun in turret.*

Right, bottom: *American armored rail gun in north Russia in White service.*

tured from the Reds in 1919–1920. Denikin's AFSR armored trains conducted a brilliant railroad offensive using the intricate railroad network in the Don Basin.

Armored trains operated by the White armies were various in crew number, fire-power, strength and configuration. Some trains were built by foreign powers, some were captured from the Bolsheviks, some other trains were composed of improvised artillery platforms (flatcar with pedestal-mounted naval artillery), and armored freight cars fitted with cannons and machine gun turrets.

White armored railroad materials were usu-ally painted gray or olive green with some-times green and brown camouflaged patterns, or white in the winter snow. They generally displayed the traditional Tsarist tricolor red, blue and white, but local particularities, im-provised and nonstandard features were para-mount.

Period 1931–1941

After the Civil War, the victorious Soviet armored train force was greatly reduced to 21 trains, with 14 kept in reserve. In 1931, due to Japanese expansion in Manchuria, Soviet Rus-sia sent two special trains to their Far East bor-ders, where tension grew high. Soviet navy guns installed on railroad cars were delivered to the port of Vladivostok for the rapid im-provement of its defense. Three railroad units were formed: Battery 1 with two 203 mm guns; Battery 2 with three 152 mm Kanet guns; and Battery 3 with three 130 mm guns. In January 1932 the guns were placed on their firing positions along the Amurskiy Gulf on the western shore of the Schkot Peninsula. During that time the Leningrad metal plants produced three railroad artillery mounts (TM-1-14) using heavy 356 mm guns from the noncompleted battle cruiser *Ismail*. These guns, mounted on special concrete platforms, had a traverse of 360 degrees. Until 1935 the defenses of Vladivostok were constantly rein-forced and improved with the construction of

concrete platforms and railroad facilities, no-tably a 1.3 km tunnel called Comrad Stalin.

In the period 1931–1941, before the Ger-man attack, the Soviet armored forces were modernized and standardized with new loco-motives, improved light and heavy artillery cars, and increasingly numerous antiaircraft wagons (as air power made spectacular ad-vances in the 1930s). These were manufac-tured at military plants and depots located at Bryansk, where Soviet military designers also experimented with new weapons. During the Civil War, the Red Army had developed a rad-ical tactic to destroy enemy trains. An expend-able locomotive and a freight car filled with explosives were sent at high speed to collide with the enemy. In 1935 this technique (wasteful of expensive railroad equipment) was replaced with a kind of railroad torpedo (designated ZhDT-3) consisting of a 220-lb explosive charge placed in a small, low, two-axle trolley. The device was battery-powered and moved in the direction of its target at a speed of 37 km/h. The ZhDT-3 went into pro-duction in 1938, and all Soviet trains were planned to be equipped with five of them. There is, however, no record of the device's use in combat during World War II, perhaps due to lack of suitable targets or the difficulty of operating the curious railroad torpedo.

During the period 1931–1941, Russian mil-itary authorities continued the development of armored scouting rail cars and draisines to accompany their trains. At the same time Stalin's dictatorial regime was greatly rein-forced. The dreaded People's Commissariat for Internal Affairs (NKVD) was created in 1934 by the fusion of all political secret and regular uniformed police forces, law enforce-ment agencies, political security troops, coun-terintelligence and military intelligence of-fices. Like Hitler's Schutz-Staffeln police forces (SS) in Nazi Germany, the Soviet NKVD was charged with protecting the total-itarian Communist state security against all opposition and real or supposed enemies.

This function was successfully carried out through massive political repression involving the use of police brutality, surveillance abuse, discrimination, persecution, intimidation and terror, political purges, blackmail, mental and physical torture, kidnapping, arbitrary arrest, detention after mock trial or without trial at all in psychiatric asylums, secret prisons and concentration camps (known as gulags), as well as executions, summary assassinations, and sanctioned political murders.

Unlike the SS, which had its own military force known as Waffen SS, the NKVD did not

Top: *Russian rail torpedo ZhDT-3*

   Middle: *Russian D-3 NKVD armored rail car. Motorized armored cars of D-3 type were developed in the USSR at the beginning of the 1930s by engineer Dyrenkov. The sloping armored hull of the car was 10–16 mm thick, and had two side doors. The commander cabin was set in the center of the vehicle on top of the roof with observation slits, and an exit hatch placed on top. Armament consisted of four Maxim machine guns, two on each side of the hull, and two 45 mm guns and DT machine guns housed in T-26 tank turrets. The D-3 was powered by a Gerkules YXC engine with capacity of 93 hp (or a Yaroslavl motor of 90 hp) placed in the center of a frame. Its gear had four speeds and a reverse device for both forward and backward movement. These armored draisines (with a crew varying between 11 and 16) were often issued to border guards and NKVD security forces. They operated independently or as scouting elements ahead of armored trains. More than 30 units were produced and a number took part in the Second World War, 1941–45.*

   Bottom: *Soviet draisine MBV-2. The armored rail-cruiser MBV-2 was a type of self-propelled draisine designed as artillery support and scout units for the Red Army and for internal security missions for the NKVD. During World War II, the series proved very useful to the point that they were refitted three times with different types of turrets and guns.*

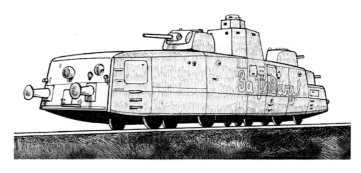

field any army, but it had armored trains and draisines manned with special armed political police crews. The NKVD's trains were tasked with various missions, like patrolling the Soviet borders, and more generally with every operation connected to the regime's internal security. The NKVD favored the use of quick and powerful armored rail-cruisers like the self-propelled MBV. Although not intended for front-line combat missions, the NKVD's motorized draisines were fitted with military weapons. The MBV had two turrets, each housing one 76.2 mm field gun, and was powered by a Hercule UXS 93 hp gas motor. In 1935 the NKVD had 40 of these self-propelled armored rail-cruisers. They were organized into seven railroad regiments, each operating three MBVs with the addition of a locomotive and supporting wagons. In 1939 a somewhat larger version was commissioned, known as MBV-2 armed with three T-28 tank turrets (two at the front and one at the rear), and a retractable antiaircraft quadruple Maxime machine gun mount. Two exemplars had been completed when Nazi Germany invaded the USSR in June 1941.

FINLAND

The Finnish Civil War

The short Finnish Civil War was fought in connection with the Russian Civil War for control and leadership of the Grand Duchy of Finland after it had become sovereign in 1917. The war lasted from January 27 to May 15, 1918, and opposed the forces of the Social Democrats led by the People's Deputation of Finland, commonly called the "Reds," and the forces of the nonsocialist, conservative-led Senate, commonly called the "Whites." The Reds, representing industrial and agrarian workers, were supported by the Russian Soviets. The Whites, representing peasants, and middle- and upper-class factions, received marked military assistance from Germany. The Reds were based in the towns and indus-

trial centers of southern Finland, while the Whites controlled more rural and central and northern Finland. In the end the Whites won the war, in which about 37,000 people died out of a population of 3 million.

Armored trains were used in Finland during the short war. Indeed, only very small numbers of motor vehicles existed in Finland during the war, and on snow-covered roads their usefulness was very limited. Besides, due to the winter weather and shortages of equipment, both sides were very much tied to the existing railroad networks. As a result, the battles were mainly fought along the railroads—the vital means of transporting troops and supplies. The Finnish Red Guards, supported by the Russians, were the ones mostly using armored trains. During the war they had about 10 armored trains in their use, while for most of the war White Army had only one somewhat proper armored train. The reasons for this were relatively simple. First, the Reds in the south had direct railroad connection with their Bolshevik ally; and second, the industry in the area controlled by the Reds included the only two railroad machine works—Fredriksberg Engineering Works (Fredriksbergin Konepaja) in Helsinki, and Viipuri Engineering Works (Viipurin Konepaja) in Viipuri.

One of the most important objectives for both sides was the seizure of Haapamäki, a railroad junction northeast of Tampere, which connected both western-eastern and southern-northern Finland. The Whites captured the junction at the end of January 1918, leading to fierce battles at Vilppula. The Whites' bridgehead south of the River Vuoksi at Antrea on the Karelian Isthmus was a constant problem to the Reds, as it threatened the railroad connection Viipuri-Petrograd. The other vital railroad junctions during the war were Kouvola, Riihimäki, Tampere and Toijala.

The structure of one of the typical Fredriksberg-built Red armored trains was: flatcar; armored artillery wagon (one or two guns plus machine guns); armored locomotive; armored artillery wagon (one or two guns plus machine guns), and flatcar. If

needed, additional closed wagons could be attached between locomotive and artillery cars for transporting additional infantry, supplies or equipment. Both sides also used improvised armored trains with cars featuring infantry breastworks made of locally available materials such as metal plates, sandbags, railroad sleepers, and combination of brick and planks.

ESTONIA

Armored trains played an important role in the Estonian War of Independence in 1918. This was a short war fought by the Estonian Army and its allies, most notably the White Russian Northwestern Army, Latvia, and the United Kingdom, against the Soviet Western Front offensive and the aggression of the Baltische Landeswehr (armed forces of the Couronian and Livonian nobility). It was also fought in connection with the Russian Civil War during 1918–1920. The campaign was the struggle of Estonia for its sovereignty in the aftermath of World War I. It resulted in a victory for the newly established state and was concluded in the Treaty of Tartu in February 1920.

The first Estonian armored train set off for the front in the War of Independence in late November 1918, the next two in December. In 1919 another ten Estonian trains reached the front. During the war, altogether six broad-gauge and seven narrow-gauge armored trains were built in Estonia. Of the latter, one was destroyed in battle. The armored

Top: *Finnish armored car 1918. Example of a typical Finnish Red roofless artillery car equipped with two 47-mm or 57-mm naval guns made at Fredriksberg Works in 1918.*

Middle: *Russian armored train used in Finland in 1918. The armored car pushed by the locomotive was armed with several Maxim machine guns and a light 76K/02 gun emplaced in a turret at the front, enabling a 270-degree arc of fire.*

Bottom: *Armored locomotive of Finnish White train named Saviour of Karelia.*

trains were organized by military commander, navy officer and politician Johan Pitka (1872–1944). The efficiency of the first three broad-gauge armored trains was remarkable throughout the war. At the critical initial stages of the war they formed the backbone of the front. Their crew was at first made up only of volunteers, whose enthusiasm was strong, but they also suffered heavy losses. Later conscripted men also operated the trains. The carriages of Estonian armored trains were based on goods carriages, but their armor was only thick planks and piles of sandbags. Later the carriages were covered with steel plates and were provided with cannons and machine guns.

Armored artillery car, Estonia, 1918.

POLAND

Rebirth of Poland

After the Napoleonic era, Poland was partitioned and a large part went to Russia. In spite of uprisings in 1830, 1848 and 1863–65, the Poles remained subjected to Russian rule until the collapse of the Tsarist regime in 1917. Between 1918 and 1922 there was a revolution and a war opposing Poland to Lithuania, Czechoslovakia, the Ukrainian Republic and Red Russia. All these states laid claims on territory occupied by Poland. The Poles liberated Wilno from the Lithuanians in 1919, reoccupied the area around Cieszyn (which had been invaded by the Czechs), and annexed a part of western Ukraine when the Ukrainian Republic collapsed under attack from Soviet forces. By then the Red Army, having crushed all White counterrevolutionary forces inside Russia, turned its attention to Poland. The chief of state and military leader Josef Pilsudski (1867–1935) sought to expand the Polish borders as far to the east as possible in an attempt to create a Polish-led federation to counter any potential imperialist intentions on the part of Russia or Germany. At the same time, the Bolsheviks started to advance westward towards the disputed territories with the intent of assisting other Communist movements in Western Europe. The border skirmishes of 1919 progressively escalated into the Polish-Soviet War in 1920. The Russians launched an offensive and by August 1920 were at the gates of Warsaw. On August 15 the Polish Army under Pilsudski, Haller and Sikorski fought the Battle of Warsaw (named the "Miracle on the Vistula"), routed the Red Army and saved Poland, and probably the weakened western Europe, from Soviet conquest. An armistice was signed at Riga in October, followed by a peace treaty in March 1921, which determined and secured Poland's eastern frontiers. In 1922 part of Upper Silesia was awarded to Poland by a Geneva Convention following three uprisings by the region's Polish population, who had been handed over to Germany at the Peace Treaty of Versailles. From 1921 to 1939, when it was invaded by Nazi Germany, Poland was a democratic republic.

Polish Armored Trains

The Polish forces further developed the concept of Pociag Pancerny (armored train, or PP) after November 1918. At the end of 1918 Poland had seven armored trains, 31 by the end of 1919, and 43 at the peak strength of 1920. They captured some 37 armored trains from Austro-Hungaria, Ukraine, and Lithuania, and from Bolshevik Russia. For example, the artillery armored car named Stzelec Kresowy served for 25 years in four different armies: Red Soviet, White Russian in 1918, Polish in 1920, and finally German in World War II.

Intended as a mobile reserve for their eastern frontier, Polish armored trains played an important role in the war against Ukraine and Soviet Russia in 1919–1921.

Polish trains operated much like the Red Army's trains. They carried some 100–150 infantrymen, and were armed with guns placed in armored rotating turrets. The Poles introduced an additional weapon to their trains: they mounted light tanks (generally a French-built Renault FT) on a flatcar fitted with ramps allowing the tank to disembark and to fight in the vicinity of the train by supporting the infantry. Each train was given a name, usually that of a national hero such as General Sosnkowski, Paderewski or Marszalek.

PP Gromobój was the name of a Polish improvised armored train from the period of the Polish-Ukrainian war (1918–1919). The train took part in the fighting in the area of the rail junction in Zagórze. Its armor was constructed from walls of brick, and river gravel. The locomotive used in the train was an ex-Austro-Hungarian kkStB Class 229. The most famous Polish armored train of this period was without doubt PP Pilsudski, named after the Polish commander Joseph Pilsudski. This train took part in the capture of the cities of Przemysl and Lwow, it supported the offensives in Ukraine and Byelorussia, and participated in the retreat in the summer of 1920, when it destroyed the Bolshevik armored train Krasnoarmiyetz in an artillery duel.

The Poles were not only fighting the Soviet Bolsheviks in the East, they were also engaged in an armed conflict against Germany in 1919–1920 in the West in the contested borderlands of Silesia and Pomerania.

After the recovery of their independence, in the 1930s peace was restored. But as the threat moved from East to West with the rise of the Nazis in Germany in 1933, the Poles continued the use and development of armored trains. They kept twelve trains: six were in reserve and six were redeployed to an area where railroad lines were more numerous, thus increasing their chance to play a role in a possible war with Germany. These trains were modernized with new rolling stock, while armament varied according to what was available at the time they were built. Their composition was standardized. For example, armored train Danuta included an armored locomotive, a command/radio car, a crew car for a raiding infantry group, and two armored cars fitted with artillery mounted in turrets. Two flat control cars were usually attached at the front and rear of the train in order to absorb any damage from mines laid on the track. The Poles continued the use of flatcars fitted with ramps carrying tanks (usually Renault FT light tanks and TSK tankettes for scouting and supporting infantry) attached to their armored trains. Like that of all armored trains, their radius of action was limited to where the rail went, and they had only few or no antiaircraft weapons, as the potentiality of ground-attack aircraft and dive-bombers was rashly underestimated.

The Nazi German invasion in September 1939 brought these two defects into sharp focus. The German ground troops easily avoided the armored trains, and the Luftwaffe easily found them and attacked them from the air. This was, for example, the fate of PP Bartosz Glowacki (aka Armored Train number 55). This armored train had been used during the Polish-Soviet War and the Polish September Campaign. In early September 1939, it was assigned to the Operational Group Wyszkow and was directed to the fortress of Brześć-nad-

Bugiem, where it fought German units of the SS-Verfügungstruppe (later to be known as Waffen SS). After withdrawal southwards to Lwow, the train was destroyed by the Luftwaffe on September 19, 1939.

In total, in the period 1918–1939, Poland

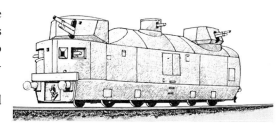

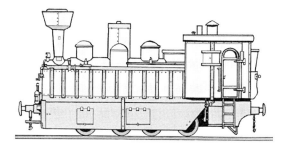

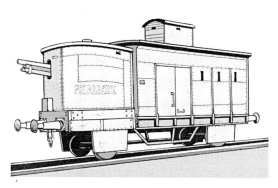

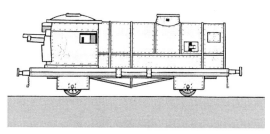

Above: Artillery armored car of train Danuta. This artillery armored car, part of armored train Danuta, was equipped with one turret-mounted 100 mm (3.93 in) howitzer, one mounted-turret 75 mm (2.95 in) gun, and a cupola fitted with a 7.92 mm (0.31 in) machine gun. Armored train Danuta was formed in Poznan in May 1919. It probably utilized some rolling stock from the German train Panzerzug 22, captured by the insurgents in February 1919. The composition of train Danuta was variable in that period. The armament of the Danuta artillery car in August 1920 consisted of a 75mm gun, 37mm gun and 10 MG's, or of two heavy guns (most likely 75 mm), two 37 mm guns and fifteen machine guns. During the Warsaw Battle in August 1920, Danuta fought within Polish 1st Army's armored train unit, which supported the 15th Division. On August 17, 1920, it took part in a successful combined raid on Minsk Mazowiecki, along with armored trains Msciciel and Paderewski. After that, Danuta was assigned to the 5th army and was fighting in the Mlawa area.

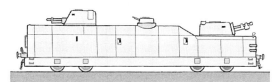

Above: Profile of armored car Danuta.

Left, top: Polish armored locomotive (series 178) used in armored train Paderewski. The train, issued in September 1919, was named after Ignacy Paderewski (1860–1941), who was a Polish pianist, composer and politician (prime minister in 1919–20)—one of the "fathers" of independent Poland.

Left, middle: Artillery wagon of armored train Poznanczyk, 1920.

Left, bottom: Armored car of train Pilsudski 1920. This rail car was armed with a 75 mm gun and several machine guns.

built 80 armored trains, and about 60 armored locomotives and 300 armored cars. Surviving Polish armored trains were taken into German service in late 1939 after the capitulation of Poland. They used them principally for security duty, patrol, and eventually as antipartisan units behind the front line in Russia after 1941.

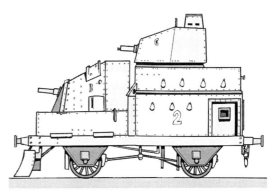

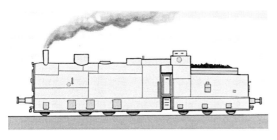

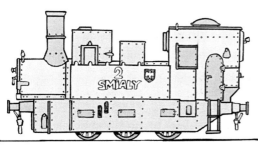

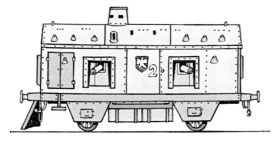

Left, top: *Armored locomotive of train Danuta.*

Left, second: *Armored locomotive Serie 180 (1920).*

Left, third: *Polish armored locomotive Ti3 (G5-3) class. Designed by the German Company Henschel & Sohns from Kassel, this type of locomotive was built in 1903–1906. Locomotive and tender had a length of 16.17 m (53 ft), and an empty weight of 80 t. Top speed was approximately 45 km/h.*

Left, fourth [Two views of PP-2]: *Top: Locomotive PP-2 Smialy. Armored train Smialy (meaning Brave or Bold in Polish) fought for thirty years, serving four different countries. It was originally an Austrian armored train that was captured by the Poles in 1918. It was then named Smialy and saw action in the Soviet-Polish War. In the interwar it was modernized, and in 1939 it fought against the Germans. After the defeat and capitulation of Poland, it was seized and impressed into Russian service and designated BP 75 of the NKVD. In 1941 it was captured and used in combat by the Germans until 1944 as the redesignated Panzerzug 10.*

Bottom: Machine gun car in PP-2 armored train Smialy in 1920. The two-axle assault car had a length of 7.90 m, and was armed with four 7.92 mm Wz08 machine guns placed in the sides. The car featured two doors (one on each side) one escape hatch in the bottom, and also doors in both ends, enabling passage between cars. It transported a complete 32-man assault platoon.

Above: *Artillery car in PP-2 train Smialy in 1920. The armor was 8–12 mm, later thickened to 40 mm. It was armed with one 80 mm M5/8 gun, and three machine guns (one in the top turret and two in casemates on both sides). The weapons were served by a crew of 12 to 15 men.*

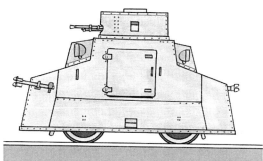

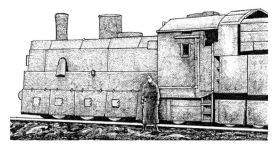

Top: *Polish D-2 armored railcar.*
   Above: *Armored locomotive PP-55 Bartosz Glowacki.*

Draisines

Poland also employed draisines in the late 1920s and during the 1930s.

The Poles purchased a number of Czech-designed Tatra T-18 draisines, which were used for scouting and also for exercises and training of armored train crews. When Nazi Germany invaded Poland in September 1939, draisines were used with armored trains Nr. 15 (Smierc) and Nr. 13 (General Sosnkowski) as reconnaissance units. One draisine of train Nr. 15 was destroyed by antitank guns near Nasielsk on September 5, 1939. The rest were apparently abandoned, some in damaged condition. All Polish Tatra draisines were captured by the Germans, but their fate is not known. Probably their weak engines, poor armament, and thin armor discouraged the Germans from front-line combat usage.

Apart from combat vehicles, draisines and armored trains, the Polish army also used road military vehicles mounted on rails. The only one to enter service by 1939 was the WZ 34 halftrack artillery tractor. For the purpose of rail riding, the truck could be equipped with a set of small rail wheels, fixed to the front

Above: *Profile, Draisine Tatra T-18. The small draisine was 3.6 m in length and 2.1 m in height. It could be coupled with other rail vehicles using a coupling rod. Standard armament consisted of one or two air-cooled 7.92 mm model 25 Hotchkiss machine guns, mounted in the turret. The riveted hull armor was 6 mm thick, and turret was 8 mm. The draisine (empty) weighted 3.7 t, was powered by a Tatra T12 2-cylinder, air-cooled gasoline engine, and had a top speed of 50 km/h and a maximum range of 700 km. The inside of the T-18 draisine was very cramped. It had doubled driver stations on both ends, and the crew included 3 soldiers: a commander-machine gunner, and two drivers.*

Above: *WZ 34 halftrack artillery tractor mounted on rail. Based on the French halftrack type Citroën-Kegresse, the Polish Wzor 34 weighed some 3,000 kg (2,205 lb). It had a length of 4.7 m (185 in), a maximum speed of 30–35 km/h (up to 22 mph) on road, and a range of up to 250 km (155 mi). It was a quite successful design, and between 1935 and 1939 some 400 units were produced in several versions.*

wheels and behind the track mechanism. Such halftracks were neither armed nor armored, so they were only used for repair by units attached to armored trains. For the purpose of reconnaissance, two such halftracks could be coupled together in order to enable faster moving in both directions.

GERMANY

According to the Treaty of Versailles in 1919, the army of the German Weimar Republic was reduced to 100,000 professional soldiers (no conscription) and those were forbidden to have tanks and armored trains, heavy artillery, airplanes, airships, and submarines (only a few warships under 100,000 t). In the years 1929–1937, however, the Reichsbahn had formed some twenty-two security trains intended not for military actions but to transport police personnel in the event of social turmoil. The locomotives and cars of these trains were lightly armored with often improvised means. The German Army had always been skeptical about the military value of armored trains even during World War I. This state of mind was shared by the Nazis, and when Hitler came to power in January 1933, he ordered the rearmament of the German Army, but no priority development of armored trains was envisioned.

In 1938 Nazi Germany annexed Austria and Czechoslovakia and captured a number of armored trains, which were relegated to the reserve. However, in 1939 the Germans changed their minds and started to believe armored trains could play an offensive role. For this purpose Hitler ordered the construction of seven armored trains using elements of the existing security and foreign captured trains. During the Second World War, Germany became one of the main users of armored trains, as will be described in Part 4.

FRANCE

August 1937 saw the creation of the Société Nationale des Chemin de Fer Français (SNCF, National French Railroad Company), which was formed by the nationalization of France's five main railroad companies by the French state with 51 percent ownership, and large amounts of funding from public subsidies invested into the system. During the period 1918–1939, France's main connection to railroads with military purposes was in the colonies, notably in the protectorate of Morocco, which was ruled by the military. Also, two locally armored trains were operated in the then colony of Indochina (today Vietnam, Laos, and Cambodia), one based in Tonkin (North Vietnam) and one in Cambodia. These were mainly used for securing the railroads during internal uprisings. The Cambodia armored train seems to have been used to patrol the narrow-gauge line between Phnom Penh and Poipet during the war with Thailand. Both of them survived until 1945, but unfortunately nothing else is known about these trains.

Militarily the great affair concerning France's defense in the 1930s was the construction of the Maginot Line. This was a barrier stretching along almost 200 miles at the Franco-German border composed of ouvrages (fortified works), many underground and consisting of interconnected combat blocks and subterranean facilities, as well as concrete artillery casemates and machine-gun bunkers, and antipersonnel and antitank obstacles.

To supply forts and bunkers, permanent military 60 cm narrow-gauge trains were used. For obvious ventilation purposes in internal subterranean galleries, cars were hand-pushed or towed by small electric-powered locomotives fitted with overhead cables, the 600-volt current being provided by underground usines (power plants). At Gros Ouvrage (Fort) Hackenberg, located east of Thionville (Lorraine), the underground electric railroad is still in use for tourists.

Outside in the open, gasoline- or diesel-engined locomotives, locotracteurs, draisines and trolleys were used. From 1930 all military trains supplying the Maginot Line were operated by sappers and engineers of the 15ème Régiment de Sapeurs de Chemin de Fer du Génie (15th Railroad Engineering Regiment) stationed at Toul.

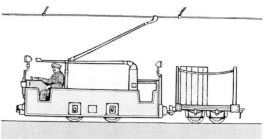

Above: *Electric locomotive for supply train inside a large artillery fort of the Maginot Line. Officially designated* locomotive électrique à trolley, *it was produced by the Société des Vehicules et Tracteurs Electriques (VETRA), and powered by two electric Alsthom motors fed by 600-volt overhead current. The locomotive had a length of 4.10 m, a width of 1 m, and a speed of 8.3 km/h. It moved small and narrow cars specifically adapted to the need of the subterranean forts of the Maginot Line.*

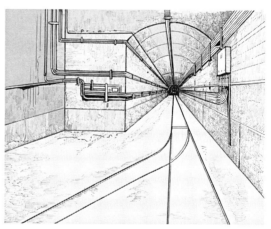

Top: *Ammunition entrance block in the Maginot Line. Note the camouflaged façade and the 60 cm gauge railroad used to supply the underground fort.*

Bottom: *Locotracteur Billard T75. The Billard Company, located at Tours, was the principal producer of diesel locomotives and draisines for both civilian and military railroads. Powered by a Panhard or Deutz gasoline engine, the 60 cm gauge T75 locomotive was used in the Maginot Line only outside the underground works.*

Above: *Subterranean gallery at fort Simserhof Maginot Line. Simserhof, located near the community of Sierstal about 4 km to the west of Bitche in the French department of Moselle, was a so-called Gros Ouvrage (artillery fort) facing the German frontier. It was a part of the Fortified Sector of Rohrbach. The entire ouvrage was provided with a 60 cm gauge electric railroad that connected the service areas at the rear with the eight combat blocks at the front, and which extended outside the position to a network of similar surface railroads behind the main line. The gallery system was excavated at an average depth of 27 meters (89 ft) below the surface.*

GREAT BRITAIN

Railroad had proved vital in World War I, but when it ended, few funds were available for military development of any kind, and transport by rail in particular had a low priority. The British Longmoor Camp railroad training base called Woolmer Instructional Military Railroad located in Hampshire, which had been created in 1903, had played an important role during World War I. It had developed into a comprehensive network and

British armored patrol car on rail. Between 1920 and 1948, Palestine was a British protectorate under a League of Nations mandate. Through the British administration period, the area experienced the ascent of two major nationalist movements, one among the Jews and the other among the Arabs. Competition and collision of those nationalist movements have had a significant impact on the history of that period, with violence peaking especially high during the Arab Revolt of 1936–1939. Among other weapons, the British used gasoline rail/road cars to patrol tracks.

full-time instructional installation including railroad lines, stations, barracks, stores, workshops, locomotive and rolling stock sheds where all railroad troops serving in France and on the other fronts had received their initial training. In the interwar years, in spite of drastic reduction of funds, the Longmoor base was not closed down, but it had to exist on whatever its staff could collect in order to keep British military railroads alive. In 1924 and 1927, new lands were purchased and gradually equipped for use as training areas. In 1930 the base was further improved and expanded by the construction of new barracks and additional facilities for training personnel and testing new materials. In 1935 the whole base was renamed the Longmoor Military Railroad (LMR). Although Britain had increased military spending and funding shortly prior to 1939 in response to the increasing and threatening strength of Nazi Germany, its forces were still weak by comparison—especially the British Army. When World War II started, British military railroads were rather unprepared.

ITALY

During the Fascist dictatorship (1922–1943) of Benito Mussolini (1883–1943), important construction and modernization programs for the Italian railroads took place. The most spectacular was the high-speed direct lines between Rome and Naples that reduced the travel time from the two cities by one hour and a half. The second high-speed line linked Bologna to Florence. Proudly announced by the regime's propaganda as "constructing Fascism," it included the second longest tunnel in the world at the time. Electrification using 3,000 V direct current was introduced, which later supplanted the existing three-phase system. Other improvements included automatic blocks, light signals, construction of numerous main stations (e.g., Milan Central, Napoli Mergellina, Roma Ostiense), and other technical modernizations.

The rolling stock was enhanced from 1933 by powerful diesel and electric Littorine locomotives, so-named from the lictorial symbols of the Fascist regime. The Italian electric locomotives in particular started the traditional vanguard position of Italy in the field. In December 1937, a type ETR 200 traveled on the Rome-Naples line at a speed of 201 km/h (125 mph) in the Campoleone-Cisterna section. Two years later the same train reached 203 km/h (126 mph) on the Milan-Florence line. In this period food trains made up of refrigerated wagons started to run from southern to northern Italy, and abroad.

On the subject of military railroads, the Fascist period was marked by conquest and construction in Africa. From 1935, Fascist Italy developed railroads with a dual role of supplying their military conquest and economic exploitation of the colonies of Eritrea and Somaliland. In Lybia few railroads were built, as the priority was given to the construction of roads, like the coastal highway named Via Balbo, for example, that ran (and still runs today) parallel to the Lybian Mediterranean Sea.

SPAIN

The Spanish Civil War

In the late 1930s Spain was torn apart by a terrible conflict. The Spanish Civil War lasted for three years from 1936 to 1939. It did not bring two parties face to face, but two heterogenic groups of radically opposed factions.

On one side there was conservative Spain, including Christian Democrats, Falangists, Monarchists and Traditionalists (former Carlists), and Ultranationalists. These factions allied with the Army, which had risen in revolt in a number of provinces against the Republican government legally elected in 1931. These conservative (aka Nationalist) parties were soon united under the leadership of General Francisco Franco (1892–1975).

The coalition opposing Franco was composed of various loose factions comprising the left-of-center Republicans, anarchists, socialists, communists (both rival Trotskyist and Stalinist obediences), as well as Catalan and Basque regional independence advocates— known collectively as the Republicans. The length of the war reflected the fact that no side really possessed the power to win quickly, and from the start both adversaries sought for and obtained help from abroad. Both Fascist Italy and Nazi Germany intervened in the Civil War, siding with Franco's Nationalists. The western democracies (notably France, Britain and the USA) discreetly supported the Republicans, but the Soviet Union substantially and openly helped the Stalinist Communist component of the Republicans by sending arms, ammunition, airplanes, and military technicians and advisors. The attention of much of the world was focused on this fratricidal struggle. Indeed, the Spanish Civil War represented the first major armed clash between the rival ideologies of the extreme right (Fascism) and Western Democracy and the left, whose mutual hatred dominated the international political scene in the 1920s and 1930s. The Spanish Civil War was a ferocious conflict, often regarded as a general rehearsal for the Second World War. Both sides gave no quarter, and exactions from one side were retaliated for by atrocities from the other. By 1939 the Nationalists emerged as victors. In an exhausted country, the chaotic victory was followed by a large-scale murderous purge, and the establishment of a Fascist dictatorship that lasted until Franco's death in 1975 when Spain became a kingdom again.

Armored Trains in the Spanish Civil War

Imbued with Marxist ideology, influenced by Soviet propaganda, and inspired by a certain mystic conviction born in the Bolshevik revolution of 1917, socialist and communist Republicans created several armored trains like those used by the Red Russians in their civil war from 1918 to 1921. In August 1936 there first appeared an improvised train with two locomotives and a few cars hastily clad with thick metal plates. Soon, another train was built by the railroad workers of the Madrid trade unions, and armed with a cannon and several machine guns. Operating on the Madrid-Escurial-Avila line, this armored train supported the Republican troops fighting around Madrid. Bombarded by Nationalist planes, the train was derailed, damaged and soon abandoned.

In the meantime other armored trains, this time better designed and better armed, had been built. One operated in the Tagus Valley on the Madrid-Caceres line, and was captured by the Nationalists while participating in the defense of Talavera de la Reina in September 1936. Two other trains were engaged, designated H and K, and used on the Madrid-Aranjuez-Valencia line. In November another train was introduced and brought into action on the Saragossa-Madrid line. In January 1937 another Republican armored train was destroyed near La Corunna by the Nationalists.

By May 1937 a Brigade de Trenes Blindados (Armored Trains Brigade) was created in an attempt to design and organize standardized trains. These were intended to include a service car carrying material for track repair; an armored car with a 70 mm gun and two machine guns; an armored locomotive; a second armored car armed with a 57 mm gun and two machine guns; and three transport wagons. However, the work of the Brigade had little practical effect, as the construction of armored trains greatly depended upon available materials and human resources at any particular place.

The Spanish Civil War was by many aspects a testing ground for new weapons (notably antiaircraft artillery, airplanes and tanks), and for the first time armored trains proved extremely vulnerable to air attacks, notably by the newly developed dive-bomber. Consequently, the existing Republican armored trains were only briefly engaged in combat from a distance, mainly providing artillery support. During daytime, wherever possible they were camouflaged with branches and foliage, hidden in forests or concealed in tunnels, and traveling only at night or by bad weather.

Nevertheless two more armored trains, designated No. 1 and No. 2, were built in 1937. Hauled by diesel locomotives, they carried on their roofs simulated tracks, complete with ballast and sleepers, to conceal them from aerial reconnaissance. Both trains were sent to the southern front and saw action in the area between Badajoz and Cordoba. By the end of 1937 both trains were ordered to proceed to Aragon, narrowly escaping capture by the Nationalists. In 1938 they saw limited action due to shortage of ammunition and increased threat from the sky. After the bloody battle of the Ebro River from July to November 1938, won by the Nationalists, the Republican command recalled its armored trains to Barcelona to help the badly mauled remnant of the Republican forces retreating in disorder to the Spanish-French border. Only one train succeeded in taking refuge in France, remaining for some time in the border station of Latour-de-Carol in the Roussillon province. In January 1939 there was only one Republican train still fighting sporadically as artillery support in the south, but by April 1939 it was all over. The surviving locomotives, cars and coaches had their armor removed and were put into civilian use by the Spanish National Railroad Company.

The use of armored trains in the Spanish

Civil War was on the whole a failure caused by the railroad lines running through a tortuous countryside, the difficulty in following the development of the battles, aimless strategy and lack of supply, and particularly the vulnerability of attacks from the air despite the use of antiaircraft weapons. The left-wing Republicans seem to have used them more for "sentimental" reasons linked with the Soviet experience than as a response to a clear tactical necessity.

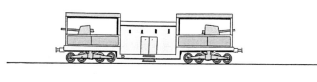

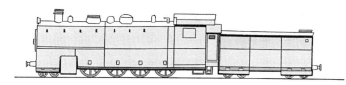

Spanish Republican armored train. Top: Artillery car. Bottom: Armored locomotive. Armored trains were often painted in camouflage disruptive patterns, and often displayed large initials indicating their owner's allegiance, e.g., UGT (Union General de Trabajadores), CNT (Confederacion Nacional de Trabajo), FAI (Federacion Anarchista Iberica), Milicias Antifascistas (Anti-Fascist Militias), or AIT (Alianza Internacional de Trabajadores). Also appearing were leftist political slogans such as UHP! (Unios Hermanos Proletarios! meaning Working class brothers, unite!) or Libertad! (Freedom!).

CHINA

The last Chinese imperial dynasty, the Qing, ruled from 1644 to 1911, when it was overthrown by Sun Yat-Sen (1866–1925), the founding father of the modern Republic of China. The new government, however, was unable to take control of the whole country, and local military governors and regional leaders began assembling their own spheres of influence. The various and differing regions of this vast country were ruled by endlessly forming, breaking and re-forming alliances of regional generals who ruled as "warlords." These warlords acted essentially as local kings, and larger power blocs emerged, sometimes fielding armies hundreds of thousands strong. Sun Yat-Sen founded an opposition government in southern China supported by his followers in the Kuomintang (the Nationalist Party).

After the death of Sun Yat-Sen in 1925, Chiang Kai-Shek (1887–1975) took control of the Nationalist Party, and quickly moved against the warlords in the North in 1927. He was quite successful in gaining control of parts of eastern China, but his efforts were complicated by the rise of the rival Chinese Communist Party, founded in 1921 by a handful of young revolutionaries inspired by the success of Soviet Russia.

In 1930 the civil war in China ended, but a new conflict erupted in 1931 when Japan occupied Manchuria. By 1937, Japan invaded a divided and weakened China, bombing Shanghai and committing horrendous atrocities on the population of Nanjing. The Nationalist government, weakened and wracked by corruption and lacking in resolve, lost many troops in battles trying to protect the coastal cities. The government eventually retreated inland up the Yangtze River, finally creating a base in Chongqing, Sichuan Province.

Meanwhile, the Communists spread their influence among peasants across northern China and penetrated behind Japanese lines using sophisticated guerrilla warfare tactics. After the defeat of Japan in 1945, Mao Zedong (1893–1976) and the Communist Peoples' Liberation Army defeated the Nationalists, and the country became the Peoples' Republic of China in 1949. By then Chiang Kai-Shek and remnants of the defeated Nationalist forces had fled to the island of Formosa (Taiwan).

The most widespread use of the armored train after the end of the Russian Civil War was in China, where the huge distances and poor road infrastructure made it an excellent area for armored train operations during the turbulent

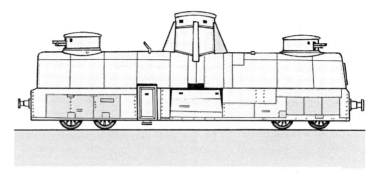

Chinese armored rail car with two gun-turrets and command tower in the middle.

1920s and 1930s. The use of armored trains in China was stimulated by the arrival of White Russian soldiers after the end of the Russian Civil War. The warlord most closely associated with armored trains was the ruthless, extravagant and colorful warlord Zhang Zongchang (1881–1932), who established control over parts of Manchuria, and proved one of the more capable generals. He introduced tanks, recruited about 4,600 defeated White refugees from the Russian Civil War, and made effective use of those who had skill and experience in armored trains. Therefore Chinese armored trains presented many similar features with the trains of the Russian Civil War.

However, there was nothing like a Chinese standardized armored train, but a lot of possible configurations including an armored locomotive in the middle; armored cars, some fitted with artillery turrets; and flatcars at both ends. These weapon systems were not threatened by the military airplane that was still in its infancy, and were particularly well suited to the size of the country and the scattered nature of combat. Zongchang had three armored trains, and all were captured by Chiang Kai-Shek's forces. The Nationalists too were deeply interested in armored trains, and in 1925 Chiang Kai-Shek had approached the Soviet government for technical support. About 1,000 Soviet advisers, including armored railroad specialists, were detached to

China and helped the constitution of Nationalist armored trains. When the Japanese seized Manchuria in 1931, they captured many of the armored trains of the Manchurian Army. Most combat between Japanese and Chinese forces took place along the railroad lines, and once again armored trains played an important role.

JAPAN

During the 1930s, the Japanese military established almost complete control over the government. When the Chinese Nationalists began to seriously challenge Japan's position in Manchuria in 1931, they occupied Manchuria. In the following year, Manchukuo was declared an independent state, controlled by the Japanese Kwantung Army through a puppet government. In 1933, Japan withdrew from the League of Nations since she was heavily criticized for her actions in China. In July 1937, the second Sino-Japanese War broke out. A small incident was soon made into a full-scale war by the Kwantung army, which acted rather independently from a more moderate government. The Japanese forces succeeded in occupying almost the whole coast of China. However, the Chinese government never surrendered completely, and the war continued on a lower scale until 1945.

Japan replaced Russian influence in the southern half of Inner Manchuria as a result of the Russo-Japanese War in 1904–05. Most of the southern branch of the Chinese Eastern

Railroad was transferred from Russia to Japan, and became the South Manchurian Railroad. This had been built as a part of Chinese East-ern Railroad in 1898–1903 by Imperial Russia according to Russian-Chinese convention and Convention of Peking 1860. Japanese influence extended into Outer Manchuria in the wake of the Russian Revolution of 1917, but Outer Manchuria had reverted to Soviet control by 1925. Manchuria was an important region for its rich mineral and coal reserves, and its soy and barley production. For pre–World War II Japan, Manchuria was an essential source of raw materials. Without occupying Manchuria, the Japanese probably could not have carried out their plan for the conquest of Southeast Asia or taken the risk of attacking the U.S. Pacific naval base of Pearl Harbor on December 7, 1941.

In the 1920s, the Japanese built some improvised armored trains converted from civilian trains, and in 1933 they made a proper train called Rinji Soko Ressha (special armored train). It was composed of twelve cars of which one was armed with a type fourteen 10 cm anti-aircraft gun, another carrying a type four 15 cm howitzer, and two cars with type eleven 75 mm antiaircraft guns. The Type 94 armored train was built in 1934 and later used by the Japanese forces in World War II. It had 8 cars (later 9) and loaded two type 14 10 cm AA guns and two type 88 AA guns. This armored train was deployed as the 1st Armored Train Unit in Manchuria.

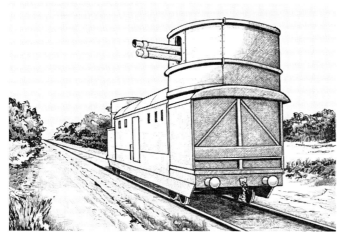

The Japanese also made use of

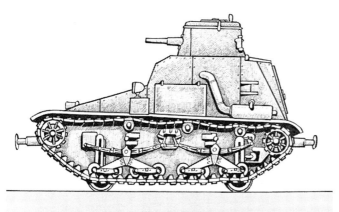

Top: *Japanese artillery railcar, Manchuria.*
Middle: *Japanese armored artillery car.*
Bottom: *Japanese So-Ki convertible tank. It had a length of 4.90 m, a width of 2.56 m, a height of 2.43 m, a weight of 8.7 t, and a maximum speed of 74 km/h on rail, and 30 km/h on road.*

small draisines and armored rail trolleys that were cheap and efficient for scouting and patrolling missions. For these purposes they developed the convertible Type 91 So-Mo armored car, which could be used both on road with conventional rubber tires, and on rail with flanged steel wheels. About 1,000 of these were produced and used throughout the wide Chinese countries. Two or more of these armored cars could be coupled together to constitute a light armored train. Another design was the Type 95 So-Ki, a railroad tank convertible to a railroad trolley owing to a conventional tracked suspension fitted with a retractable set of flanged wheels that allowed running on rail. About 138 So Ki road-rail tanks were produced between 1935 and 1943. Both So-Mo and So-Ki armored vehicles were eventually used in China and in Burma during the Second World War.

PART 4

Railroads in World War II:
Axis Powers

GENERALITIES

Roads and gasoline vehicles had greatly improved in the 1920s and 1930s. The growing competition from road transportation had decreased railroad investment during the interwar years, and companies only made a bit of modernization and refurbishment. The development of the military automobile, truck and tank in the 1930s revolutionized war at the tactical and operational levels, and railroads were expected to play a much lesser role should a war break out.

However, this assumption ignored two main advantages that railroads had over motor transport. Firstly, steam trains used coal, a product available in plentiful supply in Europe, while oil (used by gasoline vehicles) had to be imported. Should the supply of oil to Europe be cut—by war operations, for example—oil would become scarce and expensive. The USA produced some oil, but not in sufficient quantities, and neither France nor Britain nor Nazi Germany had oil. Secondly, it was obvious that long-range strategic mobility, and massive and bulky transportation on land, would continue to be carried out by rail. Indeed, the role of the railroads remained central to the logistical needs of all World War II belligerents, because they were still unrivaled for the transport of heavy loads and for distances of more than 200 miles. Cars and trucks,

to a large extent, replaced the horse rather than the railroad, but even this was not always true. The British and the U.S. armies were fully motorized by the end of World War II, but Nazi Germany, due to lack of fuel, still relied upon pack animals to transport supplies, draw ammunition carts, and tow artillery pieces onto the battlefield. The German fully motorized *Panzerdivisionen* (armored divisions) of the *Blitzkrieg* (Lightning War) period (1939–1941) were few in number compared to the average standard infantry formations with horse-drawn artillery and supply carts.

In World War II major operational movements were conducted by rail on all fronts. Most of the fighting men of all nations involved in World War II at some time in their service careers were seen off at their local railroad station or at a big-city terminus. Railroads retained their place as the key mode of transport, but their use was different than during World War I. Cars, trucks, armored and transport vehicles, and supplies were transported by trains, and then disembarked to provide the basic transport needs for short or medium distances.

Before and during World War II, tanks were transported long distances by railroad because their tracks usually lasted only about one thousand miles, many models less than that. Their dimensions, notably their width, were calculated by their ability to pass through

European tunnels against oncoming traffic. Their weight (generally under 24 tons) was limited so as to enable them to take both road and railroad bridges. For these reasons, in Germany the maximum width of a tank was 9 feet 7 inches. In Great Britain, railways had a narrower gauge, which kept British tanks to a width under 8 feet 9 inches.

In 1940 a German armored division could comprise over 3,000 motor vehicles, including the supply column, and numbered about 14,000 soldiers. Moving this force by road was a complicated and conspicuous exercise. It occupied nearly 70 miles of road space as it crawled along at about 2.5 miles an hour—in perfect dry weather, in good terrain, and without enemy action of any kind. Even in unopposed movement there was wear and tear on the vehicles, and most especially on the tank tracks. Transported by railroad, the same force required about 80 trains—each train with up to 55 wagons—but at much greater speed. So it was clear that military motorization in the 1940s did not do away with the army's dependence upon railroad. During World War II the railroad still dominated military planning as it had since the American Civil War.

The civilian network systems throughout Europe, and everywhere fighting occurred, came under enormous pressure during World War II owing to greatly increased traffic, increasing shortage of manpower, and damage from aircraft attacks. In World War I, railroads were the safest form of transport, but in World War II they were dangerously exposed, and very vulnerable. Indeed, trains, railroad tracks, yards, stations, viaducts, bridges and any other installations were favorite targets of bomber airplanes.

Aerial warfare had made tremendous advances in the late 1930s and 1940s. The period saw the appearance of aircraft with reliable, strong and powerful engines, all-metal skin fuselage and wings, aerodynamic designs, enclosed cockpits, retractable landing gear allowing for increased speed, powerful armament, and large loads of bombs. In aviation, as in the motorcar industry, the spur of competition improved not only the capability of the product, but also mechanical efficiency and reliability. In the late 1930s it had become possible for large air fleets to launch devastating surprise attacks from high above and far inside enemy land, as illustrated by the bombing of Guernica (April 26, 1937) during the Spanish Civil War. That small Basque town in northern Spain was totally destroyed by German and Italian warplanes at the request of the Spanish Nationalists. The air raid on Guernica was immortalized in June 1937 by a mural-sized oil painting on canvas by the Spanish artist Pablo Picasso (1881–1973).

As in World War I, belligerents made use of railroad heavy artillery in World War II, sometimes the very same weapons or at least their close brothers. World War II marked the zenith of heavy railroad gun development, although medium artillery was increasingly mounted on armored tracked self-propelled vehicles. Many of the railroad guns deployed at the start of the conflict were of World War I vintage, and it was the German army that made most use of heavy artillery mounted on railroad. Germany's ambitious development program saw the introduction of a number of new classes, including the world's largest, the 80 cm-caliber Schwerer Gustav and Schwerer Dora guns, which weighed in at 1,350 tons and fired a huge 7-ton shell. The German super heavy 80 cm rail gun marked at the same time the apogee and the swan song of the rail-mounted artillery.

Armored trains were used during World War II in the wide expanses of Russia and in the mountainous Balkans, but their age of glory was definitely gone as they were no match for attacking aircraft, and were more and more replaced by the versatile tank, self-propelled artillery and armored car, which efficiently combined flexibility, protection, firepower and speed.

Another use of railroads during World

War II must not be omitted: the infamous deportation of millions of prisoners and innocent people in inhumane conditions to Nazi prisons, concentration and extermination camps.

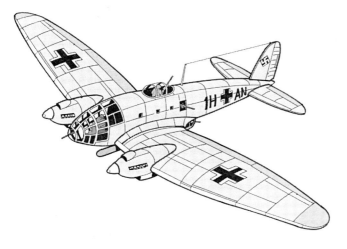

Heinkel He 111. Together with the Junkers Ju 88, the He 111, designed in 1936, was Germany's most important twin-engined medium bomber during World War II. Operated by a crew of four or five depending on the version and variant, it had a speed of 258 mph, and could carry a load of 1,000 kg (2,200 lb) of bombs.

GERMANY

After the seizure of power by the Nazis in January 1933, Hitler gradually launched an ambitious program of expanding the German armies, including the creation of a new Luftwaffe (air force) and Panzerwaffe (armored corps), as well as a rebirth and great increase of the Heer (ground forces) by conscription, and a new development given to the Kriegsmarine (navy). Hitler was enthusiastic about automobiles, and wanted a fully motorized ground force, but German industry proved incapable of fulfilling that demand. Consequently motorization remained limited, and only a few elite armored divisions were fully motorized with tanks, armored personnel carriers and transport vehicles with cross-country capacity. As for the rest of the German forces, their supplies, support artillery, heavy materials and men had to rely on horses and legwork for short and medium distances and on rail transport for long distances. In 1940, of 103 divisions, only 16 were fully motorized, and for long distances these were moved by rail. The successes of the German *Blitzkrieg* in the early years 1939–1941 largely depended on the concentration of a tremendous force of tanks supported by infantry and artillery with tactical bomber airplanes to make a quick, brutal, and decisive breakthrough. This massive gathering of forces was impossible without the backing up of trains. In spite of Hitler's dreams, and just like in former conflicts, it was the railroad that supplied the armies in campaigns.

In the summer of 1941 the invasion of Soviet Russia cruelly exposed the failings of German logistics. Operation Barbarossa (the name given to the invasion of Soviet Russia) was overwhelmed by the supply constraints, and its failure changed the course of World War II. German logistics could not cope with the size of the land, the scale and the magnitude of the task, and the weakness and inadequacy of the means available. There was no alternative to using Russia's sparse railroad network, and the speed of the advance was limited to the speed at which new railroad lines could be repaired, converted or constructed. At gauge changeovers on existing lines, there were the customary bottlenecks. Besides, Germany had the perennial problem of shortage of fuel, both gasoline and coal. From the start, the offensive had very little chance of success because of logistical problems. In Russia the German supply lines were simply overextended beyond their natural and maximum limits to the point of collapse. The

Germans had to adapt to a war of attrition, for which they were not prepared, and which ultimately would be their downfall.

German National Railroad Company

Just like in former wars, Germany's railroads were militarized, and a very efficient military rail department reappeared right before and during World War II called the Deutsche Re-

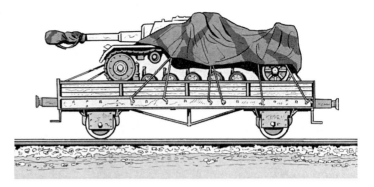

StuG III (self-propelled gun) transported on train.

ichsbahn Gesellschaft (DRG), also called Deutsche Reichsbahn (DR for short, the National German Railroad Company). This state enterprise under the Reichsverkehrsministerium (Reich Ministry of Transportation) had been created in 1920 by merging existing Länderbahnen (regional networks) from Prussia, Hesse, Bavaria, Palatinate, Saxony, Württemberg, Baden, Oldenburg and Mecklenburg into one single national company.

Since 1926, the German State Railroad Company was headed by engineer and railroad expert Julius Dorpmüller (1869–1945). After the Nazis came to power, the rail network was placed under direct government control and "coordinated" along Nazi lines within the Gleichschaltung (Nazification scheme). To emphasize this, swastikas were added to the eagle, Germany's traditional symbol of national sovereignty on the rail cars. The highly regarded Julius Dorpmüller became chairman of the Motorways Management Committee, and was appointed Reich Minister of Transport in 1937, a post he held until the fall of Hitler's regime in 1945. By laws of 1937 and 1939, the DR was further reorganized. It was made a public service, a nationally owned undertaking operating on a self-supporting financial basis with a considerable measure of administrative autonomy.

Hitler was a car fanatic, who consequently focused his country's transport infrastructure effort on the Autobahnen (motorways) and the development of gasoline vehicles, notably the cheap Volkswagen (People's Car). There was even a paramilitary branch of the Nazi party, known as the Nationalsozialistisches Kraftfahr Korps (NSKK, National-Socialist Drivers Corps) that controlled everything pertaining to automobiles.

But although Nazi Germany was profoundly motor car–minded, the railroads remained at the heart of the transportation system. In March 1938, following the annexation of Austria, the Bundesbahn Österreich (BBÖ, Federal Railroad of Austria) was integrated into the Deutsche Reichsbahn. In 1938 the railroad system covered about 35,000 miles of track of which 1,500 miles were electrically operated. The DR was a first-class railroad system, well equipped with plenty of modern locomotives and excellent rolling stock. In the 1930s, high-speed streamlined steam engines with matching cars were developed, and fast trains like the diesel-powered Fliegender Hamburger (Flying Hamburger) and the class 05 streamlined express engine reached a speed of 200 km/h (124.5 mph).

There were also a number of locomotives especially designed for military purposes during the war. Like the British "Austerity" machines, they were cheap to build and maintain, and efficient to operate. A strong workhorse was the type 52 locomotive. Used from 1942 to 1950, this 2-10-2 locomotive was produced primarily by the Floridsdorfer Werke in Vienna, by the Henschel Company, and by the Waffen und Maschinen-AG in Posen (in today's Poland). Total production was 6,303 units. The type 52 weighed 84 metric tons and had an output of 1,620 horsepower.

The 2-10-0 type 42 "Kriegslokomotive," first built in 1943, was another workhorse for the Deutsche Reichsbahn. The last type 42 ran with the Austrian State Railroads (OBB) in 1967, clearly a well-designed locomotive for such a long service life. Like most wartime products, the type 42 was designed to use only a minimum of parts and materials. Some 866 units were built in total.

Before the Second World War, the most important German rail lines ran from east to west. The most modern high-speed lines were the Prussian Ostbahn, which ran through the Polish corridor; the line from Berlin to Hamburg, on which high-speed diesel trains ran; the line from Hannover to the Ruhr; the line from Frankfurt am Main to southwest Germany; and the line from Berlin to Breslau (present-day Wroclaw in Poland).

After 1938 and during the war, owing to German conquests in Europe and Russia, the DR greatly expanded. It then operated about 500,000 miles of track and the number of employees rose from 800,000 in 1937 to 1,400,000 in 1942. In mid–1943 that number had grown to 1.7 million German men and women with an additional 250,000 foreign forced laborers employed in menial tasks. The DR was one of the most important German organizations during the Second World War. The DR played an important role in transporting supply, materials and troops from one front to another. For example, for the attack on the Soviet Union in June 1941, the German railroad company deployed some 33,000 trains to transport the Panzer and infantry divisions. By the end of 1942, the Reichsbahn had about 112,000 personnel managing 42,000 km of railroad in Russia.

Civilian life was subjected to increasing militarization, and even nonmilitary services

as the Reichspost (Postal Service) were militarized and uniformized.

To the military requirements, one also had to consider the civilian and economic needs. Raw materials from the German-occupied areas had to be brought back home so that German industry could make optimal use of them. Industry specialists had to travel from one city to another, and families also had social obligations they wanted to be able to meet.

In terms of supplementing their industrial needs, the Germans ruthlessly exploited all countries they had conquered, notably in the East. Trains were used to transport: coal from Ukraine (never shipped in sufficient quantities); manganese from Nikopol; iron ore from Krivoi-Rog; timber from Estonia, Latvia, Lithuania, and the Pripet march regions; oil-shale from Estonia (a large percentage of the Kriegsmarine's needs came from Estonian oil-shale); grains and foodstuffs from Ukraine (this was always in surplus as Ukraine was and is a very fertile region). The German economy during the war period centered thus on rail transportation, and coal was the single most important item in this equation—at least 90 percent of all coal used in Germany was transported via rail. German industry, both military and civilian, could not survive without coal and the vital railroads that carried it. Without rail, there was no coal, and without coal, the industrial might of Germany was literally doomed to failure. All other industrial necessities, as well as German passengers, goods, and freight, also required the German railroads.

It should be noted that railroad traffic between Hitler's Reich and Mussolini's Fascist Italy passed through the key tunnels of Gotthart and Saint Bernard in Switzerland. The Germans had made several plans (e.g., Operation Tannenbaum in 1940) to invade the country and secure the railroad connection between the two allies. However, they were well aware that the tunnels were defended by strong fortifications. Also they knew that in case of an attack, the Swiss would not hesitate to destroy the strategic tunnels, rendering communication impossible for a long period of time. For these reasons they respected the Swiss neutrality.

As might be expected, the Nazi government rationalized the administrative organization of the DR and introduced standardized uniform and insignia. The emblem of the DR was a rather large winged wheel. The railroad uniforms during the Nazi period of 1933 to 1945 were similar to those worn during the Weimar period (1919–1933). The basic color was dark blue and included a Prussian-style tunic and cap, jacket, greatcoat and black trousers. The belt buckle had the winged wheel above a swastika surrounded by a wreath with the words Deutsche Reichsbahn. The eye-catching DR uniform survived the war with obvious modification.

The DR was a uniformed nonmilitary company and its structure did not include a rank system based on military hierarchy. Instead,

Deutsche Reichsbahn cap. The trim on the cap was bright red.

the Company was divided into four main worker classifications (indicated by collar patches and cap cords) and subdivided into twenty-three pay categories (indicated by shoulder straps). This was modified in February 1941 when a collar patch and shoulder straps system was introduced. Old and new ranking systems and insignia, however, were mixed until the end of the war owing to lack of means for the total introduction and issue of uniform innovations. High-ranking officials had a dagger featuring the winged wheel on the guard. Laborers on the railroad wore a variety of overalls and fatigue suits, possibly with a Reichsbahn or a Wehrmacht armband. The personnel of the Reichsbahn were of important help for assisting the huge cannons of the army's Eisenbahnartillerie (E-Art, heavy artillery mounted on railroad) and Panzerzüge (armored trains).

They also contributed their experience to the Organisation Todt (OT). This was a large conglomerate of building companies working together at all Nazi construction programs, including Hitler's concrete command headquarters, and enormous concrete shelters for submarines operating from occupied French ports in the Atlantic Ocean. The OT also built bunkers for the Wehrmacht, notably the Westwall (aka Siegfried Line), and the so-called Atlantik Wall, a belt of coastal fortifications stretching from Norway down to the Franco-Spanish border intended to repulse any Allied attempt to land and invade Europe from the west.

The absence of infrastructure on the working sites often forced the OT to create communication means such as roads, paths, tracks or narrow-gauge railroads. For example, railroads were built in the Channel Islands on Jersey and Guernsey by the Organisation Todt. Jersey had a one-meter-gauge line which ran from Saint-Helier to Ronez Quarry with branches to Corbière and Tesson Mill. Another was a sixty-centimeter-gauge line which went to the Western Quarries from La Pulente

BR 64 German war locomotive. The Class 64 was developed from 1926 onwards, and it was built between 1928 and 1940. About 520 units were built, and the model was retired only in 1975. The locomotive had a 2-6-2 wheel arrangement, and a top speed of 90 km/h.

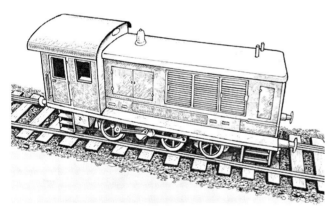

German diesel locomotive WR 360C-12. This standard Wehrmacht 0-6-0 DH locomotive was used extensively in switching, and movement of railroad artillery in rear areas. About 200 units were produced, and many were still in service in the early 1970s under the designation V 36.

Reichsbahn officer.

Security Troops

Nazi Germany was a police state and the German Railroad Company had security formations. The Bahnschutzpolizei (BZP, Railroad Protection Police) was formed in 1933 by the Eisenbahn Verwaltung (Railroad Administration) in order to assure the safety and security of rolling stock and buildings of the company in its entire network. Personnel and officers investigated trespassing on rail property, assaults against passengers, sabotage targeting the railroad, arson, pickpocketing, ticket fraud, robbery and theft

along Saint-Ouen's Bay, and a third line was a sixty-centimeter-gauge line which ran eastward from Saint-Helier to Gorey. Another example, on the island of Groix (south Brittany, France), was the construction of the large Batterie Seydlitz (four 20.3 cm SKC/34 naval guns with a range of 37 km, mounted inside two armored turrets from the German warship *Seydlitz*) also required the establishment of a railroad line to transport building materials.

of personal belongings, baggage or freight. The Bahnschutzpolizei consisted mainly of middle-aged and older men with prior police experience or service time during World War I. These men were trained as security personnel who watched over all activities of the railroad, principally in the stations, but they could also be required to operate in the trains either undercover in civilian dress or in uniform.

Captain Bahnschutzpolizei. The Bahnschutzpolizei (railroad police) were personnel responsible for railroad security. This Oberabteilungsführer (Captain) wears the light grey service uniform. Top left: Insignia of the Bahnschutzpolizei consisting of the traditional German police Gardenstern (an eight-pointed star), the DRB emblem (a winged train wheel), and a swastika.

The Bahnschutz police were organized into Bezirke (district) Abteilungen (detachments), each totaling about 150 men. These were divided into three Züge (squads or companies), and each Zug included four Gruppen (groups) composed of a dozen men. Members of the Bahnschutz were not policemen proper, but functionaries who could on occasion be called upon to assist the regular police. They were dressed originally with a dark blue uniform, but by 1941 the uniform was changed and replaced by a light blue dress with a cut title bearing the mention Bahnschutzpolizei. As the war progressed, the railroad police also checked travel papers and identity documents, and in time of crisis would take arms to defend against partisan attacks in occupied territories.

The Bahnschutzpolizei was a relatively small organization with a large responsibility. Therefore the German Army (Heer) and Waffen SS were often designated to assist auxiliary troops to the Bahnschutzpolizei to help defend the railroad and its operations. In fact, this was of vital interest to both military organizations as they relied ever increasingly so on supplies being transported through occupied territories. For this very purpose Zugwachtabteilungen (train guards units) were created. These Army troops were assigned for duty to assist security units, not only in the railroad stations, but on the actual trains. The train guards were intended to maintain order and discipline, to escort trains used by High Command Staff, and to protect convoys passing through territories that were unsafe because of partisan aggressive activities. They were lightly armed, and wore a duty Ringkragen (gorget) similar to that of the Bahnhofswache with a scroll bearing the legend "Zugwachabteilung." An armband with the same legend could be worn instead of the gorget.

The technical skills of the German Railroad personnel were also employed in the operation of Eisenbahn Panzerzüge (Eis. Pz-Z), armored trains. (See below.) Some eighty armored trains were operated during World War II by the German forces, mainly on the eastern front in Russia and in the Balkans. The Deutsche Reichsbahn-Gesellschaft saw armored trains as a way to preserve and advance its presence in military circles. By keeping a strong military face on this state-owned railroad, the Reichsbahn looked to increase both their state funding and their national prestige.

"The Final Solution to the Jewish Question"

During World War II, the Reichsbahn was an essential component of German military logistics, providing essential transportation services within the Reich and throughout the occupied lands of Europe. The company was remarkably organized, but this efficiency had a terrible and grim side. Indeed, the railroad company was also a vital part of Hitler's program of racial extermination. The participation of the Reichsbahn (and also of all railroad companies in occupied Europe) was crucial to the effective implementation of the *Endlösung der Judenfrage* (Final Solution of the Jewish Question). This euphemistic term referred to the Nazi criminal plan to exterminate the Jewish people. The genocide or mass murder of the Jews was the culmination of a decade of increasingly severe discriminatory measures. Under Adolf Hitler's rule, the persecution and segregation of Jews was implemented in stages. After the Nazi party came to power in Germany in 1933, its state-sponsored racism led to harsh anti–Jewish legislation, economic boycotts, and violent pogroms, all of which aimed to systematically stigmatize and isolate the Jewish community from society. It is not known when Hitler and the leaders of Nazi Germany definitively decided to implement the Final Solution, but in January 1942 at the Wannsee Conference, the scheme was organized along an industrial scale. Then started the development of specially designed extermination camps equipped with gas chambers and crematoria, and accessible by trains. Without railroads the *Shoah* (meaning "calamity" or "destruction" in Hebrew) would not have been possible. In peacetime the German railroad was a generator of wealth and progress, but put into evil hands it became an efficient but grim assistant to the Nazi industrial killing machine.

The Reichsbahn and its personnel, of course, were not solely responsible for this crime, but they were accomplices who were highly instrumental in the deportation of opponents to the regime to the concentration camps, and the mass murder of the Jews in the extermination camps. When ordered to transport Jews and other victims of the Holocaust from ghettoes, towns and cities throughout Europe to meet their death in the Nazi concentration camps and mass murder centers, the Reichsbahn made no objections. After all, the German company (but also all railroad companies in occupied Europe) was a business—a business ready to ship in principle any cargo in return for payment. They developed a scheme for *Sondertransport* (another euphemism meaning special transport). With a cruel irony, anyone being deported to a concentration or death camp had to pay for a one-way ticket (two Pfennig per km), with children under ten going at half-fare and children under four going free. Jews, Gypsies and other "enemies" of the Nazi regime were transported in appalling conditions in overcrowded freight cars with practically no food, no water, no or poor sanitary facilities, no heating and no ventilation, whatever the weather conditions outside. The average journey time was more than four days as the trains were given a low priority and often stabled in sidings for hours or even days. The longest recorded journey was a train of Greek Jews from the island of Corfu that took eighteen days to reach its destination in Poland. By that time all occupants of the train were dead.

Many employees of the DR Company knew about the destination and what happened there, but nobody dared protest or tried to do anything—as clearly demonstrated in the 1985 Franco-British documentary film *Shoah*, directed by Claude Lanzmann. The Holocaust was carried out on an industrial scale with extremely precise schedules and procedures. Planning and anticipated calculations were made by the railroad company to ensure that the extermination camps located in Poland received in time the exact number of people who could be "processed" or "treated"—other euphemisms for being murdered in gas chambers and having their corpses burnt in crematoria. The railroad permitted the transport of millions of victims to their deaths, and since they were locked into sealed boxcars, the Germans needed only a few guards and supervisors to carry out the operation.

It should be noted that by the end of the war—at a time of general collapse on all fronts—the scheme of extermination of the European Gypsies and the Jewish community went ahead at considerable cost to the German war effort. Death transports to killing centers such as Auschwitz continued at a time when labor and rolling stock were badly needed for armaments and troop reinforcement, as well as evacuation of casualties and refugees along a series of disintegrating fronts. By the end of 1944 and beginning of 1945, Germany was a chaotic nation with millions of civilians fleeing in haste from the eastern provinces rather than waiting for the vengeful Soviet troops. There were something like 4,500,000 displaced persons in Germany, including foreign, forced and slave laborers, plus two million prisoners of war of different nationalities. Public transport, especially the railroad, was wrecked, as were most public utilities and services. At a time when the war was already lost, the obsti-

nate, pointless and madly furious continuation of the Final Solution of the Jewish Question went on.

In its entirety, the Final Solution called for the murder of Gypsies and all European Jews by gassing, shooting, and other means. Estimations (based on DB shipping records) indicate that approximately six million Jewish men, women, and children were killed during the Holocaust, which was about two-thirds of the Jews living in Europe before World War II.

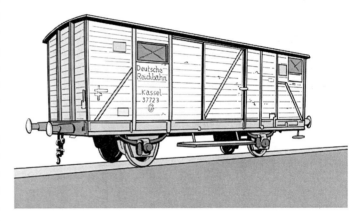

DR *Güterwagen* (Boxcar). People deported to concentration and extermination camps were transported in simple roofed and enclosed freight boxcars. In some cases 100 of them were confined in that limited space, most of the time without sanitary facilities, water and food. The only ventilation consisted of a few small windows fitted with barbed wire. Many people did not survive this appalling journey.

Armored Trains

As already said, Germany had never been enthusiastic about armor-clad trains. The army had used only a limited number of armored trains during the First World War to escort and protect supply trains through the large expanses of Poland and Russia. When the limitations imposed by the Treaty of Versailles in 1919 were rejected by Hitler's new regime after 1935, the development of armored trains had no priority. Instead Hitler favored the production of medium bomber planes and light tanks for future aggressive conquest. Nazi Germany reintroduced the concept of Eisenbahn Panzerzug into its own armies as a method of guarding their frontiers, particularly in the east, only in 1939. At the start of the Second World War, the German Army was equipped with seven standardized armored trains numbered 1 to 7. As a result of their successful diplomatic moves in 1938 and their victorious campaigns in 1939, the Germans were able to add Austrian, Czech and Polish armored trains to their own stock. By then four more armored trains, numbered 21 to 24, were available.

At first German armored trains were used as offensive weapons tasked with seizing strategic positions. The surprise attack on Poland in the early morning of September 1, 1939, which started World War II, included attempts to seize key stations and facilities in the Pomeranian corridor employing armored trains. During the May–June 1940 offensive in the west, the Germans used armored trains. For example, Panzerzug No. 6 rushed through the Dutch border at Nieuweschans in the northern province of Groningen, but the train got stuck when the Dutch blew up, just in time, a rail bridge at Winschoten. In all, ten attacks were carried out by armored trains in the campaigns of 1939–40 and only two were successful.

In spite of these failures, the number of armored trains continued to grow when German forces got involved in the Balkans and eventually in Russia in 1941. The German Panzer trains then proved their worth in the defensive and surveillance role along the huge stretches of bare lands and steppes in Russia for the protection of supply trains and dealing with the ever-increasing partisan threat. At first they included improvised armored convoys and foreign material pressed into German service. The number of crew and equipment of these trains varied a lot, from boxcars armored in a makeshift way with sandbags, concrete plates, and light weapons, to thick armor with considerable firepower used to support infantry attack.

Although many configurations were possible and frequently used, a typical early World War II German armored train would include between 12 and 18 railroad cars and one or more armored locomotives with coal tenders. Such a train usually had a command car equipped with radio, main and reserve command posts, cars for infantry, an artillery car with 7.5 cm or 10.5 cm guns, cars with 2.0 cm antiaircraft guns, and flatcars at each end of the train with equipment for mine clearing, and material for track repair.

At the beginning of Operation Barbarossa (code name for the invasion of the Soviet Union in June 1941), the Germans hoped to capture a lot of locomotives and cars so rapidly that traffic by rail would keep running. Indeed, the Russians used a broad gauge of 1.524 mm when everywhere else in Europe the gauge was 1.435 mm. Thus the German trains could not cross the borders until some extensive relaying of tracks had been carried out. In many cases, the German rolling stock was altered to fit the Russian gauge. Obviously, captured Soviet locomotives, armored trains and freight cars were used, but Germany was obliged to construct special gauge conversion yards, notably at Malaszevica (Brest-Litovsk) and Przemsyl. German rail conversion efforts were completed relatively quickly. In many cases, the Germans only had to remove one of the rails and move it closer in.

Another serious problem was locomotive maintenance, as Russian coal was of poor quality and the stations equipped with water supply were rare.

By late 1941, when the invasion of the Soviet Union got bogged down into the Russian winter, German trains were no longer weapons for attack, but progressively became defensive systems used to protect their overstretched lines of communication.

In Russia and in the Balkans, there were large areas not yet totally pacified, where partisans' activities were particularly important. For example, armored trains No. 23 and No. 24 were used in the war against Yugoslavia, and after the capitulation both trains stayed and participated in anti-partisan actions in Serbia during the winter of 1941–42. Thereafter the number of German armored trains deployed in the Balkans steadily increased, and during the rest of the war, all German armored trains participated in anti-guerrilla fighting, patrols and rail network protection.

All over occupied Europe, Germany faced a growing opposition that manifested itself, for example, by attacks and sabotage against the railroads. A notable example occurred in November 1942 in Greece, where partisans destroyed a series of three viaducts on the Thessaloniki-Athens line. Other spectacular attacks were the destruction of the 70-ft span of the Gorgopotamus Viaduct, as well as the Asopos Viaduct. In Yugoslavia the German communication system was equally disturbed by guerrilla forces' attacks.

An equally worrying situation developed in the immense and often empty Russian steppes. Behind the lines of the huge Eastern Front, large groups of elusive partisans, supported by the Soviet army and using forests and swamps as bases, made the German communications unsecure. In the early phases of the invasion, German anti-partisan efforts were relatively successful. German police and rear area units were usually able to secure and neutralize the attackers quickly. As the war progressed, partisan activities were more and more successful in disrupting rail traffic—often with disastrous consequences for the Germans. For example, during the month of September 1943, an average of 64 attacks per day were taking place against German trains. One of the consequences of the increased partisan activities was that German armored trains now found themselves more and more engaged in rear-area security duties than in supporting front-line units and direct military operations. Indeed, securing the rail network, protecting the

troop and supply trains, and actively fighting partisans became the most important tasks performed by the armored trains. They transported troops in large-scale anti-partisan operations, served as command posts and coordination centers, provided artillery support, and tried to block the partisans' retreat paths.

The need to protect long supply routes from elusive partisan actions forced first the renovation of captured trains, then the construction of new trains and armored rail cars. This happened under the direction of Colonel Egon von Olszewski, who was appointed commanding officer of all armored train troops in August 1941, and whose energy and organizational talents were of great importance in the following years. In April 1942 the Railroad Armor Replacement Department was created and established in Warsaw-Rembertov, Poland.

For this anti-guerrilla type of warfare, the Germans designed a new kind of armored train known as BP 42 based on Polish and Russian models. They introduced significant designs of a versatile and well-equipped nature, including: standardized rail cars armed with howitzers, guns, and antiaircraft guns placed in revolving turrets; flat railcars designed to carry, quickly load and unload tanks; and rail cars with complete armor protection for supplies and troops. The use of fully armored locomotives became general, and many types of equipment improving the safety of the crews were introduced. For example, angled and sloping armor (15 to 30 mm thick also covering the running gear), autonomous drives, and automatic hooks, which allowed cars to be connected without personnel exposing themselves outside the train in dangerous areas. All cars were fitted with armored doors, hatches, observation, and gun ports that could be closed by metal shutters; most cars were linked by crawl spaces to allow safe communication from one car to another. The construction program was carried out by the Linke-Hoffmann-Werke Company for building armored wagons, the Krupp Company for locomotive armor, the Rheinmetall-Borsig Company for artillery turrets, and the Gothär-Wagon-Fabrik to convert civilian rail material. The building and equipping were done on the orders of the Oberkommando des Heeres (OKH, Supreme High Command of the German Army) by the railroad engineers of the General Army Office in cooperation with appropriate branches of the Army Weapons Office. In October 1942, the Germans had twelve armored trains on the Russian front, two in the Balkans and ten in Western Europe. They were principally employed to fight guerrilla partisans behind the front lines. As we have just seen, the typical missions of armored trains were the reconnaissance of railroad lines, to clear possible obstacles, to protect installations, stations, bridges and tunnels, to escort freight trains in unsafe territories, to give artillery support, and in case of retreat to destroy all rail installations behind them. One way or another, the Germans managed to use armored trains to defend the tenuous rail links that joined the Eastern Front with the German manufacturing and supply organization at home, thus keeping the depredations of Russian partisans down to a reasonable level, but they never eradicated them.

Some German BP 42 armored trains were designated by numbers, some were given cities' names (such as Zobten, Berlin, or Stettin), names of historical figures (Blücher, Rübezahl), or simply first names (Max, Moritz, Werner). There was of course no such thing as a standard German armored train, but many possible combinations, depending upon the mission and what was available in rolling stock, locomotives and armament. No neat table of dimensions can therefore be drawn up. An Eisenbahn Panzerzug was often a mixed unit. It was a polyvalent weapon system combining potent artillery with antiaircraft guns along with a strong infantry capability. In theory a standard armored train of Type BP 42 included two Panzerlok (armored locomotives), one at each end for quick change of direction. Another possible and often seen arrangement was only one Panzerlok placed in the middle of the train with the other cars placed as symmetrically as possible around it. The Panzerlok's autonomy and range were increased by adding more coal tenders and water supply. The train generally included a Kommandowagen (command carriage fitted with radio); one or more Artilleriewagen (trucks carrying various guns, mortars or machine guns in roofed armored blockhouses or rotating turrets); several Geschützwagen (armored artillery in turret and quarter wagons provided with rifle ports); a few Flakwagen (flat wagons carrying antiaircraft MGs or flak guns); and various armored Güterwagen (freight boxcars transporting supplies and ammunition). The Germans would sometimes put a tank, such as a captured French Somua S-35 or Czech Pzkw 38-t light tank or a Panzer II, on a Panzerträgerwagen (flatbed car). The armored vehicle could be quickly offloaded by means of a ramp and used away from the range of the main railroad line for reconnaissance and combat in the train's vicinity, or for chasing down enemy partisans. Obviously an armored vehicle considerably strengthened the shock troops on foot operating outside the train. At the head and tail of the train there would be the usual pusher car, possibly fitted with a plow blade supposed to push away obstacles lying on the track. Pusher cars were loaded with track-laying materials with which the engineer unit traveling on the train could repair track damage that hindered the unit's movement. Of course, armored artillery cars and tank-carrying cars were used only when heavy mobile enemy forces were likely to be encountered in some strength, as they were not so well adapted to dealing with pinprick attacks by small groups of lightly armed and elusive partisans. Armored trains were very often supported by small reconnaissance airplanes (e.g., Fieseler Fi 156 Storch), but also by rail vehicles, scouting railroad-wheeled armored cars, and draisines, which will be described further below.

There were also repair and recovery units, including one or more locomotives, supply wagons, personnel cars, a crane suitable for the load it would have to recover (for example, an SSt 662 six-axle heavy steam crane), and a security detail. Damaged bridges took longer to repair. Portable bridges, ferries or other trans-shipment methods were used until the bridges had been repaired. But with few exceptions, most of the bridges destroyed by the Soviets were quickly made operable again by the Germans. Some examples: The bridge at Kaunas was destroyed on June 24, 1941, and repaired by July 17, 1941. The bridge at Riga, destroyed on July 2, 1941, was repaired ten days later. The bridge near Petseri, destroyed on July 9, 1941, was repaired by July 24, 1941. In addition, Soviet yard and line switches had to be rebuilt, and German traffic signals, placards and bills had to be installed.

As a rule most armored trains were self-contained for independent operations. They had thus their own medical equipment, power plant, supplies, kitchen and food, ammunition, fuel and water. The number of soldiers manning a Panzer train could obviously vary greatly, between 40 and 200 men. The crew was composed of two sorts of personnel. First, the fighting troops, who were gathered from volunteering infantry, artillery, antiaircraft gunners, railroad engineers, intelligence, smoke screen and sanitary units. Second, the technical crew included many civilians such as railroad inspectors, technical leaders, locomotive drivers, firemen, track watchmen, servicemen and wagon masters provided by the Transportation Ministry and the national railroad company Deutsche Reichsbahn.

After mid–1943, the partisans, fighting a guerrilla war behind German lines in Russia and in the Balkans, seriously crippled transportation and gave the situation a threatening new dimension. As a response, German armored trains were pushed more and more into a defensive stance. By that time armored trains offered a large and easily vulnerable target, notably by Allied planes, which gradually had air supremacy on all fronts. As a result a new standard armored train was designed, known as BP 44, featuring heavier artillery and more antiaircraft weapons than on the BP 42. At the beginning of 1944, the number of armored trains operating in occupied Europe had

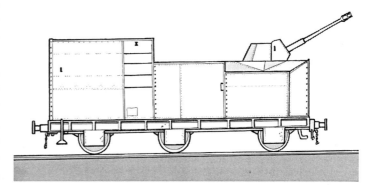

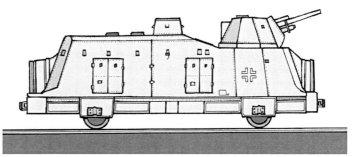

Top: *Artillery rail car of German armored train No. 3 with 7.5 cm L/41 gun, 1940.*

Bottom: *German armored rail car with 10.5 cm howitzer in turret.*

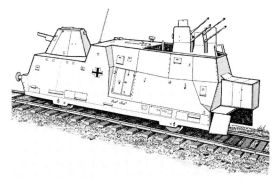

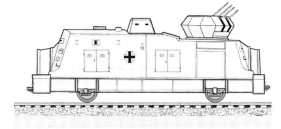

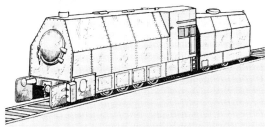

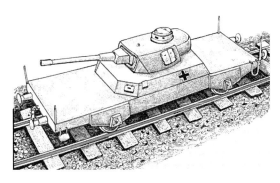

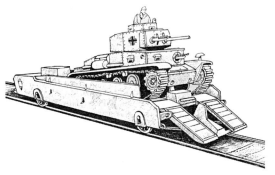

Left, top: *German armored rail car with 10.5 cm howitzer in turret and Flak Vierling.*

Left, middle: *German armored railcar with Flak Vierling in turret.*

Left, bottom: *Panzerjägerwagen. Introduced in 1944, this weapon system included the turret of a German PzKfw IV ausf. H tank armed with the long 7.5 cm KwK L/48. The turret of a captured T34 tank was also used. It was intended to be placed at each end of a train in order to replace the earlier pusher car (it had a plow blade and reinforced armor at the front), and at the same time provided additional all-around firepower.*

Right, top: *Panzerjägerwagen with T-34 turret.*

Right, middle: *German Panzerlok BR 57 (BP 44).*

Right, bottom: *Panzerträgerwagen with Pz 38 (t). Many German armored trains included one or more light tanks—often captured French Somua or captured Czech Pz 38 (t). Tanks were carried on a Panzerträgerwagen (special flatcar with ramps) for infantry support in case it was decided to pursue attackers or when a reconnaissance of the surrounding area was launched. The loading ramp was folded up when the train was in motion and often stowed on a pusher car.*

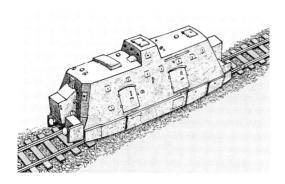

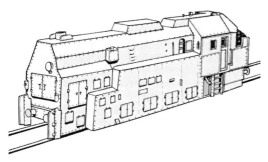

Top: *Armored command car BP 42.*

Middle: *Armored locomotive type BR3-41.*

Bottom: *G-Wagen. This Geschützwagen (artillery wagon) was part of German armored train type BP 42. Usually a BP 42 train included two of these turreted armored cars. They were often placed in the 4th and 5th positions symmetric from the locomotive (located in center point). The turret was armed with a captured Russian 7.62 cm 295/l(r) cannon. Safe communication between cars was made by using armored crawl spaces placed at both ends of the wagons.*

grown to thirty, but they could not turn the tide of the war. By that time the lack of materials, the scarcity of fuel, the loss or destruction of steel mills, as well as the loss of many trained and skilled personnel, had led to a crisis that only grew worse. In August 1944 the construction of armored trains was moved to the second-highest priority (equal to Panther and Tiger tanks), showing how important they were considered. However, attempts to produce the needed quantities of steel failed and the program could never be completed. The men on the battlefront had to use what was at hand and improvise. Only three BP 44 trains were delivered in late 1944, and older trains were re-equipped. In 1945 the Wehrmacht had 55 operational armored trains, most of them deployed on the Russian front, but they could not do much to hold their ground when the Allies started their general offensives on all fronts in 1944 and early 1945. By then their fate was sealed. The trains were destroyed, or captured and later scrapped for reprocessing, and crews were taken prisoners of war.

Scout Cars and Draisines

The Germans also developed diesel, armored railcars, trolleys, armored scout cars (*Spähwagen*, SP for short) and self-propelled armored coaches for patrol and reconnaissance. Light scout cars (e.g., the light Steyr SP) could be used as individual units, or coupled together to form a train. The fact that every car had its own engine was a great advantage; no longer could a direct hit on the locomotive cripple the whole convoy. Some armored reconnaissance road vehicles (e.g., captured French Panhard Type 178 armored cars, or captured Russian BA-20) were also employed in a scouting role after replacement of the rubber road tires with steel rail wheels. Following the same principle, heavy trucks (e.g., Henschel 6J2, MAN 4500, or Faun ZR) were used on rail for transport, towing or switching.

There was also a project by the Sauer Company from Vienna called Schienenkampfwagen SK1 (rail tank) composed of a PzKpfw III tank fitted with train wheels to drive on railroad. The rail running gear was retractable owing to a lifting device, and was driven by the tank's engine via four screw spindles. Only a few prototypes, intended to secure railroad lines in partisan areas in the Soviet Union, were produced in late 1943.

Similar small rail wheels (Eisenbahnrädern) could also be fitted under the chassis of a six-wheeled SdKfz 231 Panzerspähwagen (armored recce six-wheel truck) for use on rail.

Light scout cars were well suited for patrol, but not adequate for real combat because of their limited armor and weak armament. Therefore heavier units were designed and used, called rail-cruiser or Panzertriebwagen (self-propelled armored car, PzTrWg for short) or sometimes Panzergeschütztriebwagen (artillery rail-cruiser) because many of them included rotating turrets armed with cannons. There were fifteen such vehicles when World War II started, but the number was increased during the war by new construction and captured enemy (mostly Russian) draisines.

Panzertriebwagen No. 15 was issued in the late 1930s to the German Bahnschutz (Railroad Protection) for use in track surveillance duties. When World War II broke out, rail car No. 15 saw service in France, later in Russia, in the Balkans and in Greece. The PzTrWg Nr. 15 operated together with armored trains 6, 7, 25 and 65. Armament included six 7.92 mm MG 34 machine guns, but no heavy weapon. It had a crew of 17 men, 8 NCOs and one commanding officer, who were captured in May 1945 at Graz, Austria.

Panzertriebwagen No. 16 was designed and built by the Schwarzkopff Company and issued in December 1942. It was a large vehicle based on the WR550 D14 diesel locomotive with two armored units attached to each end, each armed with two captured Russian 7.62 cm FK 295 guns emplaced in rotating turrets. Armor thickness was from 31 to 84 mm. PzTrWg 16 saw combat on the Russian front, in 1943 as patrol in guerrilla-threatened areas, in 1944 assigned to Army Group Mitte with combat at Rawa Ruska, Lublin, and Kielce. In 1945 it was captured by the Poles and used in 1944–47 against Ukrainian partisans. Today the impressive motorcar is displayed at the Skarzysko-Kamienna railroad station in southern Poland.

Panzertriebwagen No. 17 was a captured Russian rail-cruiser armed with two 7.62 cm guns placed in turrets, entering German service in December 1943.

Subsequent rail-cruisers No. 18 to 23 reached the troops in 1944. It is not clear whether they were of Russian origin or German copies. Their armament featured two captured Russian 7.62 cm guns in turrets and four machine guns. The armor was 20 mm thick, they had a weight of 34 tons, a crew of 21, were powered by an eight-cylinder 180-hp engine that gave a speed of 60 km/h and a range of 500 km. They operated in conjunc-

Panzer III Mark N armed with a 75 mm KwK L/24 gun equipped with special railroad running gear designed by the Sauer Company in 1943.

tion with armored trains as additional artillery or were sent ahead alone for reconnaissance duty.

Panzertriebwagen 51, designed in early 1945, was not completed. It would have been a self-propelled armored rail-cruiser with two long 7.5 cm KwK L/48 guns, each emplaced in the turret of a German tank mark IV/H.

Left, top: Steyr scout car. This self-propelled German Schienenpanzerspähwagen (scout rail car) with PzKpfw III tank turret mounted a 75 mm L 24 short-barreled gun. Designed by the Steyr Company; there was also a variant with a turret armed with two machine guns, and another command-car variant with a rail aerial on the roof for short-range radio. Introduced in late 1943, these scout cars were intended to secure railroad lines against partisan attacks in the Balkans. The concept was to permit an armored train consisting of 12 cars with varying armament: four cars with Panzer III N turret mounting a 75mm L/24 cannon, two cars carrying a quadruple 20mm antiaircraft gun, and six cars armed with machine guns carrying infantry, command, communication, and medical sections. Since each car was powered by a 76 hp Steyr motor, disabled units could be assisted by other operating cars, an improvement over other armored trains generally powered by a single steam engine. Due to material shortages, only eight trains were operational; these contained only eight scout cars (two cars with Pz III turrets, two command cars with fixed antenna, and four infantry cars). Six other cars were also included: two flak cars carrying the quad 20 mm guns on a flatcar, two Panzerträgerwagens (tank carriers) with a Panzer 38 t tank, and two flatcars carrying track maintenance equipment, which was used to detonate mines on the rail bed. Each train could be operated as two sections of four scout cars each, depending upon the mission.

Left, middle: Panzerspähwagen Panhard Type 178. After the defeat of France in June 1940, the Germans captured a batch of about 190 brand-new Panhard armored scout cars. Some 43 units were converted as Schienenpanzer for railroad protection duties by replacing rubber road tires with metallic flanged rail wheels. Originally designed in 1934 and introduced in 1936, the four-wheel drive Type 178 had a crew of four, and was armed with a 25 mm SA 35 gun and one 7.5 mm Reibel machine gun. It was powered by an SK 105 hp engine and had a maximum speed of 72 km/h. With a heavily riveted armor of 20 mm, the vehicle weighed 8.2 metric tons.

Left, bottom: SdKfz 231 six-wheel Panzerspähwagen. The armored reconnaissance truck was fitted with small additional metal wheels for rail use.

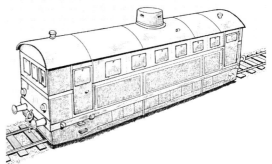

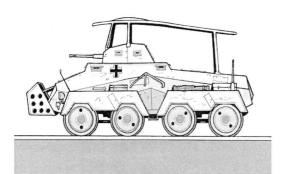

Left, top: *Heavy truck Henschel 6J2 on rail.*

Left, second: *German MAN 4500 truck on rail.*

Left, third: *Heavy reconnaissance armored vehicle SdKfz 241 (8 wheels) with radio on rail.*

Left, fourth: *Heavy SdKfz 231 (8 wheels) on rail.*

Right, top: *Tatra T-18 draisine in German service. Designed in 1925 by the Czech Ringhoffer-Tatra Works, this little armored rail vehicle was purchased by Poland in the late 1920s. After the bloodless annexation of Czechoslovakia and the defeat of Poland in 1939, Tatra T-18 draisines were captured and some of them were perhaps used for a short while by the Germans, possibly as training vehicles.*

Right, bottom: *Panzertriebwagen Nr.15. Its appearance obviously displayed the descent from passenger car.*

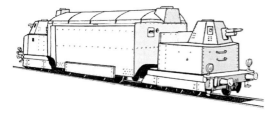

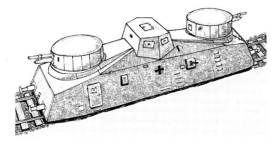

Left, top: *Panzertriebwagen No. 16. Issued in December 1943, this was a large vehicle with two captured Russian 7.62 cm FK 295 guns emplaced in turrets.*

Left, second: *German Panzertriebwagen 17-23.*

Left, third: *Panzerjägertriebwagen 51. The heavy reconnaissance and antitank artillery carrier self-propelled rail-cruiser 51 would have been armed with two turrets from PzKfW IV Ausf. H, each armed with a 7.5 cm KwK L/48 gun and protected by Schürzen (spaced armored skirts). PzTrW 51 is unlikely to have ever seen actual service, only being listed as ordered in December 1944. Only one unit seems to have been fully completed by the end of World War II.*

Left, bottom: *Improvised draisine. Along with the (more or less) regular Panzertriebwagen, there were also improvised railcars designed locally by the troops themselves.*

These railroad patrol cars were hastily built out of whatever was available, including truck parts, captured Soviet reconnaissance vehicles, and parts and armor plates of partly destroyed tanks. According to the U.S. War Department Intelligence Bulletin on Railroad Car (Armored) from September 1943, the unorthodox result was known as an "armored Zepp." The depicted draisine featured a captured Russian tank turret armed with a 4.5 cm KwK cannon.

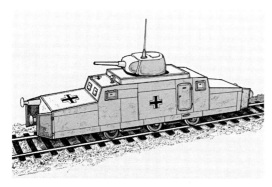

Protection Measures

Draisines and other armored reconnaissance vehicles were attempts to have a flexible weapon in order to strengthen firepower, increase mobility, and cover a much wider area of the track network.

To increase security, whenever possible, supply and troop trains traveled in convoy within sight of each other. Other protection measures against partisans and saboteurs included the constitution of security formations composed of police auxiliaries and anti-insurgency units, and Jagdkommandos. These were special "hunting" commandos (long-range patrols) whose thorough and rigorous training enabled them to carry out unconventional and difficult tasks, and high-risk missions like infiltrating, hunting and striking at partisan units and their bases. Although natives and local auxiliaries were recruited in these special forces, Jagdkommandos were always too few in number. Besides, they suffered from a disproportionately high casualty rate, and the loss of men who required such extensive and expensive training limited their operations to only the most critical ones.

A more conventional approach was the construction of static fortified posts, strongpoints, blockhouses and bunkers at scattered intervals along the lines and in the vicinity of strategically vulnerable spots (such as stations, marshaling yards, supply depots and dumps, bridges, viaducts, tunnels and other key installations) with enclosing barbed wire fences, sentries, constant patrols by guards on foot with watchdogs or in draisines or light armored trains. Such posts also provided shelter from bad weather. It must be noticed that on the Russian front the worst enemy was the terrible winter cold.

In forested areas the Germans cut back several hundred meters of trees on both sides of the track, creating a large clearing or glacis—a broad empty space offering no cover for ambushing parties. People without permission were banned from approaching the glacis and the railroad lines. In some areas the German army established restricted zones on either side of the railroad line that could be as wide as five kilometers in the countryside and two hundred meters in populated areas. Villages along the lines were evacuated and "death zones" were created where trespassers were to be summarily shot on sight without any warning. However, these protection and anti-guerrilla measures had limited results. They were costly, not always feasible, and highly unpopular, thus generating even more hostility among the local populations. They only inflamed hatred, fueled support for the partisans, and in the end proved noneffective in eradicating partisan attacks and sabotage actions.

Top: *Bunker protecting tunnel. Such small fortified posts were established in Russia, in the Balkans, and in Greece and Italy as protection against partisan sabotage and attacks.*
Bottom: *Patrolling the track. The use of first-line troops and combat units in the fight against partisans presented the disadvantage of diverting and tying down a great number of combat divisions far behind the battlefront.*

Flak Trains

The Germans used their tactical air force (notably the

dive bombers) as an extension of their artillery, and therefore were fully aware of the possibility of having the same weapon used against them. From 1943 onwards the Allies gradually won the domination of the skies, and German rail transport was considerably hampered, exhausted by minimum maintenance, and suffering from bombing from the air and sabotage by local partisan and resistance groups. After the successful landing in Normandy and the invasion of Europe in mid–1944, military railroad clearly showed its vulnerability to an enemy with air superiority. Whole German divisions being rushed forward by trains to conserve on wear and fuel found themselves strafed and bombed mercilessly by Allied airplanes. They were also sidetracked by uncooperative civilian railroad men or halted time and time again as partisans and maquisards blew up tracks in front of them. When they actually managed to reach the front, German units were often disorganized, already mauled and often too late.

To protect against air attack, some armored trains were exclusively composed of flat wagons armed with flak guns to constitute powerful and mobile antiaircraft batteries. During World War II, military supply convoys, VIP passenger cars, railroad artillery and armored trains always included Flakwagen (flat wagons) carrying antiaircraft machine guns as well as light and heavy flak guns. As the air war above Germany increased, a special antiaircraft artillery mounted on railroad was created, known as Eisenbahn-Flak, allowing mobility to flak batteries. Converted passenger coaches and standard freight cars with part of the roof removed were often used instead of freight cars—a measure probably dictated by the need to economize in specially constructed cars. Any flatcar could, of course, house a flak gun, but there were several standardized Geschützwagen (gun carriages) especially adapted to flak defense: Geschützwagen I and II were intended to carry light weapons (e.g., 2 cm, 3.7 cm or quad 2 cm guns); and Geschützwagen III and IV were stronger designs for heavy pieces (e.g., 8.8 cm, 10.5 cm and 12.8 cm guns). The latter were fitted with armored sides that could be folded down when in action, allowing a larger working platform for the crew, and movable outriggers arms, which could be deployed for stability when firing. Safety fences on all four sides of the gun ensured that it was not fired below a safe angle. These measures made it impossible for the gun to strike obstructions such as tunnels, signal posts, or other trains. Other safety measures included the posting of lookouts to prevent firing, which might damage telegraph wires, signal posts, tunnels, or other obstructions, and a complete prohibition of firing on electrified lines with overhead cables. In addition a flak train usually included armored passenger cars for the crews, and other carriages carrying field kitchens, supplies, ammunition, power plants, searchlights, range finders, radar, and other related equipment.

The powerfully armed, self-supporting,

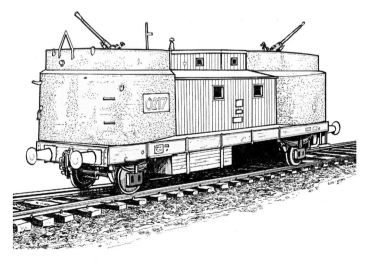

Concrete flak car.

and mobile flak trains fulfilled several distinctive tasks. They defended strategic railroad

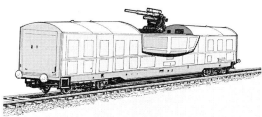

tracks, important junctions and stations, bridges, tunnels and marshaling yards. They enabled the transport of heavy guns and ponderous equipment, which otherwise were complicated to move by road. They allowed the rapid distribution of flak firepower in strategically important areas with little anti-aircraft defense (for example, a newly conquered region), and reinforced flak fire in the most often attacked or threatened military or

Left, top: *Concrete flak car II with flak quad.*

Left, second: *Heavy Flakwagen with 8.8 cm gun.*

Left, third: *Würzburg radar on rail car. The Würzburg radar (FuMG 62) was designed by the Siemens Company in 1934. Taking its name from the city of Würzburg in Franconia (a town famous for its university and electronic productions), the device entered service in 1940. During the Second World War it was produced by the Telefunken Company, and became the standard ground-based gun laying radar system for both the Heer (German Ground Army) and Luftwaffe (Air Force). The radar had a maximum range of 29 km (18 mi.) using low-UHF band and a 3 m paraboloid dish antenna. For transport Würzburg was placed on a wheeled trailer with the dish tucked along the horizontal midline. The basic Würzburg radar had a weight of 1.500 kg, and could also be installed and operated on a railcar for mobile use with Flak artillery units. Over 4,000 Würzburg radars of various improved models (A, B, C, and D) were produced during World War II.*

Left, fourth: *Reichsbahn car for VIPs with 2 cm quad flak gun.*

Above: *Heavy 12.8 cm flak gun mounted on flatcar.*

Top: *2 cm Flak Vierling mounted on flatcar.*
Bottom: *Panzerlok BR 57. This type was used for both armored and flak trains.*

industrial centers. Although railroad flak units were part of the German Air Force and were administered through Luftwaffe channels, train protection detachments were operationally subordinate to the transport authorities. In certain circumstances, flak guns on railroad mount could also be manned by Heer (ground army) personnel.

German Railroad Artillery

In German artillery mounted on railroad carriage was called Eisenbahnartillerie, and shortened as E-Art or just E. Like military armored trains, railroad artillery was an attractive weapon to continental armies since both allowed heavy support weapons to be moved rapidly across countries in time of need. The First World War had seen the large-scale use of railroad guns, usually as heavy front-line artillery. The Germans were one of the few nations to develop railway guns after the Nazis came to power in 1933. They had a good experience with long-range guns. As already said, in 1918 they had built the so-called Paris Guns, and in the interwar years, there was a widespread opinion that rail guns would form a useful addition to field and coastal artillery.

Between 1918 and 1933, the German heavy industry was dismantled and heavy weapons were forbidden. The Treaty of Versailles in 1919, imposing on the Reichswehr severe limitations, ensured the German military authorities would not be burdened with obsolete World War I stocks of weapons and ammunition. After the Nazi accession to power in January 1933, rearmament was launched in a fresh start, at first in secret. When the expansion of the Wehrmacht began again in the mid–1930s, new designs of modern guns were immediately called for. In 1935 railroad guns got the go-ahead with the creation at Berlin of a design office called the Deutsche schwerste Artillerie (German Heaviest Artillery, or Dessart for short). In 1936 the so-called Sofort-Programm ("immediate" program) was initiated, and huge long-range cannons were ordered from Krupp (Essen), Rheinmetall-Borsig (Düsseldorf and Kassel), and Hanomag (Hannover).

In 1939 Nazi Germany had a large fleet of railway artillery. The diplomatic annexations in 1938 and the victorious military conquests in 1939–40 allowed the German armies to capture a large number of foreign railroad heavy artillery pieces, notably French ones, which formed a reserve for the German rail artillery. French captured railroad guns included the 30.5 cm M93/06 Batignolles; the 32 cm M74 Schneider, which had a weight of 162 t, a length of 25.9 m, and a gun that could fire a shell of 388 kg to a distance of 25 km; and the 34 cm L/47 M12, which weighed 270 t, had a length of 33.72 m, and could fire a projectile weighing 430 kg to a range of 37.6 km.

German railroad guns came in two main types. First, those in which the gun was pivot-mounted on a flatcar, allowing it to fire in any direction relative to the line of track. These guns often required stabilizing outriggers and rail clamps to resist the firing stress and recoil. Second, those pieces in which the weapon (usually above 20 cm/ 8 inches caliber) was trunnioned (rigidly fixed and aligned in its mounting), and thus capable only of a very small amount of traverse by moving the mounting bodily across the supporting bogies. These guns demanded that special preparation was done before the weapon system could operate: either a curved sidetrack or a Drehscheibe (track turntable) to allow them to point over a wider arc of fire. An Eisenbahn battery was generally composed of two, three or four heavy railroad guns. Each gun was accompanied by one or two trains for transport and operation, which included freight cars for carrying the turntable, one or more cranes to assemble it, a command car, ammunition cars, coaches arranged as living quarters and field kitchen for the crew and personnel, service cars, and several cars carrying motor transport. The battery's convoys also included several flatcars armed with flak guns for defense against air attacks.

Germany's World War II heavy railroad guns were remarkable technical achievements and looked highly impressive, but that is all there is to say about them. There were far too many designs, and on the whole their effectiveness on the battlefields of World War II was not worth the investment in time, money and personnel. Besides, in the 1940s railroad artillery (and this applies to armored trains as well) was an obsolete weapon system compared to the speed, range and payload of bomber airplanes. It had also become a vulnerable weapon, which was then at the mercy of fast and powerfully armed attacking airplanes. The fact that so much effort, research and funding were wasted to develop such old-fashioned weapons is without doubt due to Hitler's conservative ideas about warfare and to his megalomaniac love for gigantic and prestigious weapons.

In 1944 an experimental railroad launch system for the guided ballistic missile Aggregat 4 (A-4, aka V2) was tested. However, it was rejected because of the vulnerability of the European rail network to Allied air attack.

15 cm Kanone in Eisenbahnlafette

Introduced in 1937, the 15 cm (E) was mounted on two 6-wheel flatcars with four outriggers allowing a complete 360-degree traverse. It was a sound design with good performance. A projectile of 43 kg (94.82 lb) could be fired to a distance of 22.5 km (24,606 yards), but 15 cm was actually too small a caliber to be worth the trouble of a railroad mounting. Eight units were built in 1937 and another ten in 1938 when production was ended and replaced with heavier caliber.

15 cm railroad mounted gun.

17 cm Kanone in Eisenbahnlafette

The German 17 cm K (E) railroad gun—dating from c. 1901 and designed as artillery of the Deutschland class pre-dreadnoughts—was intended to replace the 15 cm. It was placed on the same pivot-mount on the same two six-wheel bogies flatcar. It could fire a high explosive 62 kg (138.47 lb) shell to a maximum range of 27 km (29,527 yards). Six units were issued in 1938, but like the 15 cm, its production was dropped in favor of bigger weapons.

17 cm Kanone in Eisenbahnlafette (shown here in traveling position with outriggers folded).

21 cm K 12 (E)

In the 1930s, the Krupp Company designed the heavy 21 cm K 12 railroad gun. The barrel had a length of 33.3 m (109.25 feet), and had to be externally braced to prevent the tube from bending under its own weight. The K 12 fired a 107.5 kg (237 lb) projectile to a range of 115 km (71.46 miles). The shell had curved ribs matching deep rifling grooves in the barrel, a special sealing ring behind it, and a powerful charge. Wear and tear on firing was so great that the barrel had a maximum life of only 90 rounds. The whole weapon weighed 302,000 kg (297.28 tons), and was placed on a railroad truck mounting. In order to allow the gun recoil at high elevation without striking the track, the carriage was jacked up from the bogies before firing. It could fire a HE shell weighing 105.50 kg (237.04 lb) to a distance of 45 km (27.96 miles). Two heavy 21 cm K 12 railroad guns were completed. Originally designed to smash the fortifications of the Maginot Line, they were placed in Pas-de-Calais (northern France) in 1940 and engaged against England. Contributing very little to the German war effort, the battery was withdrawn in 1941 and never seen again. The heavy 21 cm K 12 railroad gun was a remark-

able technical achievement, but militarily totally pointless.

24 cm Kanone in Eisenbahnlafette Theodor Bruno

Design by Krupp in 1936, this railroad gun used the naval 24 cm SK/L35 barrel mounted on a World War I two eight-wheel bogies box-girder structure. It could fire a projectile weighing 148.50 kg (327.44 lb) to a maximum range of 100 km (10,936 yards). Only six were built and issued in January 1939. Another gun using the same naval equipment mounted on a slightly different cradle was the 24 cm Theodor, of which three were manufactured in 1937.

28 cm Kanone in Eisenbahnlafette Bruno

A series of four 28 cm types designated Bruno was started by Krupp in 1936. All mountings were rather similar to that of the 24 cm Theodor Bruno. The series included rail gun "kurz Bruno" with a short 28 cm SK L/40 naval barrel (eight produced); "lange Bruno" with a long ex-naval 28 cm SK L/45 barrel (only three built); "schwere Bruno" with a heavy discarded naval 28 cm Kusten Kanone L/42 (only two manufactured); and "Bruno neue" (new), a clean design from 1939 intended to have better performance than all 28 cm Brunos and K5s. Only three "new Brunos" were completed between 1940 and 1942, when the project was canceled.

28 cm Kanone 5 (E)

The 28 cm Kanone 5 (E) or K5 was a brand-new design by Krupp in the early 1930s. It was accepted for service in the German army in 1936, and eight were operational by 1940. The 28 cm K 5 (E) was the best workaday railroad gun ever built, and formed the backbone of the German Eisenbahnartillerie.

The deep-groove barrel was 21.539 m (70.08 feet) long and fired a conventional 255.5 kg (563.38 lb) high explosive ribbed shell. A rocket-boosted shell was developed, which increased the maximum range to 86.5 km (53.7 miles). Another improvement was the fin-stabilized dart-shaped shell, known as Peenemünde Arrow Shell, and a special propelling charge, which gave a range of 151 km (93.8 miles). The shell was 75.2 inches long it had four fins at the rear end, and a 31 cm sabot or discarding ring around the center of gravity. When the shell was fired, this sabot fell away outside the gun muzzle, and the shell attained a velocity of 5,000 ft/sec.

The K5 gun was placed on a 29-m-long carriage, a simple box-girder assembly carried on two six-axle bogies, with the front bogie slung so as to allow the front of the box-girder to be swung across it for aiming the gun. For large angles the whole weapon was mounted on a special portable turntable built at the end of a short spur of track laid at the desired firing point. For firing, a crew of ten artillerymen was required, but installation and maintenance demanded hundreds of soldiers. The 28 cm K5 (E) railroad gun was also called *Schlanke Bertha* (Slim Bertha, referred to as "Anzio Annie" by the Allies in Italy). By 1940 eight 28 cm K5 (E) were in service, and production continued during the war. In all, twenty-five of them were manufactured, plus a small number of experimental 31 cm smooth-bored pieces which could fire sophisticated arrow shells designed by the Rocket Research Establishment at Peenemünde.

Some heavy 28 cm K5 (E) railroad guns were deployed in the summer of 1940 in the Pas-de-Calais (northern France) in order to support the invasion of the British Isles (Operation Seelöwe). After Operation Seelöwe was canceled, long-range batteries were kept and reinforced as the nucleus of the Atlantic Wall coastal defense batteries. Secondary tracks were then constructed leading to Bettungen, or huge concrete round firing turntables. Each Bettung contained one gun and was fitted with a complex installation permitting a 360° angle of fire; the positions included service and ammunition bunkers, concrete shelters for the gunners, observation posts, and a Feuerleitstand (fire control station) connected to radar installations. Examples of such bunkers still exist today in France: in Brittany, navy batteries Plouharnel near Lorient and Bégot near Quiberon; in Normandy, army battery Auderville-Laye near La Hague.

An Eisenbahnartillerie battery could also be concealed from air attack in existing tunnels or might be stored in huge concrete garages specially designed for this purpose. These installations, called Dom-bunker (cathedral-bunkers), featured heavy armored doors, 70 to 80 m long and 10 m high, as one still can see today at Lorient (Brittany, France), in Hydrequent and Fort Nieulay near Calais in northern France.

The Germans also employed 28 cm K5 (E) railroad artillery guns in Italy, notably at Anzio: for four months two 28 cm K5 (E)— taking turns to emerge to fire from a railroad

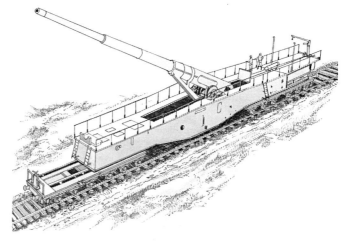

Railroad gun 28 cm K5 (E).

tunnel on the Rome-Nettuno line—made life hell as they shot a constant hail of shells all over the landing beach areas. A number of K5s were also engaged on the Russian front, at Stalingrad and Leningrad. The last recorded firing took place in 1945 when a K5 gun placed near Bonn fired on Maastricht (in the Netherlands). A well-preserved specimen of a German 28 cm K5 Eisenbahnartillerie is exhibited

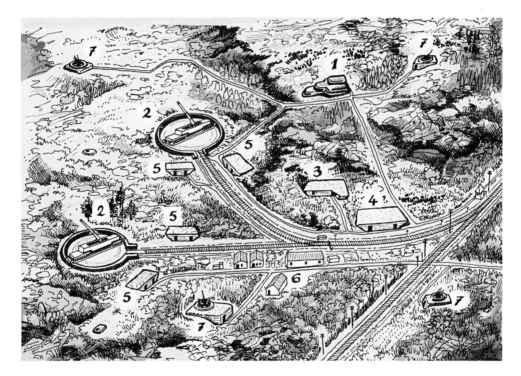

Top: *German Dom-Bunker at Lorient.*

Bottom: *German permanent railroad battery. A long-range permanent coastal railroad battery (as could be encountered in the Atlantic Wall, for example) generally included the following elements:*

1: Fire-control station (for example, Type M157);

2: Concrete emplacement with revolving turntable housing the railroad gun;

3: Power plant (for example, Type V192);

4: Ammunition store (for example, Type S448a);

5: Shelter for personnel (for example, Type M160 or M151);

6: Various non-concrete magazines and service buildings;

7: Bunker armed with flak guns (for example, Type FL242 or FL247).

The guns, bunkers, tracks and buildings were, of course, camouflaged, and the whole complex was arranged as a Stützpunkt (stronghold). The battery was connected to a radar station and to a fire command center. It was protected by a barbed wire fence and mine fields. The railroad line was heavily guarded, and the whole position was defended by various bunkers and Tobruks armed with antitank guns and machine guns.

in the Musée du Mur de l'Atlantique in the ancient battery Todt at Haringzelles near Cap Gris Nez in northern France. Another K5 Anzio Annie railroad gun is now displayed at the Aberdeen Proving Ground (APG) in Harford County, Maryland, U.S.A.

38 cm Kanone in Eisenbahnlafette Siegfried

Designed and based around eight available naval 38 cm SK C/34, the project Siegfried was launched by Krupp in 1938. During the war, four guns were emplaced in Norway as static coastal defense, and the other four were mounted as conventional railroad guns trunnioned on the side plates of a box-girder riding on two sixteen-wheel undercarriages. They were first deployed on the Hel Peninsula in Poland and in 1942 moved to France as mobile coastal artillery in the Atlantic Wall. They could fire a projectile weighing 495 kg (1091.48 lb) to a maximum range of 55,700 km (34.61 miles).

On the same mounting as Siegfried, the Krupp Company produced a super heavy rail gun (code name Adolf) using one discarded ex-naval 40.6 cm SK C/34 gun.

80 cm (E) L40 Dora/Gustav

Another technically remarkable but militarily pointless German design was the enormous 80 cm Kanonen (E) L40. Designed by Dr. Erich Müller in 1935 and produced by the Krupp Company in 1937, this monster, the biggest gun ever built, represented the culmination of Nazi megalomania. Intended for the destruction of heavy ferro-concrete fortifications (notably the large bunkers of the French Maginot Line), the 80 cm gun was quite a conventional design, except for its immense size. The whole affair weighed 1,350,000 kg (1328.9 tons); the length of the barrel was 32.48 m (106.56 ft). The projectiles used were of two sorts: either a 4,800 kg (4.73 tons) high explosive, or a 7,100 kg (6.99 tons) concrete-piercing high explosive. Muzzle velocity was 820 m/sec (2690 ft/sec) for the high explosive shell. It had a range of about 47 km (29.2 miles) and a rate of fire of two rounds per hour. A long-range hyper-speed "Peenemünde arrow shell" was developed for the monster 80 cm gun, but, so far as is known, was never fired; this was to weigh 2,200 pounds and range to 100 miles. There was also a proposition to mount a 520 mm gun on the same carriage to fire rocket-assisted shells and Peenemünde arrow shells to a range of 118 miles for cross-channel bombardment, but this project never got past the drawing board.

The barrel was mounted in a huge cradle and housed on a box-girder structure featuring no fewer than eighty wheels. For ammunition handling there was a long working platform extended backwards from the gun breech with two powerful hoists at the end to lift and deliver projectiles and propellant charges to the breech. The whole equipment was 7 m in width and was mounted on four huge rail undercarriages; these ran on parallel tracks, with each pair locked together to form a double unit. The monster gun was moved piecemeal in 25 trainloads to its firing emplacement, where a dual track had to be laid and the gun mount was reassembled with the aid of two massive 110-ton overhead cranes. It took six weeks to lay the tracks and put the weapon together. The 80 cm gun needed its own headquarters, and a crew of no fewer than 1,420 for assembling, maintaining, and guarding, plus an antiaircraft gun unit for air protection. For firing alone, a crew of 500 men was required. The equipment was demonstrated at the Rugenwalde testing ground in March 1943, in the presence of a jubilant Hitler.

Two huge 80 cm guns were built, named Dora and Gustav (after the designer Gustav von Bohlen-Krupp). Originally these monster rail guns were intended for attacking British-held Gibraltar in southern Spain. However, the autocratic dictator General Francisco Franco (1892–1975) refused to join World War II on the Axis side, maintaining an official policy of strict neutrality. Therefore the Spanish Caudillo (chief) did not allow the Nazis to cross Spanish territory. As a result, both 80 cm guns proved of very limited usefulness. The only record of the use of Gustav was at the siege of the naval base at Sevastopol, in Crimea in the Soviet Union, where it shot about 48 shells, and during the Warsaw uprising in Poland in 1944 where it fired about 30 rounds. The second 80 cm gun, Dora, so far as is known, never left the proving ground. The subsequent history of both guns is unknown. Just like the 1918 Paris Guns, Dora and Gustav just disappeared, and their disappearance is one of World War II's mysteries. It is strongly believed that Soviet forces probably captured them in 1945 and later scrapped them.

Top: *Shell fired by 80 cm Dora/Gustav.*

Bottom: *Captured French Saint Chamond 400 mm rail gun. A veteran of World War I, the Saint Chamond 40 mm was one of the largest rail guns captured and used by the Germans. It had a maximum range of 17,500 yards and could fire several different types of shells varying in weight between 1,410 lbs and 1,980 lbs.*

Nazi VIPs' Private Trains

Hitler and Nazi senior leaders had special trains for their own travels. Hitler had a personal Führersonderzug (Leader's Special Train), which he frequently used when traveling and visiting various headquarters throughout Europe. Hitler's special train was also used as a headquarters code-named Führersonderzug Amerika in 1940. In the spring of 1941 it was redesignated FHQu Frühlingssturm (Spring Storm HQ) at Mönichkirchen, Austria,

Rail gun 80 cm Dora/Gustav. The 80 cm project proved to be a very expensive exercise in futility, as revealed by comparing the millions of Reichsmarks spent to the poor results on the battlefield.

during the Balkan campaign. The train was later re-codenamed Führersonderzug Brandenburg. After the Balkans campaign, the train was no longer used as headquarters, but Hitler used it throughout the war when he traveled between Berlin, Berchtesgaden, Munich and other headquarters and destinations. The configuration of Hitler's train varied, but it often included the following: two locomotives; two Flakwagen flatcars armed with antiaircraft weapons, one at each end of the train; a baggage car; the Führerwagen, Hitler's Pullman private car with own laundry and bathroom; a Befehlswagen (command car) that included a conference room and a communication center; a Begleitkommandowagen for Hitler's SS bodyguards and agents of the Reichssicherheitsdienst (SS, Security Service); a dining car; one, two or more cars for guests, depending on who was invited to travel with the Führer; a Badewagen (bathing car) for the guests; another dining car for the personnel; two sleeping cars for the personnel; and a Pressewagen intended to receive and release press reports and messages.

Since tunnels were the most convenient places for trains to hide from air attacks, Hitler and his staff always made sure there was a tunnel in the vicinity when the Führer's train made a halt. For example, the meeting with the French Marshal Philippe Pétain on October 14, 1940 (with the infamous handshake that sealed the official start of the organized state collaboration of Vichy France with the Nazi regime) was held at the small and spruce place of Montoire-sur-le-Loir (Département of Loir-et-Cher in central France) just because of the nearby tunnel in Saint-Rimay, where both the Führer and the Marshal's trains could shelter in case of an air attack. When no tunnels were available, Hitler frequently ordered the construction of the large concrete shelters known as Dom-Bunkers. Several of these impressive shelters (sometimes covered with a thick layer of protective earth and closed at both ends by enormous armored doors) were

built by the Organisation Todt in the flat and bare Polish plain, notably at Tomaszow Mazowiecki, Strzyzow, and Konewka. At Cieszyna-Stepina, the Dom-Bunker (386.6 m long and 14.4 m wide with a vaulted ceiling 8.76 m high) included a gas lock and emergency side exits. The structure was built on a rail spur running parallel to a low hill for extra protection. The site gradually became a small base with a road access, auxiliary and support buildings including a power plant and underground gallery for the cables connected to the tunnel, a kitchen, an infirmary, bunkers housing ventilation and heat-producing devices, and barracks for the escort troops. The site was enclosed with a barbed-wire fence and mine fields, guarded by armed security personnel, and defended by antiaircraft artillery. In the vicinity there was an airstrip. The "cathedral" tunnels in Poland were built at enormous cost for Hitler's sole protection, but they were seldom or never used.

Other Sonderzüge (special trains) used by Nazi bigwigs and prominent German officials included the following:

Sonderzug Asien (Asia), also code-named Pommern (Pomerania), was used by Hermann Göring (1893–1946), Chief of Luftwaffe, and No. 2 within the Nazi hierarchy. Göring's private train was part of the Reichsmarschall's splendid lifestyle. It included two heavy locomotives; one car designed with luxury taste as a bedroom for him and his wife; a car arranged as a pleasant living room/study; a rail car arranged as a modern cinema; a car equipped as a command post with communications and a map room; a dining car with kitchen; and a varying number of carriages intended for senior commanders and for guests. All cars were specially suspended to provide a smooth ride. Sometimes there were several additional freight cars for Göring's "shopping"—e.g., artworks plundered from European museums or stolen from private collectors. At the front and back of the train there were special flatcars armed with flak guns, although whenever possible the train halted near tunnels as protection against possible air attacks.

Sonderzug Steiermark (Styria), also called Heinrich (Henry) or Transport 44, was used by the infamous Heinrich Himmler (1900–1945), Reichsführer SS, Chief of the German Police, and Minister of Interior from 1943 to 1945. Himmler's train was stationed at Angerburg (East Prussia), near Hitler's HQ "Wolfsschanze." From there Himmler often inspected his SS and police units in the east.

Ministerzug (Ministers' Train) and *Sonderzug Westfalen* (Special Train Wesphalia) were used by Foreign Minister Joachim von Ribbentrop (1893–1946).

Sonderzug Afrika (Africa), also code-named Braunschweig (Brunswick), was used by the senior officers of the Armed Forces High Command (Oberkommando der Wehrmacht, or OKW).

Sonderzug Atlantik (Atlantic), also called Auerhahn (Grouse), was used by senior commanders of the Kriegsmarine (Navy).

Sonderzug Atlas (Atlas), also code-named Franken (Franconia), was a command train used by the Wehrmachtführungsstabes (Armed Forces Operations Staff).

Sonderzug Enzian (Gentian Violet) was a special command train used by the chief of the Nachrichtenwesens der Luftwaffe (intelligence service of the Luftwaffe).

Sonderzug Ostpreußen (East Prussia), also code-named *Sonderzug IV* (Special Train 4), was used by the Oberkommando des Heeres (OKH, or Army General Staff).

Sonderzug Robinson 1 was used by the chief of the Command Staff of the Luftwaffe.

Sonderzug Robinson 2 was used by the chief of the General Staff of the Luftwaffe.

Sonderzug Württemberg was used by the Generalstabs des Heeres (Ground Army General Staff, or Gen. St.d. H.).

Hitler's Broad-Gauge Train

Adolf Hitler was a megalomaniac tyrant who loved gigantism, and whose Third Reich was meant to last for thousand years. The dictator had a delirious project to build new railroad lines for both freight and passengers, intended to link industrial centers and major cities in Europe. The new railroads were to be built after Nazi Germany had won the war. They would have a gauge of 3 m, and be powered by a new generation of electric engines allowing train speed between 200 and 250 km/h. Freight cars would be composed of two floors and equipped to carry goods in standardized containers easy to load and unload. Passengers' cars would be designed with great comfort, similar to that of elegant hotels and palaces. They would include two floors divided into roomy compartments with wide panoramic windows, large first-class restaurants, and luxury sleeping rooms.

A line was planned from Berlin to Rostow-on-Don in southern Russia. Another line was planned to connect Berlin to the industrial region called Ruhrgebiet, then running to Aachen (Aix-la-Chapelle in North Rhine-Westphalia) and ending in Paris, France. A number of lines were also planned for connecting south and north Germany. There was also an ambitious commercial project to directly connect the port of Rotterdam in the Netherlands to Berlin. Railroad experts regarded Hitler's plans as crazy dreams that would only waste funds, time and labor. These grandiose schemes, of course, never got off the ground, but until the end of the Third Reich in 1945, teams of engineers, designers and artists worked on planning Hitler's extravagant giant trains.

Rail Wolf

Before closing this section on the use of railroads by Nazi Germany during the Second World War, it is interesting to conclude with a device called Schienenwolf (Rail Wolf), sometimes also referred to as Schwellenpflug (sleepers' plow or hook) or rail wrecker. This odd rail vehicle was designed to destroy railroad lines in the eventuality of a retreat, in order to make the Allies' advance as difficult as possible by destroying as far as they could the lines of communication and hamper their build-up of supplies. The Rail Wolf consisted of a large and strong down-pointing hook that could move up and down. It was mounted on a flatcar and provided with a coupling for attachment to one or two locomotives, as the device needed an enormous amount of energy to operate. The hook was positioned over the track and its point was lowered into a hole dug between the sleepers. Rollers placed at the car's rear were then adjusted to press on the railhead, and then the whole assembly slowly went into motion. The strong hook grabbed up the sleepers, but at the same time the rollers prevented the rails from lifting. Hence the wooden sleepers, being the weaker element, were broken in half, thus wrecking the track completely. The apparatus was subjected to a pronounced swaying movement, which necessarily slowed the operation, and the speed of the track destroyer was only about 9 miles per hour. Rail Wolf's equipment included one or two locomotives, a flatcar, a freight car for explosives, a freight car for personnel, and a hook car. The crew usually consisted of one noncommissioned officer and 12 men. Such railroad track destroyers were used fairly extensively in the years 1943–44, when Nazi Germany was forced to retreat on the

Russian and Italian fronts. They were also used in Germany herself in the last months of the war in accordance with Hitler's scorched-earth policy of total destruction, the so-called Nerobefehl (Nero's Order) intended to deny the Allies any use of the already seriously damaged railroads into Germany.

ITALY

Italy in World War II

When Germany invaded Poland in 1939, Mussolini's Fascist Italy was in no way ready for an offensive war. However, the megalomaniac Duce (Leader) Benito Mussolini (1883–1945) desperately wanted to participate in the redrawing of the map of Europe, so he overlooked the state of Italy's military-industrial complex in order to feed his obsessive ego. Italian industrial power was a mere fraction of that of Britain, France or Germany. It was not ready to produce the airplanes, guns, ammunition, artillery, tanks, and trucks on the scale that was needed. When Italy entered the war, its forces were equipped more in line with the First World War rather than the Second.

Artillery included vestiges of the previous century with a contingent of horse-drawn artillery and many leftovers from World War I. The most modern models, while very effective, were never made in enough large numbers. Heavy battle tanks were non-existent, and Italy's armored weapons were lightly armored vehicles and tankettes. By the time Italy started producing better tanks and mobile artillery that could compete with the Allied weapons, it was too late to make a difference. Small arms, such as Beretta pistols and automatic rifles, were very capable, but several machine and submachine gun types were often poorly made. Even the shoddy models were always in short supply. The Italian

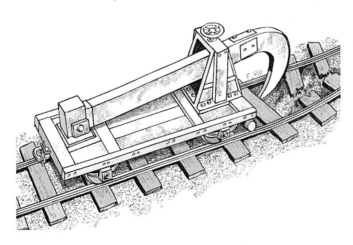

Schienenwolf (rail wolf).

shipyards produced (or retrofitted) fast and well-designed ships, but they had the fatal flaws of being too lightly armored and not equipped with radar. Italian air power looked good on paper, but in fact it was weak, with only a few thousand aircraft at the start of the war, many of them old-fashioned biplanes. The few modern aircraft created were underpowered, poorly designed and no match against modern Allied fighters. The Regia Aeronautica (Italian air force) also had made the deplorable and criminal mistake of dropping poison gas during the conquest of Ethiopia in 1935, to the disgust of the international community. Of all the major military forces involved at the start of World War II, Italy by far had the least competent high command. Mussolini granted the top staff positions to men whose only qualifications were their unconditional adherence to Fascism and their personal loyalty to him. On the subject of military railroads, too, there were very few achievements.

Colonial Railroads

In Libya, Italy built less than 400 km of railroads with 950 mm gauge. There were only five small lines all around the country's two most important cities: Tripoli-Zwara (118 km); Tripoli-Gharian (90 km); Tripoli-Tagiura (21 km); Benghazi-Soluk (56 km); and Benghazi-Barce (108 km). In Libya the first locomotives were the steam locomotives R.401 and R.301, gradually replaced with the modern R.302. The Italian authorities had given priority to the construction of roads in Libya, notably the Via Balbia, as said before. This was a fully paved highway running parallel to the Mediterranean coast and connecting all cities, towns and ports in northern

Libya. The coastal highway was named after the Fascist air force officer, Minister of Aviation and General-Governor of Libya Italo Balbo (1896–1940). Balbo had made himself famous in 1933 when commanding a fleet of twenty-four seaplanes from Italy to the United States for the Chicago Exhibition. After 1926 no more railroads were constructed in Libya. During World War II the need of rail transport to the frontier with British Egypt changed this approach. In spring 1941 the Italian authorities started the construction of a new railroad connecting Tripoli to Benghazi. By the end of 1942, however, all work was stopped when the Italians were defeated in North Africa.

In the Horn of Africa, the Eritrean Railroad was constructed between 1887 and 1932 for the Italian colony of Eritrea, and connected the port of Massawa with Bishia near the Sudan border. In 1935 the line carried large quantities of supplies for the Italian war effort in Ethiopia with about 30 trains daily. Until 1941 the Italians used the railroad, but the fortunes of war allowed the British to take control. After 1942 the railroad (damaged during the British occupation and by Italian guerrillas) was abandoned from Agordat to Biscia. By that time the British moved some diesel locomotives and materials to Eritrea when they dismantled the Railroad Mogadiscio-Villabruzzi of Italian Somalia. In 1944 the British (as a war compensation) dismantled

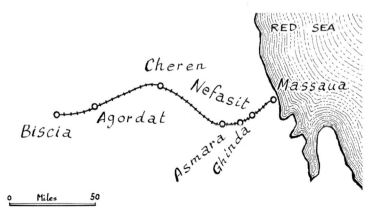

Map of the Eritrean Railroad in World War II.

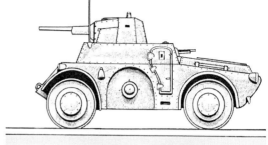

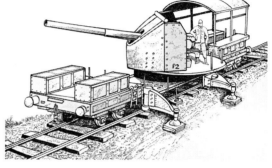

Left, top: *Italian Libli. Like the German Pan-zertriebwagen No. 15, the Italian armored Libli's appearance showed the descent from civilian passenger car.*

Left, bottom: *Profile Italian Libli. The illustration depicts a variant Libli with two tank turrets at both ends of the vehicle, and a Breda model 35 heavy antiaircraft machine gun placed in the middle of the roof.*

Right, top: *Italian Autoblinda AB 41 Ferroviaria. The 4 × 4 car, designed in 1938 and issued in 1941, was intended to replace the obsolete vintage 1915 Autoblinda Lancia I.Z. It had a range of 400 km (250 miles), and a speed of 78 km/h (48 mph). It had a crew of four, comprising a commander, gunner and two drivers, as there was a dual steering system, one in the front and the other at the rear for quick change of direction. The conversion from road tires to railroad wheels could be carried out by the crew in about 30 minutes.*

Right, bottom: *Italian rail gun. The Italian army only had a few heavy guns mounted on rail cars. These were generally smaller caliber of 76, 102, and 152 mm for coastal defense, operated by the Navy.*

the Italian-built Asmara-Massawa Cableway that supplemented the railroad as a means of transportation inland.

Italian Rail Cruiser Libli

Italy used only a few armored trains during World War II. The ALn-56 Littorina blindata (armored rail-cruiser Libli for short) was a self-propelled diesel armored rail-cruiser. It had a length of 13.6 m (44 ft 7.4 in), and was powered by two 115 hp diesel engines giving a maximum speed of 118 km/h (73 miles per hour). The Libli was fitted with two M 13–40 turrets, each armed with one 47 mm Ansaldo 47/32 gun. Additional armament included two 20 mm Breda Model 38 cannon, six 8 mm Breda Model 38 machine guns, and only on a few models, two Type 40 flame throwers. There were also variants with single or twin 47 mm gun placed on the roof. Armor thickness ranged from 6 mm in the first cars to 11.5 mm in the last eight vehicles. A Libli had a varying crew size of 18 to 23 men, which included an operator for the RF 3M radio set, a commanding officer, as well as drivers, mechanics, artillerymen and machine gunners.

Fiat-Ansaldo produced 16 units of the Libli, and these were used in the Balkans from late 1942 until 1944. They were used in anti-partisan roles, including patrolling of railroad lines, which were target of sabotage by the partisans, and for the protection of installations, facilities, convoys and personnel. Armored and semi-armored railroad cars with a pronounced improvised nature (civilian cars with reinforced sides and armed with various machine guns) were often added to trains for protection against partisans' attacks, while locomotives' cabins tended also to be protected by light armored plates for the same purpose.

The Italians also used standard armored cars type AB40 called Autoblinda Ferroviaria, whose wheels could be stripped of their rubber tires and used on rail for escorting, patrolling and scouting railroad tracks—particularly in the Balkans. Types AB 40 were replaced on the production line with the improved AB 41. The new version was actually the same vehicle, but it featured a new and better-armed turret based on that of the L6/40 light tank, armed with a 20 mm Breda automatic cannon.

JAPAN

In 1940, Japan occupied French Indochina (Vietnam) and joined the Axis powers Germany and Italy. These actions intensified Japan's tension with the United States and Great Britain, as both countries reacted with an oil boycott. The resulting oil shortage and failures to solve the conflict diplomatically made Japan decide to capture the oil-rich Dutch East Indies (today Indonesia). To achieve this aim, they had first to neutralize the U.S. fleet based in Hawaii, which of course meant starting a war against the U.S. and Great Britain. On December 7, 1941, Japanese airplanes attacked the U.S. fleet based at Pearl Harbor. The surprise bombing killed more than 2,300 Americans. It completely destroyed the American battleship USS *Arizona* and capsized the USS *Oklahoma*. The attack sank or beached a total of twelve ships and damaged nine others. One hundred sixty American aircraft were destroyed and 150 others damaged.

December 7, the "date which will live in infamy," brought the United States into World War II. The U.S. was already close to joining the war, but in an attempt to preserve its stance of isolation and neutrality, it had only committed to sending war supplies on loan to Great Britain. Within days, Japan's allies, Germany and Italy (known collectively as the Axis powers), declared war on the United States. Within the following six months after Pearl Harbor, Japan was able to expand her control over large territories from the border of India in the West and New Guinea in the South.

The turning point in the Pacific War was the Battle of Midway in June 1942. From then on, the U.S. and Allied forces slowly won back the territories occupied by Japan. In 1944, intensive air raids started over Japan. In spring 1945, U.S. forces invaded Okinawa in one of the war's bloodiest battles. In July 1945, the Allied powers requested Japan in the Potsdam Declaration to surrender unconditionally, or destruction would continue. Although they had no chance to win the war, the Japanese vowed to fight to the bitter end. In order to bring the war to a quick end (and to put the United States in a dominant position to determine the course of the postwar world), President Truman took the difficult decision to use new weapons of mass destruction. Only after the USA dropped two atomic bombs on Hiroshima and Nagasaki on August 6 and 9, 1945, did Japan surrender unconditionally on August 14.

In the Far East war opposing Japan to the Allies, railroads played a less important role than in Europe. The war in the Pacific Ocean was fought on islands and many campaigns took place at sea or in tropical jungles. Nevertheless, when battles were fought in vast continental Asia, railroads were, of course, significant means of transporting troops and supplies.

Although the railroad played a comparatively minor part, it did produce the most notorious railroad of the Far East war—the infamous "Death Line" in Burma. To maintain their forces in Burma, the Japanese were required to bring supplies and troops by sea through the Strait of Malacca and the Andaman Sea. This route was vulnerable to attack by Allied submarines, and a different means of transport was needed. The obvious alternative was a railroad through Thailand. This new line was a connection between the Thai and Malaysian systems in the south and the Burmese railroads in the north. Linking Bangkok to Rangoon, it was needed to support the Japanese armies intending to attack British India. The line was built between June 1942 and October 1943 by Allied prisoners of war (about 60,000, most of them captured after the fall of Singapore in February 1942)

and local native press-ganged forced labor (about 180,000) under appalling conditions. Hard and long working days, broiling sun, bad food, poor accommodations, lack of medical attention, and Japanese guards' brutal behavior, harsh discipline and cruel punishment caused the death of thousands of prisoners: 16,000 Allied PoW and 90,000 Asian forced

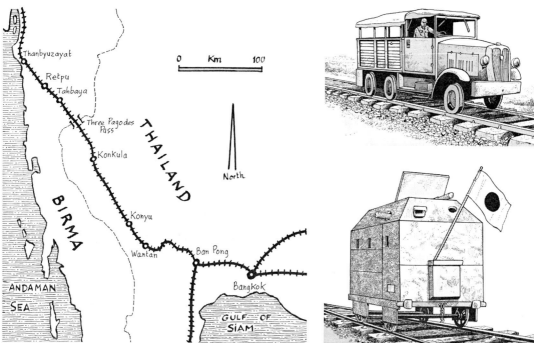

Left: *Map of the Japanese "Death Railroad" in Thailand and Burma.*

Right, top: *Japanese armored car on rails. The standard Japanese 6-wheel Type 91 So-Mo armored truck could be converted to rail use owing to dismountable wheel rims. The vehicle had 4-wheel drive to the rear axles, weighed 7.5 tons, was powered by a 6-cylinder 40 hp engine, and had a speed of 25 mph on road and 37 mph on rail. It had a crew of six and was armed with one machine gun.*

Right, middle: *Japanese Type 98 truck for use on road and rail.*

Right, bottom: *Japanese armored draisine.*

laborers. The line was ready in October 1943, but was so repeatedly bombed by the Allied air force that it was never really used. After the war most of the line was abandoned, and only some eighty miles remain in use today. The Burma Death Line was immortalized by Pierre Boulle's novel *Bridge on the River Kwai*, published in 1952, and by the 1957 film adaptation directed by David Lean and starring William Holden, Jack Hawkins, Alec Guiness and Sessue Hayakawa.

Another much less known "death railroad line" was built by the Japanese in present-day Indonesia, across the thickly forested island of Sumatra, linking the capital city of Padang to the port of Siak on the Malacca Strait. Called the Pakanbaru Railroad, this line too was built with local forced laborers from Indonesia and Dutch and British Commonwealth prisoners of war. Here, too, prisoners and workers were overworked, underfed, provided with little medicine, and subjected to constant physical and mental abuse by their Japanese overseers. So horrible were the working and living conditions in the deep tropical jungle that about 60 percent of the 5,000 men died. The death railroad line was ready for use in August 1945, just when Japan surrendered after the American attacks with nuclear weapons on Hiroshima and Nagasaki.

During World War II the Japanese had only a few armored trains, and they used the previously described armored road/rail vehicles as well. There were also conventional trucks—for example the Type 98 and its successor the Type 100—that could be used as small locomotives by replacing the rubber tires by a set of steel wheels.

Railroad Gun

Japan possessed only one large caliber railroad gun, the 240 mm Type 90, which saw service between 1930 and 1945. Japanese military advisors in Europe during World War I had noted the development of heavy artillery mounted on railroad for front-line combat. However, despite this interest, other projects had higher priority, and nothing was done until funds were found to purchase a single sample unit from the Schneider Company in France in 1930. Only the barrel was purchased from Schneider, and the railroad carriage and auxiliary equipment were all produced locally in Japan. The completed assembly was designated as the Type 90 240 mm railroad gun. The large gun was emplaced on two eight-wheeled undercarriages. It had a weight of 136 tons, a barrel length of 12.83 m (42 ft), a caliber of 240 mm (9.4 in), and an effective range of 50 km (31 miles).

The weapon was initially deployed as a coastal artillery battery at Futtsu, Chiba, as part of the defenses guarding the entrance to

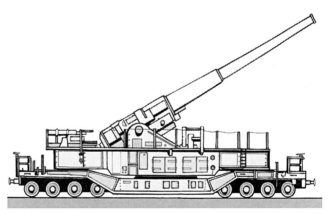

Japanese railroad gun Type 90 240 mm.

Tokyo Bay. It was redeployed to Manchukuo in 1941, and based in the Hulin area of Heilongjiang, as part of the defenses against the Soviet Union, where it remained for the duration of the war. When the Soviet Union invaded Manchukuo in the closing days of World War II, the gun was sabotaged and abandoned by retreating Kwantung Army forces, and later reprocessed to scrap metal.

CROATIA

Following World War I and the demise of the Austro-Hungarian Empire, Croatia became a part of Yugoslavia. The Axis occupation of Yugoslavia in 1941 allowed the Croatian fascist Ustashi Party to come into power, forming the Independent State of Croatia, led by Ante Pavelic, who assumed the role of Poglavnik ("Head-man" or Leader). Following the pattern of other fascist regimes in Europe, the Ustashi enacted racial laws, and entered the war on the side of Nazi Germany. At the same time, the country was in a state of civil war. Indeed, the Communist-led Partisan movement emerged in 1941. Headed by the revolutionary Croatian-born Josip Broz Tito (1892–1980), the Communist, anti–Fascist guerrilla movement spread quickly into many parts of Yugoslavia.

In April 1941, an Ustashi governmental decree created a home defense force (Hrvstako Dombranstvo) consisting of an army, navy, air force, and police. The force was largely officered by former members of the Yugoslavian army. By November 1941, six divisions were formed, and this would expand to sixteen by the end of the war. The Ustashi Party formed an armed force along the lines of the German Waffen SS that was to earn a similar reputation for ruthless brutality.

Croatia depended heavily on its wealthier Axis partners for military assistance. Even Finland contributed surplus army uniforms, which the Croatian army was happy to receive. Croatian military forces and volunteers (Croats who joined foreign armies) fought largely in the east against the Russians and at home against Tito's Communist Partisans.

As far as military trains were concerned, the first measure to develop improvised (or provisional) armored trains stems from the period of August and early September 1941. An improvised Croatian armored train is known to have been attached to the Croatian Bosan-

ska Division and was operating along the tracks in the Maglaj-Doboj area in East Bosnia in September 1941. It was still being used there during the second half of November 1941 in support of Croatian operations to encircle groups of partisans in the Ozren Mountains between the Bosna River and Tuzla. In January 1942, two Croatian armored trains are known to have been operating in the Doboj-Maglaj-Trbuk area under the control of 4th Infantry Division. During this period until approximately late spring 1942, crews for the armored trains were provided by the Croatian Railroad Battalion.

In April 1942 the Croatian Defense Ministry ordered the railroad car factory in Slavonski Brod to establish a department for the construction and repair of armored railroad cars, and in July 1942 the government placed an order for 20 of them. Concurrently, the Ministry of Defense started forming armored train companies as special units within several of the infantry regiments. By 1943, a typical Croatian armored train had 4 to 7 armored railroad cars manned by a half-company of infantry, and was armed with two stationary Renault FT Model 17/18 tanks (each with a 3.7 cm gun), one medium mortar, two heavy machine guns, and four light machine guns. The tanks were stationary in the sense that they could not be disembarked from their carrying flatcars.

At first, the Croatians had total control over their armored trains, but when the Germans set up a special command designated Railroad Security Staff Croatia in November-December 1942, this control was lost at the higher and tactical levels, although the Croatians continued to exercise administrative authority over their units. By September 1943 there were at least two armored train companies with a total strength of 364 officers and men operating 7 or 8 armored trains and improvised armored trains.

PART 5

Railroads in World War II: Allies

GENERALITIES

Mobility offered by road vehicles had not made the train obsolete in World War II. It was perhaps a paradox, and something that many experts, including even some railroad men, had not expected, but the value of the railroad in war was even greater in the age of the motor vehicle and the aircraft than it had ever been before. Railroad indeed showed itself a harsh master, imposing on the railroad men even more complex and more dangerous duties. The quantity of provisions and equipment needed to supply World War II armies in the field increased enormously. While airplanes, tanks and motor vehicles opened up new possibilities in the tactics, and indeed in the strategy of operations, their successful use depended on logistical demands that only railroads could fulfill. That is to say, assured and regular delivery over comparatively long distances of supplies and fuel in such huge quantities that the armies could not only live on what they were receiving but could build up reserve stocks for their next move. Beyond a certain distance of haulage, road transport consumes almost all fuel it can carry, and it is of course wasteful of manpower. So in every World War II campaign where a railroad could be made to provide transport, it was brought into use at the earliest possible moment. Civilian lines were of course pressed into military service, and where railroads did not exist, they were often built, including narrow gauge tac-

tical tracks. Military railroads were in action behind almost every one of the widely scattered battle areas in World War II, and the national railroad systems and the personnel who operated them were submitted to heavy pressures and great dangers.

Experiences with armored trains during World War I and the interbellum did show the need for light armored vehicles running on the railroad tracks for reconnaissance tasks usually 10–15 km in front of the train to support supply and communication tasks. Many nations thus had such vehicles to accompany armored trains, either specially designed or adapted cars with interchangeable wheels for operation on both road and track.

Besides troops and supplies, the railroads in war-engaged countries carried civilians to save their lives—refugees and evacuees by the millions. In almost every involved land, a more or less well-organized exodus was carried out to evacuate people from cities and regions likely to be bombarded from the air, and large numbers of people had to leave their home territories when these were menaced with capture by vengeful enemies.

The two world wars of the first half of the 20th century claimed lives at a rate unimaginable in former ages, and civilian populations were largely involved. In both conflicts, blockade and large-scale starvation were used as weapons, while gunfire and high explosives caused havoc at the front. In World War II, the predicament of civilians became even worse with the development of massive and long-range air bombardments. Indeed, area or "carpet" bombing wiped out whole cities, and the use of nuclear fire in 1945 added yet more suffering to the horrors of war as it led to long, slow deaths from atomic radiation sickness for those who had survived the blast of explosion.

Yet some good occurred in the medical domain. Major discoveries were made and existing knowledge was refined and expanded. For example, new drugs helped ease the problem of wound infection, epidemics could be tackled by vaccines in mass immunization programs, and prepared blood or plasma could be transfused to wounded persons. And of course, when medical evacuation was possible without delay, the death rate was somewhat lowered by adequate and rapid transport of casualties in well-equipped ambulance trucks and relatively comfortable sanitary trains.

GREAT BRITAIN

Transport

Just as in the First World War, the British army found itself rather ill-prepared in 1939 so far as provision of military railroad was concerned, although preparation for war had started as early as 1937. Just as in 1914 Britain immediately organized a convenient military adaptation that would fulfill its requirements with a minimum of modification of the existing civilian network. When World War II broke out, Britain had 19,463 locomotives, 1,241,711 freight cars and 45,838 passengers cars, and a total rail mileage of 19,273 miles. In World War II the transportation service of the Royal Engineers and the Indian and Dominion forces numbered nearly 150,000 men at its greatest expansion. Between 1939 and 1944 the British railroads at home were subjected to more than 9,000 bombing raids, but despite this the Germans were never able to successfully paralyze the network.

In 1939 the British railroads

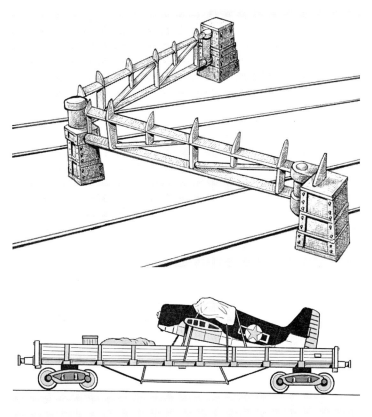

Top: Dutch railroad obstacle. Several such strong steel obstacles intended to block (armored) trains were placed on tracks at strategic positions in the neutral Netherlands in late 1939 and early 1940 when a German attack was feared.

Bottom: Warflat. A warflat was a standard railroad bogie wagon that could carry various kinds of loads including, for example, armored tracked or halftracked vehicles, trucks or vans, or airplanes with dismounted wings.

smoothly dispatched contingents of the British Expeditionary Forces (BEF) to France. In May 1940 the Southern Railroad network organized the return of evacuees and injured of the BEF after the debacle of Dunkirk.

During the Blitz (strategic bombing of the UK by the Luftwaffe from September 1940 to ca. May 1941), the British railroads greatly helped the evacuation of 1.3 million children and other vulnerable people as well as cultural heritage out of London and other large cities likely to be attacked by the German air force. Artifacts were stored, e.g., in especially adapted disused mines in Wales.

From the start of the war in 1939, there was a labor shortage due to the mobilization of men in the army. As a result, women were recruited in great numbers, with more than 100,000 employees by 1943, representing one-sixth of the workforce.

After the United States joined the war, the British railroads, although heavily burdened, also made possible the gigantic logistics buildup of Allied forces gathered in Britain for the invasion and liberation of Europe in 1944. In fact, Britain was for a while a huge arsenal and a springboard for an invasion of the European mainland, packed with U.S. troops and equipment, but also with Commonwealth soldiers and war materials. Up to late 1942, movement of heavy military matériel by rail was vulnerable to Luftwaffe air recce and attacks. Therefore various subterfuges and camouflages were used, for example by placing large canvas dodgers on platforms carrying tanks. All sorts of rail vehicles were used, ranging from standard civilian rail cars and tankers to newly U.S.-built cabooses, and warflats especially designed to carry heavy loads like tanks.

During World War II, Britain produced many standard locomotives, mostly based on prewar freight designs. These "austerity" machines were designed in a minimalist style to ensure they were relatively cheap to build and maintain, and efficient to operate. In 1941 the 2-8-0 Stanier freight locomotive was chosen

as the basis for a military machine. This fairly simple and rugged engine was produced by the hundreds and served in most theaters of war. The British War Department also acquired a number of civilian diesel locomotives (e.g., WD 0-6-0 DE) and used them in conjunction with some American Lend-Lease equipment (e.g., the double-undercarriage Whitcomb B-B). These diesel locomotives conjunctionally useful for switching, or for use around dumps and explosive works, or in desert conditions where coal and water were in shorter supply than gasoline at times.

Considering the "austerity locomotives" were designed for a short and hard life for wartime, they lasted surprisingly well, as a number were still doing useful civilian work well into the 1970s.

Compared to other railroad networks on the European Continent, which had been overworked and greatly damaged by war operations and air attacks, Britain's railroad network suffered no extensive damage from the war, but it was put under extreme pressure, worked to exhaustion, and poorly maintained. Still under private ownership, British rail networks faced a difficult and laborious post–1945 period of patching up and making up in an attempt to reach their former prewar capacity, standards of efficiency, and level of security. British Railway, part of British Transport Commission, was created in January 1948.

Quite apart from their massive use on the home front, railroads were also employed by the British military authorities in the various World War II fronts in Asia, the Middle East and Africa. Most were civilian networks taken over, or partly controlled, improved, or extended, by the military. Let us take for example the forgotten campaign in Eritrea in east Africa. The Eritrean Railroad, as already discussed in Part 4, had been built by the Italians in the 1930s. It was also used by the British in their war against the Italians in 1941. The British possessed a fairly extensive rail system in the Sudan, which they used for logistical purposes. The system was a network of narrow-gauge, single-line tracks dating from the 1890s, having been built to support Kitchener's campaign against the Mahdi Muhammad Ahmad of Dongola (1843–85). An important line for the British ran from Port Sudan inland to Haiya, where it split in two. From Haiya, one line went further inland to Atbara and then down to Khartoum and places beyond. The second line from Haiya went almost due south to Kassala, then on to Gedaref and other points, including Sennar, from where it looped back up to Khartoum.

About three weeks after Italy declared war in June 1940, the Italians took Kassala in early July. But it appears for some reason they had placed a limit of 40 km or so on their incursions into the Sudan, and they never really threatened the Sudanese rail line. Thanks to the railroad, in January 1941 the British retook Kassala, and on February 1–2, 1941, they captured Agordat and Barentu. The victory at Barentu was as important as that of Agordat, and the conquest of the little

town opened an important route between the British railhead at Kassala and Agordat. During this period, the Italian forces withdrew to Keren and the surrounding hills. On March 15, 1941, the British resumed the attack on Keren. Twelve days later, on March 27, they took the city.

After the loss of Keren, which was regarded as the end of Italian East Africa, things went

Top: *British WD 0-6-0 ST. The standard switching locomotive for the British Army was the War Department Austerity 0-6-0 designed by the Hunslet Engine Company from Leeds. Some 378 were produced, and after the war many continued serving civilian railroads until the 1970s.*

Bottom: *British Bedford MWD truck. In 1940 the British Army had dispensed with the horse apart from ceremonial duties. In the late 1930s several special military vehicles were designed. The GS Bedford MWD truck consisted of a 4x2 chassis cab and roadster wooden box with a powerful engine and a relatively low overall silhouette with the hood tilted in order to increase the visibility of the driver. Its strengths were its engine (Bedford 6-cylinder in-line gasoline OHV, 3519 cc, 72 hp), and its excellent handling. Engaged for the first time during the battle of France in 1940, it became the workhorse of the British army, equipping also the Royal Air Force and Commonwealth units. From 1943, the models were equipped with half doors and a folding windshield. The Bedford MWDs were used during all battles of World War II, filling all kinds of logistics missions.*

The vehicle had a length of 4.38 m, a width of 1.99 m, a height of 1.93 m, and an empty weight of 2,100 kg. It had a maximum speed of 80 km/h, a range of 430 km, and could transport either 10 infantrymen or 800 kg of matériel or supply.

very fast in Eritrea—the British were in Asmara four days later on April 1 and in Massawa by April 11. Although it was another month until the capture of the Duke d'Aosta and a sizable Italian force at Amba Alagi, the decisive victory was Keren.

The British had also built a railroad line in Egypt running parallel to the Mediterranean coast and linking Alexandria, El Alamein and Mersa Matruh. This line proved of great importance during the battles fought against the Italo-German Axis in the North African campaigns in 1941–43. The highly strategic line from Alexandria to Mersa Matruh (294.4 km) was decided upon in late 1935. The first 74 km were opened to traffic in January 1936 with the remainder following suit three months later. That part of the line was a normal one, i.e., properly ballasted and with normal infrastructure with a planned capacity of 600 tons daily. During the war, it was extended to Sidi Barani, which it reached in December 1941, and Bir Suesi (near El Adem about 10 km south of Tobruk) in June 1942. When Rommel's Afrika Korps had to receive supplies, weapons, ammunition and fuel, tanks and vehicles from Germany and Italy across the Mediterranean Sea (where cargo ships were repeatedly attacked by the British based on the island of Malta), the convenient Alexandria-Mersa-Matruh railroad line was an important trump for the build-up of British forces in the North African theater of war.

Armored Trains

The Longmoor Military Railway in Surrey (created before World War I, and until 1935 known as the Woolmer Instructional Railway) was used by the British military for training purposes. Its usage increased during the Second World War and at its peak it had seventy miles of lines and siding with a large array of locomotives and rail cars offering varied experience to the trainees. The British Army opened numerous similar railroad lines both for training purposes and to transport supplies

and ammunition. The largest was the Bicester Railway at Eastriggs near Carlisle. Existing lines were also used for military roles, notably in southern England.

After the collapse of France and the evacuation of Dunkirk (May 27–June 4, 1940), a weakened Britain stood alone facing a victorious Nazi Germany. By that time many thought that an invasion of the British Isles was imminent, resulting in anti-invasion measures being taken and quickly carried out. The Home Guard was raised, soon comprising 1.5 million local volunteers otherwise ineligible for military service, usually owing to age, hence the nickname "Dad's Army." General Edmund Ironside, C-i-C Home Forces, designed a defense plan consisting of concentric zones and stop lines in case of a German breakthrough in southeast England. These hastily built lines included natural obstacles such as rivers, canals and embankments, as well as man-made features including concrete pillboxes, gun emplacements, antipersonnel and antitank obstacles, mine fields, combat trench systems and barbed-wire entanglements.

Neither France nor Great Britain had used armored trains in the 1940 campaign, and for the first time since the Boer War, the British re-used them in their anti-invasion preparation. The Southern Railway (having a number of lines running parallel to the Channel coast) was used for improvised armored trains. Around Wadebridge in Devon, a part of the Bodmin and Wadebridge line was upgraded and then used to allow trains from west Cornwall to use the South Railway route to Exeter to avoid the bombing in Plymouth. An armored train was created to patrol the line and possibly to participate in fighting against a German invasion. It was composed of a non-armored locomotive running push-pull between four 4-wheeled concrete and steel armored cars. Each car featured two parts. At the outer end was a compartment housing a shielded two-pounder gun. Behind it was a walled compartment provided with apertures for infantrymen's rifles.

Around Romney Hythe in Kent, the quasi-miniature 15-inch narrow-gauge Romney Hythe and Dymchurch Railway line was patrolled by a small military train composed of one locomotive fitted with armor sandwiched between two solidly built and armored steel undercarriage wagons built for mineral haulage on the Ravenglass and Eskdale Railway. Each wagon housed two Lewis guns and one Boys anti-tank rifle. This micro unit actually shot down one German airplane during the Blitz. Fortunately the German invasion never materialized, and by 1943 the British coastal armored trains were disbanded. The Romney Hythe-Dymchurch line, however, continued to be extensively used by the military, notably during the building of PLUTO (Pipe Line Under the Ocean), which ran over 130 km (70 nautical miles) from Shanklin Chine on the Isle of Wight through the English Channel to Cherbourg, Normandy, France, in order to supply fuel to the Allied forces in Western Europe in 1944–45.

It should be noted that in 1941 a few special armored railcars were made by the London, Midland & Scottish Railway for the protection of the royal family.

During the Anglo-Iraqi campaign in May 1941, the British captured an Iraqi armored train near Basra.

The British used an armored train in December 1941 during the Battle for the Ledge, an operation to move into southern Thailand following the Japanese invasion of Malaya and of Thailand. This armored train, carrying 30 men from the 2/16th Punjab Regiment and some engineers, advanced into Thailand from Padang Besar in Perlis. It reached Khlong Ngae, and successfully destroyed a 200-foot-long bridge before withdrawing back to Padang Besar.

Railroad Artillery

As far as Great Britain was concerned, the railroad gun had had its day. However, the veteran guns of World War I, which had been greased and tucked away in 1918, were dragged out and cleaned in 1939 as part of the British anti-invasion scheme. The railroad guns were deployed in Kent in order to fire across the Strait of Dover and hit German positions in the region of Calais, northern France. These ex–World War I weapons included three 13.5-inch (342.9 mm) railroad mounted guns on the East Kent Light Railway, located around Lydden and Shepherdswell. These were known as Gladiator, Scene Shifter and Peace Maker. Several 9.2-inch Mark 13 guns were emplaced near Canterbury and Hythe. One World War I 18-inch howitzer, designated Boche Buster, was emplaced on the Elham Valley Railway, between Bridge and Lyminge. Around Guston, 12-inch howitzers Mk III and Mk V were sited. The role played by these rail guns would have been very limited, as their fire control and sighting systems were not suited to engaging moving targets such as ships. It can hardly be said that British railroad guns had gone to war. Besides the rise of the bomber airplane effectively ended their usefulness. Just like armored trains, rail guns were too

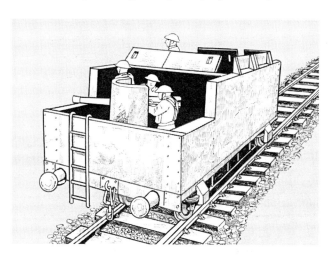

Armored car, Wadebridge armored train.

massive, too expensive, and too easily destroyed or immobilized from the air. In fact, in 1940 rail-mounted heavy artillery had already become obsolete.

AUSTRALIA

As a British dominion, Australia entered World War II in September 1939. About one million Australian soldiers served in the armed forces, whose military units fought primarily in the European theater, North African campaign, and the Southwest Pacific theater. In addition, Australia came under direct attack for the first time in its post-colonial history. Australian forces played a key role in the Pacific War against Japan, making up the majority of Allied strength throughout much of the fighting in the Southwest Pacific.

World War II marked the beginning of a long period of Australian economic growth. The war greatly increased the size and importance of the Australian manufacturing sector and stimulated the development of more technologically advanced industries.

Rail transport played a vital role in Australia's war effort. It was the main means of shipping service personnel and military equipment around the country. However, Australian railroads were not up to the demands of war. Each state used a different gauge, much of the rolling stock was unsuited for the task, and not until early 1943 was rail transport centrally organized. And yet the demand for quick and efficient means of transport only increased as coastal shipping was diverted for use by the armed forces or reduced by losses to Japanese actions.

The rail network in Queensland (in the northeast) was closest and thus most exposed to the fighting. In 1942 the army had effective control of transport in Queensland. This led the Queensland Railway Commissioner and the federal Minister for Transport to clash with the Minister for the Army, a dispute only solved through the prime minister's intervention.

By the end of the war, hundreds of thousands of Australian and Allied soldiers, and even enemy prisoners, had traveled millions of kilometers on Australian trains.

UNITED STATES

Transport

In the 1920s and 1930s, in spite of the Great Depression that started in 1929, the United States grew steadily as a global economic and military power. Although the United States had embraced the automobile age more firmly than any other nation, the railroads were at the heart of their transcontinental transportation system, carrying virtually all war traffic, both supplies and men. In June 1930 the U.S. government had established an Army military base called Camp Claiborne near Forest Hill and Rapides Parish in central Louisiana. It was principally used for basic training and artillery practice, and was also the home to the U.S. Engineering Unit Training Command. In September 1942, in order to simulate wartime demolitions and repairs of railroads for special service forces, Claiborne Polk Military Railroad was enlarged to include 23,000 acres (93 km^2), 50 miles (80 km) of railroad tracks, and 25 bridges. Much of the line was intentionally built over the very unstable mud of the Louisiana swamplands and had numerous wooden trestles. The intent was to train soldiers and railroaders in the most adverse conditions in order to prepare them efficiently for war. Derailments would be staged, and trains were followed by a big hook and work train to see how fast the derailed engines and cars could be re-railed, and the track repaired and returned to operation. Trestles would be intentionally blown up and work crews raced around the clock to rebuild them and reopen the line as soon as possible. Backshop forces were trained to repair locomotives and cars in intentionally very primitive conditions.

The Japanese surprise attack on the U.S. fleet at Pearl Harbor, Hawaii on December 7,

1941, propelled the USA into the war, and the whole country was quickly put on a war footing. The transportation of troops and supplies to build up and maintain the force of millions of soldiers deployed overseas by the U.S. Army in World War II involved operations of unprecedented magnitude and complexity, both across the Atlantic and Pacific Oceans and within the military theaters. In March 1942 the urgent coordination of ships, railroads and motor vehicles within the U.S. armed forces resulted in the creation of the United States Army Transportation Corps (USATC), to deliver men and goods where and when they were needed to defeat Germany, Japan and their allies. Thanks to much better coordination and cooperation with the rail companies, there occurred none of the bottlenecks that had forced the government to take over the railroads in 1917 and 1918 during the First Word War.

By the end of World War II, the Transportation Corps (including its railroad branch called Military Railroad Service, or MRS) had moved more than 30 million soldiers within the continental United States, and 7 million soldiers plus 126 million tons of supplies overseas. The total strength of the Military Railroad Service in June 1945 was 44,084 officers and men, of whom 28,828 served in the European theater of operations. One of the greatest feats of the Transportation Corps and Military Railroads Service was the rebuilding of France's shattered railroad network after D-Day (June 6, 1944) and the transportation of many locomotives and railroad cars specially built for the lighter French track system starting with D-Day +38. To speed up the process, and to avoid delays caused by the sabotage and destruction of French channel ports and docks by the retreating Germans, the Transportation Corps developed ingenious and improvised schemes. For example, they installed rails on the beaches, and shipped the heavy railroad stock across the Channel in specially converted landing ship tanks (LST, with open-

ing bow doors) equipped with rails in their holds. As LSTs were in scarce number, they also used a number of peacetime purpose-built ferryboats whose normal cross-Channel runs had been abruptly terminated in 1940. Indeed, civilian ferryboats had clear car or train decks and could easily be modified and adapted for military shipping use.

To sustain the war effort, the United States produced 748 steam locomotives of a type designed by the Corps of Engineers that came to be known as "Mikado" or "MacArthur," after General Douglas MacArthur (1880–1964). These heavy 2-8-2 wartime locos were used in many theaters of war including Europe, Africa, India, Burma, and even Australia. Other steam locomotives, notably type 030 and type USATC S100, built in the USA in the period 1942–1944, as well as numerous rolling stock, were also brought to Europe. After the war, some of this American railroad equipment was purchased by European countries, for example, the French Société Nationale des Chemins de fer Français (SNCF, or French National Railroad Company).

After the landing in Normandy in June 1944, in order to make up for the lack of sufficient railroads, an emergency transportation system by trucks on roads was set up to supply the rapid advance of the Allied army in France. Known as the Red Ball Express, this scheme (carrying all kind of supplies, and principally POL = petrol, oil, lubricants) included 6,000 trucks continuously running almost nose to tail at 35 mph (56 km/h) with full priority, operating night and day through a strict set of rules and a demanding schedule, carrying some 12,500 tons of supplies per day at its peak. At first, in July and August 1944, the Red Ball Express started at Arromanches and Cherbourg, then ran via Saint-Lô, Vire, Argentan, and Laigle to the temporary U.S. logistics base of Chartres.

On the way back, empty trucks returned via Alençon, Mortain, Saint-Hilaire du Harcouet, Saint-Lô, and Carentan to Cherbourg. When the Allied and the 1st and 3rd U.S. Armies advanced eastwards in September 1944, the route was extended to Versailles and Soissons (northeast of Paris), while a second branch (east of Paris) ran to Juvisy, Dourdan, Melun, Mormant, Esternay and Sommesous. A few weeks later, when the Channel and North Sea ports were liberated and repaired, other truck convoy supply routes were established, e.g., the White Ball Express connecting Le Havre to Paris, and ABC in Belgium linking Antwerp to Brussels and Charleroi. For a couple of months the cargo road service schemes were remarkably efficient operations as vital parts of the Allied lines of supply. However, when the Allied armies progressed to eastern France in the direction of Germany, the system became self-defeating, since the trucks consumed more gasoline than they could transport. Thereby they highlighted the severe limitations of automobile transport by road for long-distance haulage. Fortunately railroad lines were more rapidly repaired than the withdrawing Germans could destroy, and portable gasoline pipelines were installed, so more men, cargo and supplies were transported by trains. The Red Ball Express cargo service was discontinued on November 16, 1944.

The rapidly repaired French rail network also played an important role during the Battle of the Bulge, fought in the densely forested Belgian Ardennes in appalling winter conditions from December 16, 1944, to January 25, 1945. The secretly prepared operation was the last major German counteroffensive in the West, taking the Allied forces completely off guard. The objectives of Hitler's last gamble were extremely ambitious: first, to stop Allied transport over the Channel to the port city of Antwerp; second, to split the British and American Allied line in half; third, to encircle and destroy them; and then to force the Western Allies to negotiate a peace treaty. Once that was accomplished, Hitler could fully concentrate and win on the Russian eastern theater of war. At first the Germans attacked a weakly defended section of the Allied line, taking advantage of heavily overcast weather conditions, which grounded the Allies' overwhelmingly superior air forces. However, fierce U.S. resistance at Elsenborn Ridge and around Bastogne blocked the German advance. Soon, running out of fuel and ammunition, the German offensive bogged down. In great haste the Americans managed to bring fresh troops, armor and artillery owing to a railroad line that was available. At the same time, fortunately improved weather conditions allowed for attacking the Germans from the air.

By late January 1945, the failure of the ambitious offensive was sealed, and the invasion of Nazi Germany started, opening the last chapter of World War II in Europe. The German strength totaled around 450,000 troops, of whom between 67,200 and 125,000 were killed, missing or wounded. As for the 610,000 U.S. troops who bore the brunt of the Ardennes attack, 89,000 were casualties, including up to 19,000 killed.

When the Soviet-Nazi nonaggression pact was violated by the launch of a massive German invasion of the Soviet Union in June 1941, Stalin joined the Western Allies. Supplying the Soviet Union's war effort was another difficult challenge for the Allies. The waters around the northern Russian ports of Archangel and Murmansk were frozen during the winter months, and ships' convoys sailing in the summer were attacked by German submarines and bomber airplanes based in Norway. The other way to help supply Stalin's armies was a railroad line to the south across Persia and Azerbaijan. Build between 1927 and 1938 by German and American private companies, the 865-mile Trans-Persian Railroad was an ambitious and remarkable achievement through difficult mountains and deserts. During World War II, under very demanding conditions the Anglo-American Allies managed the part of the line between the Persian Gulf port of Bandar Shapur and Teheran, while the Russians took care of the northern part of the line between Teheran and the Caspian Sea. British and American rolling stock proved strong enough to cope with the difficult climate, and the war matériel transported on this lifeline was a welcome addition to the Soviet combat against Nazi Germany and her allies. The Trans-Persian Railroad was protected by Anglo-Indian troops, particularly in the bandit-infested mountain sections. It transported millions of tons of supplies to the Soviet Union in under three years with a peak of 6,490 tons per day in 1944. Aid to Soviet Russia ceased by May 1945.

Transport lines were used by American forces in all theaters of operations, including in the Pacific. For example, on the islands of Saïpan and Tinian (Northern Marianas) there were narrow-gauge railroads intended to haul sugar cane in peacetime to the central processing plant in Chalan Kanoa. The lines were built by the Japanese engineer Haruji Matsue in the 1930s, and helped develop a prosperous sugarcane industry. After the battle for the control of these islands (June 15–July 9, 1944), the Americans Seabee (CBs or NCBs, from U.S. Naval Construction Battalions) refurbished the tracks, locomotives and rolling stock, and used them to transport supplies to the Asito airfield. The historic Saïpan railroad was restored in the 2010s as a popular tourist attraction.

Railroad Artillery

During World War II, the U.S. forces had no armored trains and only a few guns mounted on railroad cars, e.g., 14 in. guns, 12 in. mortars, and 8 in. Mark VI guns based on the earlier model M1888. For the most part surplus World War I, these weapons were adapted to coastal defense. When World War II broke out, mobile railroad artillery was deployed temporarily to protect harbors with inadequate defenses until permanent modern coastal fortifications were built. For example, batteries were placed in 1943 at Fort Miles, Cape Henlopen, Delaware, and Cay May, New Jersey, at the mouth of Delaware Bay. They included mobile 155 mm guns and 8 in. railroad guns protected by large circular emplacements

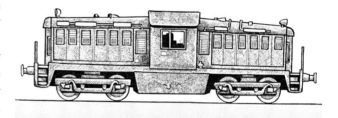

Top: *Whitcombe B-B. This was the standard World War II U.S. Army diesel locomotive. It was a double-undercarriage design powered by two 325-hp diesel-electric motors. It had a length of 49 ft 9 in, an undercarriage wheelbase of 7 ft, and a wheel diameter of 3 ft 3 in. It was manufactured in quantity and was used in North Africa, Italy, and after D-Day in northwest Europe.*

Bottom: *U.S. S100 0-6-0 USATC locomotive. The S100, designed by Colonel Howard G. Hill, was a side-tank switcher in which water was contained in rectangular tanks mounted on either side of the locomotive, next to the boiler instead of carried in a tender. In 1942, the USATC ordered 382 S100s from Davenport Locomotive Works of Iowa, H.K. Porter, Inc., of Pittsburgh, and Vulcan Iron Works of Wilkes-Barre. They were shipped to Great Britain in 1943, where they were stored until 1944. After D-Day, they were shipped to Continental Europe.*

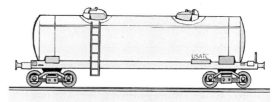

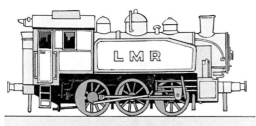

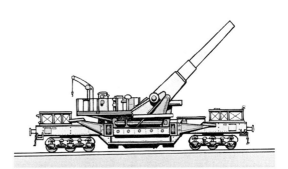

Left, top: Insignia of the USATC. The winged car wheel symbolizes rail transportation, the mariner's helm stands for transport by water, and the U.S. highway marker shield is for land transportation.

Left, middle: USATC 0-6-0 side-tank locomotive.

Left, bottom: USATC caboose with 40 mm Bofort gun on platform.

Right, top: MacArthur 2-8-2 S-200 war locomotive.

Right, middle: USATC tanker rail car.

Right, bottom: U.S. 8 in. naval gun on railroad mounting. Manufactured by the Baldwin Locomotive Works, the 8 in. (20.3 cm) caliber gun was in U.S. service from 1941 to 1946. It had a range of 35,300 yards (32 km) and a rate of fire of two rounds per minute. In firing position the railroad gun was stabilized with outriggers. Some 24 units were built during World War II, of which eight were positioned at Fort Miles on Cape Henlopen near Lewes, Delaware.

made of thick earth revetment. Another example would be the coastal batteries established at Fort Dawes, Deer Island, Massachusetts, to defend Boston Harbor. When World War II ended in 1945, railroad guns were discarded. Indeed, the U.S. Air Force had demonstrated that when it came to delivering enormous quantities of high explosive at long range, large four-engine bombers (e.g., B-17, B-24, and B-29) were a reasonable, if not always quite accurate, substitute for railroad guns.

FRANCE

Following the campaign and defeat of May-June 1940, France was occupied by Germany. All French weapons and military railroad equipment, at least everything that could be useful, were captured and pressed into German service. In 1940 France had about 16,000 locomotives, of which 4,320 were taken to Germany as compensation. The French National Railroad Company (SNCF) civilian network was requisitioned to support Germany's war effort. A special overseeing organization was created in August 1940 known as the *Wehrmacht Verkehrs Direktion* (WVD, Direction of Traffic of the Armed Forces).

Top: *GMC truck. Although many vehicles were in use by the Allies in World War II, it was the General Motors Company's CCKW two-and-a-half ton 6x6 cargo truck (popularly known as the "deuce-and-a-half" or just "deuce" or "Jimmy") that made an outstanding contribution. The nomenclature CCKW means: C, designed in 1941; C, conventional cab; K, all-wheel drive; and W, dual rear axles. This truck was the most widely used tactical transport vehicle of the U.S. and Allied forces in World War II. The Allies' superior ability to move mountains of supplies was recognized as one of the keys to victory. No vehicle was more important in creating that superiority than the GMC CCKW. Some 800,000 were produced, seeing widespread service in all theaters of operation, including of course the Red Ball Express. The basic chassis could be fitted with a multitude of specialist bodies including troop carrier (with a capacity of 16 fully equipped men), stock rack, tanker, dumper, mobile repair workshop, ambulance, command post, radio vehicle, and many others. The cabin was either open, with canvas cover and doors, or completely enclosed. Some CCKW trucks were equipped with a winch at the front. Others featured a ring mount for a 12.7 mm (0.50 cal) machine gun above the cab, both for antiaircraft fire and defense in the event of an ambush, the gunner standing up on the passenger's seat to operate the weapon. The basic GMC CCKW 352 was powered by a 6-cylinder GMC 270 gasoline engine generating 104 bhp. It had a maximum speed of 75 km/h (45 mph) and weighed 4,585 kg (5.175 tons). Length was 5.86 m (21 ft 4.25 in); width was 2.24 m (7 ft 4 in); and height was 2.80 m (9 ft 2 in).*

Bottom: *Locomotive on the narrow-gauge railroad at Saïpan (Mariana Islands).*

Like all railroad companies in occupied Europe, the SNCF was used to transport military goods and German troops. It also transported thousands of Jews and other Holocaust victims to Nazi extermination and concentration camps. The French National Railroad Company charged the victims third-class tickets although passengers were transported in appalling conditions in cattle cars. After the liberation of France, these scandalous deportations became the subject of historical controversy and lawsuits until 1992, when the SNCF commissioned a group of French academics and historians to write a history of the company's activities during World War II. Their report was published in 1996. The same happened in other lands then occupied by the Nazis. In the Netherlands, for example, the leadership of the *Nederlandse Spoorwegen* (Dutch Railroad) in 2005 made an official and public apology for the role the company had played in the deportation of Jews to Nazi extermination camps in the period 1941–1945.

In 1941 the puppet government of Vichy revived the project of constructing a trans-Sahara railroad in order to connect Mediterranean North Africa to Dakar in Senegal. For a while, prisoners and foreign internees were put to work in appalling conditions; their suffering was similar to that suffered by the workers on the Japanese death railroad in Burma, only on a far smaller scale. The project was abandoned in 1942 when its sheer unreality became apparent, and when colonies in West and Central Africa rallied to General de Gaulle's Free French Forces that were fighting along with the Allies.

The French railroad company, at least some of its personnel, also took part in the fight against Nazi Germany and against the Vichy government. In early 1943 two SNCF employees, Jean-Guy Bernard and Louis Armand, created *Résistance-Fer* (Railroad Resistance), intended to fight the Nazi occupiers. An underground organization composed of railroad workers was set up. At first the secret movement only used passive resistance like amending paperwork to ensure that freight was sent to the wrong destination, and using any other tricks that would delay services. They also collected and transmitted to the Allied forces in London information and intelligence about strength, positions and movements of German troops. In late 1943, the Résistance started to carry out daily sabotage actions, as well as guerrilla attacks intended to thwart German transportation.

Preparing for the D-Day landing in Normandy in June 1944, the Allies asked Résistance-Fer to make an all-out effort to disrupt the occupiers' rail transport. In coordination with the Allied headquarters in London, Résistance-Fer played an important role by taking an active form of combat like sabotaging lines, materials and railroad infrastructures with explosives to slow down and delay German movement, supply and communication. As a result, the German military formations sometimes spent days and even weeks making their way to the front line, and even then arrived piecemeal and somewhat battered. For example, in May 1944 the 2nd Waffen SS Armored Division Das Reich was deployed in the region of Montauban near Toulouse in southwest France about 700 km from the beaches of Normandy. When it became clear that Normandy was the place of the main Allied landing, the division was ordered to move north to take part in the fighting. Because of the pressure on the rail transport network with ambushes by armed partisans, sabotages by railroad men and the constant danger of attack by roving Allied aircraft, Das Reich arrived in Normandy only on June 26, 1944—much too late to repulse the Allied invasion. On its way Das Reich left a track of devastation and blood as retaliation, notably at Tulle, where 99 civilians were hanged and 149 arrested and deported to Dachau concentration camp. At the small village of Oradour-sur-Glane, the entire population (some 642 civilians, including 207 children) were massacred, allegedly because two SS officers of the 2nd Division had been kidnapped by French maquisards. Only six persons survived the slaughter.

Before D-Day the activities of Resistance-Fer and the Allied aerial interdiction campaign by strategic bombers had devastated the French rail network, bridges, installations and other military positions. The Allied air attacks on the communications were on a staggering scale, and indeed the French railroad system was crippled. The offensive involved every kind of air activity possible: large-scale carpet-bombing by heavy bombers (e.g., U.S. B-17 Flying Fortress, B-24 Liberator, and British Avro Lancaster) and medium bombers (e.g., U.S. B-25 Mitchell and Douglas Boston); precision swoops by fast fighter-bombers (e.g., U.S. P-47 Thunderbolt, P-38 Lightning, and British De Haviland Mosquito and Hawker Tempest); and fighter sweeps and low-level reconnaissance (e.g., U.S. P-51 Mustang and British Spitfire). Allied fighter-bombers and fighters were widely used for strafing—attacking targets on the ground with small bombs, machine guns, automatic cannons and rockets. The term strafing comes from the German verb *strafen* (to punish), specifically from the humorous adaptation of the World War I German catchphrase "Gott strafe England" (May God punish England). It was not necessary to attack the defended trains. Judicious and repeated bombing of strategic bridges, marshaling yards, switching points and junctions continually forced the Germans to divert their trains or halt them while repairs took place. The German Army in France needed one hundred trains a day for its supply. By April 1944 the available number was down to sixty, and in May down to thirty-two. For these results, the French railroad Résistance paid a heavy toll. Nearly 1,700 SNCF workers were killed or deported for resisting Nazi orders. About 150 Résistance-Fer agents were shot without trials for their acts of sabotage, and about 500 of them were deported. Half of those deported died in concentration camps.

So after the Normandy landing, there was effectively very little left of the railroad system

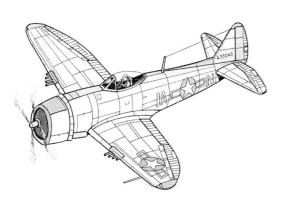 

Left: P-47 Thunderbolt. The Republic P-47 was a very effective single-seat airplane, used either as a short-to-medium range escorter or fighter in high-altitude air-to-air combat, or as a fighter-bomber in both the European and Pacific theaters. Powered by one Pratt & Whitney R-2800 Double Wasp radial engine, it had a maximum speed of 697 km/h (433 mph). Its armament included eight .50-caliber machine guns, four per wing. In the fighter-bomber and ground attack role it could carry ten 127 mm (5 inch) unguided rockets or a significant bomb load of 1,134 kg (2,500 pounds)—over half the weight the four-engine Boeing B-17 Flying Fortress bomber could carry.

Right: SNCF 141R. At the end of World War II, there was a shortage of locomotives, and to quickly obtain the large number needed, locomotives were ordered in North America under the Lend-Lease Program. The main American and Canadian locomotive builders (e.g., Baldwin Locomotive Works, Pennsylvania; American Locomotive Company, New York; and Lima Locomotive Works, Ohio; Montreal Locomotive Works, Quebec; and Canadian Locomotive Company, Ontario) produced a total of 1340 141Rs. These locomotives were powerful, competent and rugged; they became maids-of-all-works, and remained in service in France until 1974. The 141R had a 2-8-2 configuration, weighed 115.5 t (113.7 long tons), had a length (without tender) of 14.64 m (48 ft), and a maximum speed of 100 km/h (62 mph).

in France because of Résistance sabotage, Allied air bombardments, and destruction by the retreating Germans. The Allies, however, needed the railroad, and a process of rapid reconstruction began, as just discussed in the previous paragraph.

SOVIET UNION

Stalin, unlike Hitler, had long recognized the value of the railroad and had ordered a large program of investment in the interwar era. The smooth running of the Soviet railroads was instrumental in enabling the quick transport of supply and troops, and also the withdrawal of a part of the nation's industry away from threatened western areas to the safe and remote east. The Russians laid a staggering 4,500 miles of new tracks during World War II, and regauged thousands of miles of track. In a country where mud in autumn and ice in winter represent an insurmountable obstacle to smooth transport by road, railroads played a crucial role in supplying armies on the field, notably the defenders of Moscow, Leningrad and Stalingrad. Owing to their good use of railroads, the Red Army managed to check the German advance before Moscow, and stabilize a continental-scale front stretching from the Baltic Sea in the north to the Black Sea in the south. After the defeat of the Nazis at Stalingrad in early 1943, the German forces lost the initiative, and then the Soviet Armies constantly went on the offensive, starting a giant westward push that brought them right to Berlin, the very heart of the Third Reich, in April 1945.

Armored Trains

Despite the growing menace of air power, the wide-open spaces of the Soviet Union ensured that transport by rail and armored train as weapons would remain important factors through the war against Nazi Germany between 1941 and 1945.

The Soviet rearmament plan that brought out a series of new tanks in the early 1930s also called for new purpose-built armored trains. The standard BP-35 armored train used many components from the tank program (for example, the same 76.2 mm turret as the T-35 heavy tank). When Nazi Germany attacked the Soviet Union in June 1941, the Red Army had 34 light and 19 heavy armored trains, while the NKVD (Narodnyi Komissariat Vnutrennikh Del: Stalinist police commissariat of internal affairs) had another 25 armored trains (many of them surplus from the 1919–1921 Civil War) and 36 self-propelled armored wagons (a large locomotive sporting one or several tank turrets), which were intended for maintaining order within the Soviet Union. Armored trains proved extremely useful in covering the Red Army's retreats during the summer of 1941. All of the rail lines ahead of them were in friendly hands, and they could unleash their massive firepower from secure locations. However, they suffered such heavy losses, notably from air attacks by the German Luftwaffe, that the Commissariat of Communications ordered the increased use of antiaircraft weapons aboard armored trains, and the creation of entirely antiaircraft artillery trains, as described in the following paragraph.

Soviet workers achieved considerable feats and industry began producing more trains as quickly as possible. A great advantage of military railroad was that it could run even in the worst weather, such as heavy rain and mud that brought road traffic to a standstill. This was a great asset in a country like Russia where autumns are usually rainy and muddy, and winters particularly snowy and freezing cold.

The early World War II Russian armored trains of Types NKPS-42 were rather crude and simple, being easy to manufacture under great pressure. Soon as there was a desperate need for mobile firepower, large and heavy armored trains were produced. However, they proved vulnerable to German air attacks, and in January 1942 Soviet factories began turning out a new design code-named OB-3. After the heavy losses of 1941, this program was intended to reconstitute the Red Army's railroad force quickly and cheaply. Cars were often simple two-axle wagons with only one armed turret carrying one field or antiaircraft gun. This would allow the crew to jettison damaged cars without losing as much of the train's firepower, and their lower profile would make them more difficult to hit. But armor quality was poor (often a pair of steel plates with several inches of concrete poured between them), and the weapons were the leftovers from the Red Army's depots—guns of French and Polish manufacture captured during the Civil War. Twenty of the sixty-five OB-3 trains built were lost in action. Each OB-3 armored train consisted of one armored locomotive (usually an OV or OK series steam locomotive with 30–50 mm armor) with an antiaircraft machine gun placed on the tender, and four armored wagons. Each of these cars had 30–80 mm armor (often laminated or concrete-filled, as described above) positioned at an angle of 30 degrees. Each car had a crew of 12, and was armed with one

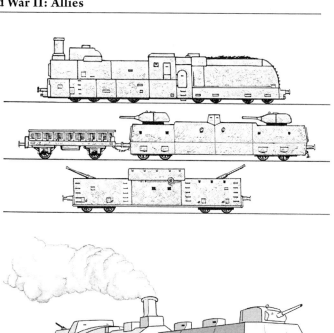

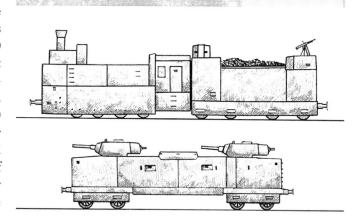

Top: *Soviet armored train "Ilya Muromets." The armored train Ilya Muromets (named after a Ukrainian medieval folk hero and knight-errant) was built from October 1941 to February 1942. Its armament consisted of two armored cars, both with two T-34/76 turrets with 76.2 mm machine guns; and two armored cars with two 37 mm antiaircraft guns and one M-8 rocket launcher.*

Middle: *Soviet armored train "Fascism Fighter."*

Bottom: *Soviet armored train No. 1 "Baltic." This train was composed of an armored locomotive with a heavy antiaircraft machine gun emplaced on the tender; two artillery wagons armed with six machine guns and two KV-1 tank turrets with 76 mm guns; and two flat pusher cars. No. 1 train fought near Stalingrad in 1942.*

gun in a hexagonal turret and five machine guns (four in the corners of the wagon and one in the turret). The car did not include any optical devices (except the gun sight), so all observation was made through small openings, slits, and hatches. OB-3 trains began to participate in battles in the spring of 1942.

They proved themselves in the oncoming heavy battles, such as Voronezh, Kharkov, Stalingrad and the Northern Caucasus.

The final Soviet armored train design was the BP-43, another attempt to flesh out the

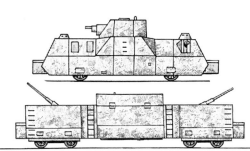

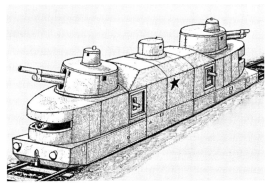

Left, top: *Soviet armored locomotive Type OB-3. Armored locomotive standard type OB-3 was developed for armored train in the first months of World War II. However, there were some differences between units, like the setup of the commander's post, armoring of the pipe, presence or lack of air-defense turret on the tender, etc. Typical units of this kind of locomotive were armored with steel plates: boiler, tender and moving parts were 40 mm thick; machinist and commander posts about 45mm thick; air defense turret 36 mm thick. In total 60 steamers of type OB-3 were manufactured in 1941–43.*

Left, bottom: *Armored cars of train type OB-3. Upper—gun in turret; lower—antiaircraft guns placed in open pits.*

Right, top: *Armored locomotive Russian BP Nr. 77. The BP Nr. 77 of the 77th NKVD Regiment was the former Polish armored train Nr. 51, which had been abandoned by its crew in September 1939. The train was captured by the Russians, then repaired and reused under the designation Bepo (Bronyepoyezd, or BP, Armored Train) of the 77th NKVD Regiment.*

Right, bottom: *Russian BP Nr. 77 artillery car. The NKVD BP Nr. 77 included two turreted artillery cars armed with original Polish armament (four 75 mm WZ. 02/26 guns, 7.92 mm and WZ. 08 Maxim machine guns). Interestingly, the train's artillery cars were actually Soviet former wagons of a standard type built in Krasnoye Sormovo plant in Nizhny Novgorod (Gorki) in 1919 during the Russian Civil War, and captured by the Poles in 1920 during the Polish-Soviet War.*

Red Army's railroad forces in an expeditious manner. A BP-43 train was a modified OB-3 with real armor and tank turrets from the T-34 production line. It had light, two-axle PL-43 armored wagons armed with one T-34 tank turret. The number of machine guns was decreased to three per armored car (one in the turret and two in each side of the wagon with a better field of fire than in previous designs). Each BP-43 armored train also included two antiaircraft armored wagons, plus one antiaircraft machine gun, usually mounted on the locomotive's tender. Overall twenty-one BP-43 armored trains were produced for the Red Army, plus an unknown number for the NKVD.

In all, the Russian Army had 143 armored trains during World War II, but their tactical value was greatly decreased due to their vulnerability to air strikes and the greater versatility offered by tanks and self-propelled artillery.

Anti-Aircraft Trains

The other branch of the Soviet armored train family were the PVO type (anti-aircraft, AA for short), used to protect supply and troop trains as well as important railroad hubs, junctions, bridges and all military, industrial and economic facilities. The first were built in early 1942 when it became obvious that mobile anti-aircraft batteries were badly needed. Typically PVO trains consisted of one armored locomotive and five two-axle platform wagons with 12–15 mm armor. Three cars were armed with one 76.2 mm AA gun, the other two with one 37 mm AA gun and one 12.7mm DShK machine gun each. Sometimes 37 mm guns were used instead of 76.2 mm MGs. Anti-aircraft weapons mounted on armored trains were capable not only of firing from the platforms, but could also be disembarked for use from the ground. The second operation was the norm when guarding railroad or industrial objectives, while the first was used when German planes were encountered when the train was running. There were eight PVO trains concentrated at the Battle of Stalingrad, and thirty-five at Kursk. Overall during World War II about 200 such trains were built and used in various configurations as powerful mobile anti-aircraft batteries.

Draisines and Rail-Cruisers

For the purposes of reconnaissance and patrolling, the Russians used standard wheeled armored vehicles that, with minimum modification, could be adapted to rail use.

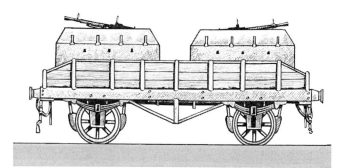

Anti-aircraft artillery car. In the beginning of World War II, Russian armored trains suffered considerable losses due to insufficient air defense capability—usually twin 7.62 mm Maxim machine guns placed on the tender. To resolve this issue, armored trains began to receive special air-defense (PVO) armored cars that were put in production at the end of 1941. A common type featured a platform model car equipped with twin 12.7 mm DShK heavy machine guns on special pods inside armored boxes with hinged roof shields. It was manned by 6 to 10 troops and carried an ammo load of 10,000 rounds. Addition of these platforms enabled the Soviets to decrease losses due to air attacks. Experience gained led to more advanced 4-axle cars with armored chassis and armed with automatic 25 or 37 mm guns. A variant designed for the same purpose in the same period included a standard flatcar fitted with a fixed octagonal armored box with a sliding movable roof armed with a quad Maxim 7.62 mm served by 3 soldiers.

The vehicles were the common armored cars (e.g., D-2, BA-6, BA-10, and BA-20), which had spare metal wheels and special lift devices, so after a small modification in field conditions, they were able to run on rail. The armament remained the same as the original road model. Older models (such as D-2) were mostly used by NKVD troops by 1941.

For the same purpose the Soviet Army pro-duced a number of self-propelled armored draisines and rail-cruisers. These vehicles of various types were often attached to and op-erated together with armored trains.

The MBV self-propelled armored wagon was designed in 1936–1937 at S.M. Kirov's Factory in Leningrad. Its construction in-cluded many of the details and features of the T-28 medium tank (which was designed and produced at this factory too). It was an orig-inal vehicle with a specially designed five-axle

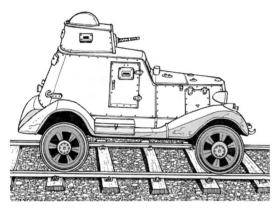

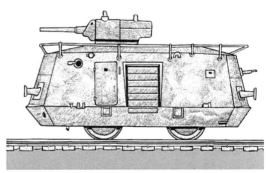

Left, top: *Russian BA-20. The armored BA-20 (short for BroneAvtomobil, meaning armored car) was based on the GAZ-M1 car, and was developed in 1936 as scout vehicle. It was also used by the Soviets to accompany armored trains. Equipped with flanged metal railroad wheels, it was designated BA-20Zhd (Zhd standing for railroad). Some 4,800 BA-20 were manufactured in the early stages of the war and production ceased in 1941. The Germans captured a lot of these armored cars and, although the design was obsolete, used them as training and reconnaissance vehicles. Captured Rus-sian BA-20 used by the Germans as patrol rail cars and training vehicles were designated Panzer-spähwagen 202 (r), or PzSpWg 202 (r) for short.*

Left, bottom: *Experimental draisine D-2.*

Right, top: *Rail car BDT. The rail car BDT was developed in the USSR in 1934. It was armed with one 45 mm 20K model 1932/34 gun with a coaxial DT 7.62 mm machine gun mounted in the T-26 tank turret and three on-board Maxim machine guns. The crew consisted of 9 men. About 10 were produced and some were still in service during World War II.*

Right, bottom: *Profile, rail car BDT.*

frame. It weighed 79.8 tons, had an armor thickness of 16–20 mm, and its engine allowed a maximum speed of 120 km/h. The armament was three fully armed T-28 (later T-34) tank turrets and five machine guns placed in the hull. The MBV self-propelled armored series had a very successful design and were used throughout the war.

The self-propelled armored trolleys (D, BD and PL series) were smaller in size and less

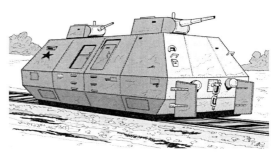

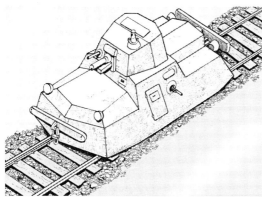

Left, top: *Draisine type D-37. Armored self-propelled railroad car D-37 with D-38 turret was developed in the USSR in 1932. It was designed for railroad track protection as well as a scout car for armored trains. D-37 had a unibody welded from 6–12 mm armored plates. The 40 hp Ford engine was located in the lower part while armament was located at the top. It was manned by 6 troops. D-37 was able to move with the same speed forward as backwards. Armament consisted of 76 mm (1927) gun and two side machine guns (DT). An anti-aircraft weapon station with twin Maxim machine guns was fitted in the rear of the compartment closed by a two-part hatch. The hatch was opened for combat and the station was raised up. It never entered production but served as a base for more advanced armored car DT-45.*

Left, bottom: *Self-propelled armored rail car DT-45. Railroad car DT-45 was developed in 1933 by modernization of the earlier type designated D-37. It was designed for railroad track protection as well as a scout car for armored trains. A cylindrical turret from a T-26 tank with 45 mm gun was fitted to the unchanged hull of D-37. Radio set 71TK with rail antenna was also installed. It was manned by 6 troops. To improve mobility, special equipment was installed to allow DT-45 to be easily transferred on to a parallel track. It was successfully tested but never went into production because of shortage of manufacturing abilities. However, experimental units were used for training up to the beginning of World War II.*

Right, top: *Russian draisine. This rail car featured sloping armor and two T-26 tank turrets. Each turret was armed with one 45 mm 20K model 1932 cannon.*

Right, bottom: *Self-propelled armored railcar "Leningrad."*

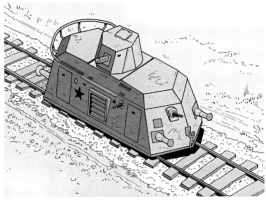

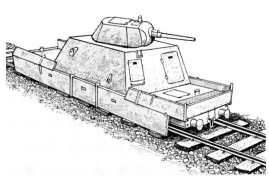

Left, top: *Soviet DTR.*

Left, bottom: *PL-43 armored rail car. Intended to equip the new armored train Type BP-43, platform PL-43 was developed in 1942. It was built from a 20-ton two-axle rail car with a turret from a T-34 tank armed with a 76 mm gun mounted on top. Three additional 7.62 DT machine guns were mounted in ball mounts. The front and side armored shields were 45 mm thick, turret 45–60 mm, and roof and chassis were 20 mm. The vehicle was manned by a crew of six or eight. Some eighty units were produced and effectively used on every front during World War II.*

Right, top: *T-28 tank. In the first year of the Second World War, damaged tanks were often used at construction of armored trains. For example, on the basis of the T-28 tank were built Bepo "Fascism Fighter" (one armored platform) and "Dzerzhinets" (four armored platforms). The armament of such armored platforms consisted of 76 mm gun (KT-28), and six DT machine guns (four in turrets and two in boards) with a crew varying between twelve and fifteen men.*

Right, bottom: *Soviet BA-64 ZhD. The BA-64 (nicknamed Bobik) was a small, lightly armored, four-wheeled scout car. Produced between 1942 and 1946 by the Soviet State Manufacture GAZ, the number built was 9,110. The fast and flexible vehicle came in several variants including the basic scout car as well as staff and liaison vehicle, halftrack with skis for use in snow, and rail scout car (ZhD). The BA-64 saw service during World War II and the postwar period in the Soviet Red Army, but also in the armies of China, North Korea (in the Korean War), Poland, Romania, and Yugoslavia. It had a weight of 2.36 tons, a length of 3.66 m (12.0 ft), a width of 1.69 m (5 ft 6.5 in), a height of 1.90 m (6 ft 2.8 in), and was operated by a crew of two. It was powered by a 4-cylinder liquid-cooled GAZ-MM 50 hp (37 kW) engine, and had an operational range of 300–600 km, and a maximum speed of 80 km/h on road. Its main drawbacks were the light armor thickness that varied from 4 to 15 mm, and the weak armament that featured either one 7.62 × 54mmR DT Degtyaryov machine gun with 1.260 rounds or one PTRD anti-tank rifle placed in a small turret.*

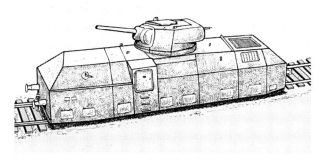

Russian draisine Krasnaja Zvezda (KZ-1, Red Star).
This motorized train vehicle intended for reconnais-
sance, scouting, track patrolling and other auxiliary
combat tasks, usually belonging to armored trains, but
also operating alone. It was designed in late 1941 and
entered service in March 1942. It used the heavy tank
KV-1 turret armed with 76.2 mm gun and a V-2K diesel
engine.

armed than the MBV. The series was used for reconnaissance, cover and support. There were many types of them, e.g., D-2, D-3, D-37, DT-45 with T-26 tank turret, BDT with T-26 tank turret, T-28 tank on rail, PL-43 with T-34/76 tank turret, and several others.

Some were captured and used by the Germans from 1941 to 1945.

Railroad Guns

During World War II, the Red Army had several heavy guns mounted on railroads, mostly original naval guns; for example, 130 mm-B-13-2, 152 mm B-38, 203 mm TM-8 and 356 mm TM-1-14. There is little point in describing them all, and two examples should suffice.

There were three railroad units (TM-3-12) each equipped with one naval 305 mm (12 inch) Obukhovski 12/52 model 1907 gun from the sunken battleship *Imperatritsa Mariya*, which had been lost to a magazine explosion in Sevastopol harbor in October 1916. The type 12/52 naval gun had a rate of fire of 2 or 3 rounds per minute, and could fire a 471 kg shell to

a maximum distance of 29,340 m (32,080 yards). The rail guns were used in the Soviet-Finnish Winter War in 1939–1940. In June–December 1941 they took part in the defense of the Soviet naval base on Finland's Hanko Peninsula. They were sabotaged by Soviet personnel when the base was evacuated, and were later restored by Finnish specialists using guns from the withdrawn Russian battleship *Imperator Aleksander III*. After World War II these were handed back over to the Soviet Union, and they were maintained in operational condition until 1991. They were discarded in 1999, and a survivor is displayed today at the Central Museum of Railroad Transport at Varshavsky Rail Terminal in Saint Petersburg. Another survivor is displayed at Poklonnaya Gora Museum in Moscow.

Another rail gun used by the Red Army was the model TM-1-180. Designed in 1934, it was composed of a 180 mm naval gun B-1-P placed in a turret on a rail car. In June 1941 there were four batteries, each with four TM-1-180 guns, at Tallinn, Hanko, Libav and Novorossiysk. During the siege of Leningrad all available

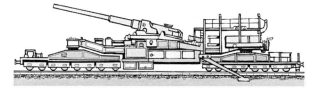

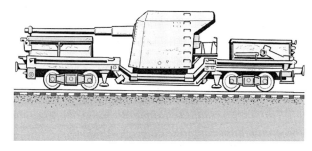

Top: *Soviet T.M.3-12 305 mm rail gun.*
Bottom: *Russian TM-1-152 rail gun.*

TM-1-180s were organized in the 101th naval railroad gun artillery battery. Today one TM-1-180 is displayed at Sevastopol in Ukraine, and another at the Victory Park Museum in Moscow.

SLOVAKIA

The Slovak National Uprising (August-October 1944) was an armed uprising instigated by the Slovak resistance movement during World War II. It was an attempt to defeat German troops that occupied Slovak territory and the removing of the collaborationist government of the pro–Nazi Jozef Tiso (1887–1947). However, the insurgents were weakened by internal dissension and political rivalry, and insufficient and inadequate external support. As a result they were defeated by German forces (including four Waffen SS divisions). Guerrilla operations continued until the Soviet, Czechoslovak and Romanian armies liberated Slovakia in 1945.

During the uprising, the Slovak resistance deployed three improvised armored trains named *Hurban*, *Stefanik* and *Masaryk* to fight against the better-equipped German forces. These trains were produced in the Zvolen railroad manufactory following prewar Czechoslovak regulations and based on German and Soviet army experiences. However they were not fully armored in the full sense of the word as metal was scarce. Instead they included 8 mm steel plates, heavy wooden planks and pounded stones with gravel filler between the panels.

The armored train *Stefanik* was built in September 1944. It was armed with a Czech 75 mm vz. 15

mountain gun, two 37 mm caliber cannons, and ten 7,92 mm machine-guns. The train had a crew of 70 commanded by Captain F. Adam.

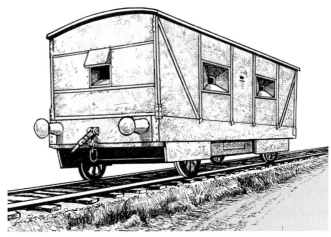

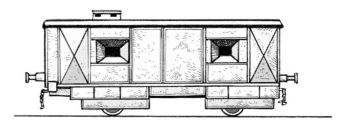

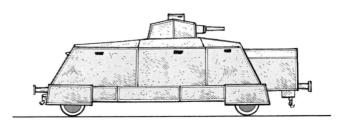

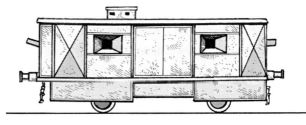

Top: ***Machine gun car of Czech armored train Hurban.***
Bottom: ***Czech armored train Stefanik, 1944; upper—profile of machine gun car; middle—profile of tank turreted car; bottom—profile of artillery car (guns placed at both ends).***

It saw action in the region of Stara Kremnicka in September and October 1944, when it was badly damaged and rendered irremediably useless. Its crew sabotaged all weapons and continued the war as a partisan unit on foot.

The armored train *Hurban* was built in September 1944. With a crew of 71 placed under the leadership of Captain J. Kuklis, its main armament included one 8 cm vz.17 artillery piece installed on an armored car, four 37 mm guns emplaced in discarded tank turrets as well as eleven heavy 7.92 caliber machine guns. The armored train Hurban saw action in the region of Brezno and Cervena Skala area against the Germans particularly the 18th

Waffen SS division Horst Wessel. In October 1944 it participated to combats on the upper Hron River. Despite a damaged locomotive its crew warded off all German assaults. The train was subsequently towed to Harmanec, where it was left in a tunnel, the crew fighting from then on as a guerilla infantry formation. Some Hurban armored cars have been preserved and restored, and replicas have been made. Together with World War II German and Soviet weapons, artifacts and armored vehicles, they are displayed since 2009 near the Zvolen castle in the open-air museum of heavy weapons, which is a part of the Museum of Slovak National Insurrection.

PART 6

Post-1945 Military Use of Railroads

GENERALITIES

The end of World War II found European railroads in a worse state than they had been in 1918 at the end of the First World War. In Germany, worst hit of all, even coal trucks had to be pressed into use for emergency passenger services while trains of battered motley rail stock worked gingerly across temporary or badly shored-up engineering works. As after World War I, much of the best equipment and rolling stock was requisitioned by the victors as reparation and compensation. All over the world, everywhere battles had been fought, reconstruction was carried out, and railroads were rebuilt and re-equipped, sometimes with discarded military materials—often of American origin.

Everywhere in Europe where the war had raged, railroads had been worked to exhaustion; many had been severely damaged or totally destroyed. It took a hard and laborious period of patching up, making up general arrears of maintenance, and rebuilding in an attempt to quickly reach prewar capacity and standards of security and efficiency. The destruction was sometimes so large-scaled that it offered the opportunity for a totally new fresh start. For example, the Dutch railroad network was so badly damaged that the Kingdom of the Netherlands was able almost to start from scratch, electrifying their lines and adopting new diesel-engined locomotives. In 1956 the Netherlands was one of the first countries to dispense entirely with steam power.

The massive use of military railroad was discontinued after the end of World War II because modern road vehicles had become much more numerous, more reliable and more powerful, and offered more flexibility than before. When a road convoy is attacked, some of the individual vehicles are likely to get through. But a disabled locomotive or a destroyed section of track render a whole train motionless and vulnerable.

Railroads were no longer the fundamental war-winning means of transportation. Large-scale conflicts involving massive armies of millions of soldiers have become impossible. Today the trenches of the First World War would be smashed and destroyed in a matter of hours by missiles or rockets. Today's armies are much smaller but they are extremely well-equipped with sophisticated high-tech weaponry, vehicles and gear giving enormous firepower, mobility and efficiency. There is no longer any need for massive use and general mobilization of the railroad in case of war. Indeed, in many cases, transport methods have greatly improved, and large carrying aircraft and transport helicopters can ferry soldiers with remarkable speed. Once in the war zone, soldiers can be rapidly deployed in modern trucks, armored personnel carriers, combat helicopters or hovercraft, while being supported by a fleet of ground-attack airplanes and artillery mounted in tracked vehicles.

After 1945 armored trains and artillery mounted on railroads were totally obsolete, because their large size and weight made them cumbersome and much too vulnerable to track sabotage as well as to attacks from the air. Besides, enormous payloads can now be delivered with amazing precision by bomber aircraft, e.g., rockets, bombs or missiles both for long-range strategic offensives and for short-range tactical attacks.

However, despite the growing sophistication of aircraft, helicopters and weapons, notably jet airplanes, rockets and missiles, the railroads still played a part in several conflicts of the second half of the 20th century. After 1945 military trains, notably armored trains, draisines, and armored road-vehicles on rail were used on several occasions, typically in a number of colonial wars or regional conflicts, but more in support and anti-guerrilla insurgency roles than as decisive offensive weapons. They could help to secure a railroad track, provided the insurgents did not have access to modern antitank weaponry. Indeed, postwar colonial conflicts have clearly shown that, even with air superiority, it is the attitude of people that determines whether a railroad line is viable.

The Cold War (1947 to 1991) was a period of sustained political and military tension between powers in the Western Bloc, dominated by the United States with NATO among its allies, and powers in the Eastern Bloc, dominated by the Soviet Union along with the Warsaw Pact. The use of railroad as means of transportation for troops, supplies and war materials remained essential for both blocs only in strictly controlled areas. Railroad indeed remains the only way to move heavy tanks and bulky equipment rapidly over long distances and preserve their battle worthiness prior to combat. Both in the NATO bloc and in the Warsaw Pact bloc, tanks' dimension and weight were determined by the capacity of European flatcars and bridges, as well as the height and width of tunnels. During the Cold

War, in the eventuality of an armed conflict both, sides made preparations. For example, a large park was created at Amersfoort-Vlasakkers in the Netherlands where NATO tanks and other vehicles could be loaded onto platform rail cars and shipped to the front at short notice. Seedorf near Bremen was another of these NATO military transport bases. In the East Bloc, similar bases existed and mobile nuclear rocket launching trains were developed. When Russia began removing its forces from East Germany at the end of the Cold War, they of course went by rail. Railroads are still the most efficient carriers of military supplies in bulk, but they can only operate in pacified areas.

After the end of the Cold War, military transport trains continued to play a significant role, for example during operation Desert Shield against Saddam Hussein in 1990–91, and during the wars in the Balkans following the breakup of Yugoslavia in the 1990s.

One armored train that probably remains in regular use today (in 2016) is the private train of North Korea's dictator Kim Jong-un, whose father Kim Jong-il had received as a gift from the Soviet Union.

THE NETHERLANDS

The huge archipelago of Indonesia (then known as Dutch East Indies) had been a Dutch colony since the 16th century. The Japanese occupation during World War II ended Dutch rule, and encouraged the previously suppressed Indonesian independence movement. Two days after the surrender of Japan in August 1945, Sukarno, an influential nationalist leader, declared independence, was appointed president of the new republic, and severed the connections of four centuries of Dutch oppression. The Netherlands tried to re-establish their rule, and started an armed repression known as *Politionele Acties* (Police Actions). The words "independence war" as well as "colonial war" were avoided because the Dutch refused to acknowledge that it was a conflict between two states, regarding it as a rebellion—a purely internal problem of public order. There were two major police actions spread over a three-year period during which 120,000 young Dutch men were sent on a mission to bring back "order and peace" to the Indies. The war involved sporadic but bloody armed conflicts, internal Indonesian political and communal upheavals, as well as brutal guerrilla and equally brutal anti-guerrilla warfare. Dutch military forces were able to control the major towns, ports and industrial assets on the islands of Java and Sumatra, but could not always control the wide countryside. After two major international diplomatic interventions, pressure on the Netherlands became such that the Dutch were formally forced to recognize the independence of the United States of Indonesia in December 1949.

Many battles between Indonesian freedom fighters and Dutch soldiers occurred over the railroads in the main islands of Borneo, Java and

Dutch rail Braats. The Braats was a Dutch **Overvalswagen** *(assault vehicle) designed in the late 1930s for the Dutch colonial army. The Braats was composed of the chassis of a Chevrolet 4 × 2 cab over truck and a sloping armored hull designed and produced by the Braats metalworks manufacture in Surabaya, Eastern Java, whence its name. Armor was 20 mm at the front, 12 mm at the sides and rear, and 6 mm for the bottom plate. The vehicle was open-topped, though some versions included a roof cover plate. It weighed about 6 t, had a maximum speed of 90 km/h, and was generally armed with one or more light machine guns. It had a crew of two (driver and gunner), and could carry up to twelve soldiers. During World War II, after short combat on Java Island, most Dutch Braats were captured and pressed into Japanese service. After World War II, by order of the Dutch colonial army, several surviving armored Braats were converted by the Manggarai Workshops into railroad draisines known as* **schietwagens** *("firing cars"), and used as fighting and scouting rail cars against nationalist natives during the Indonesian Independence War. Other vehicles used on rail by the Dutch during that period included U.S.–made armored Jeeps and Dodge WC.*

Sumatra. Often the lines (built by the Dutch from 1867 for economic reasons, but also for military and peacekeeping purposes) became the demarcation line between Dutch-held and Republic-held areas. In general, there was an atmosphere of insecurity and war, and on railroad lines held by the Dutch, sabotage was an almost daily occurrence. There was a kind of battle of the rail as trains were used to smuggle firearms and transport freedom fighters. On the other hand, the Dutch used armored vehicles on tracks to prevent attacks. While the struggle raged on, the civilian railroad service was, however, kept running. Passenger trains ran between significant cities and towns in the territories held by the Republican independence fighters, and some of the lines removed by the Japanese were restored. In the territories they controlled, the Dutch did the same.

After Indonesia's full independence in 1950, the railroad was in an appalling state. Years of neglect, World War II, and the Independence War had caused much destruction or damage to the rolling stock, tracks, signals

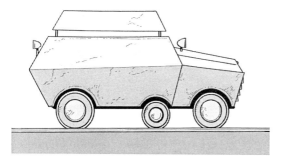

Left, top: *Profile, armored rail jeep. Built by the Leger Technische Dienst (LTD, Army Technical Service), this small armored reconnaissance rail vehicle was used by the Dutch in South Sumatra during the Indonesian War of Independence.*

Left, middle: *Dutch armored rail jeep.*

Left, bottom: *Dutch KNIL soldier, 1947. The Koninklijk Nederlandsch-Indisch Leger (Royal Dutch Indies Army, or KNIL) was founded in 1819 and officially formed by royal decree in March 1830. It was not part of the Royal Netherlands Army, but a separate military arm specifically created, trained and equipped for service in the Netherlands East Indies. It was disbanded after the independence of Indonesia in 1950. During the "police actions," KNIL soldiers wore a mishmash of World War II vintage uniforms and equipment, including camouflaged U.S. Marine fatigues and gear, and British webbing. Headgear included various caps, berets, and bush hats, as well as U.S. or British steel helmets. Weapons too were U.S. and British vintage, including Garand and Enfield rifles, as well as Lanchester, Sten, Grease Guns or Thompson submachine guns.*

Above: *Emblem of the KNIL (Royal Dutch Indies Army).*

and other structures. The Indonesian railroad had to be rebuilt, but that took time because the early independence years were marked by ethnic troubles, turmoils and tribal rebellions in several areas, and inevitably the railroad was affected.

POLAND

After the end of World War II there still existed a state of war in some areas in southeast Poland. Various Polish army and police units fought against Ukrainian nationalist partisans of the UPA (Ukrainian Insurgent Army) who had fought both Soviet forces and the Nazis during World War II. When Ukrainska Povstanska Armiia (UPA) partisans attacked stations, bridges and railroad tracks, Poland reacted by creating special units called the Sluzba Ochrony Kolei (SOK, the Railroad Protection Service) commanded by Captain Marian Jarosz.

In the autumn of 1945, SOK started to form improvised armored trains with the Army's help. In the period 1945–47 there were four trains in SOK service, some featuring vintage World War II German captured and repaired vintage armored artillery cars. The mission was to patrol the tracks and protect transport trains in dangerous areas in southeast Poland. The SOK units also operated an ex–German armored draisine (Panzerdraisine) type Steyr K 2670, known in German as leichte Schienenpanzer (le. SP for short, or Panzersicherungswagen), used for reconnaissance, security patrol and scouting. The railroad units were based at Zagorz near the town of Sanok in southeast Poland, and some SOK trains took part in combat against UPA in the Bieszczady Mountains.

Train No. 1 Szczecin was formed in the end of 1945 with crew and SOK guards from Szczecin (Stettin), hence its name. The train operated in the area of Medyka near the Polish-Soviet border on the Lubaczow-Rawa Ruska line.

In October 1945 train No. 2 went into service, code-named Grom (Thunder). The train operated mainly on the Sanok-Lupkow and Sanok-Ustianowa lines. It took part in a few skirmishes against UPA partisans. It was composed of: two flatcars placed at both ends protecting the train against derailment; an ex–German fully armored steam locomotive

series Tw-1; two or three infantry (assault) wagons, two-axle (probably armored freight wagons); a flat artillery car with Soviet 76.2 mm wz.43 (Model 1943, OB-25) regimental infantry gun; one ex–German armored 4-axle artillery wagon of BP-44 standard, armed with two 10.5 cm (105mm) howitzers leFH-18/40, each placed into a rotating turret. Currently this wagon is preserved in the Railroad Museum in Warsaw, along with Panzertriebwagen 16 (self-propelled draisine).

In October 1946 train No. 3 Huragan (Hurricane) was formed. In 1947, like the other Polish armored trains, it was based at Zagorz and used in combat against UPA. In 1948 Huragan was used for training purposes at the SOK Officer School in Torun. It included: one unarmored heavy freight locomotive series Ty2 (ex–German standard wartime locomotive series 52 "Kriegslok"); two or three armored infantry wagons, 2-axle, former German non-standard infantry wagon with AA-gun emplacement (in Polish service it was equipped with a searchlight); and two flatcars. Later composition included one ex–German standard artillery car and Flakwagen type BP 44 with quadruple 2 cm flak gun.

In December 1946 the last train, designated No. 4 Blyskawica (Lightning), was formed, mainly with ex–German rolling stock repaired in railroad workshops in Ostrow Wielkopolski. The crew consisted partially of No. 1 train's crew. Until June 1947, train No. 4 was stationed at Zagorz near Sanok, and operated on the Zawada-Zwierzyniec-Belzec and Zawada-Hrubieszow lines. After the combat against the UPA had come to an end in 1949, the train was moved to Zawada near Zamosc. No. 4 train included: a locomotive of unknown type; one 2-axle artillery wagon with a rotating turret of a BT-7 light tank, armed with 45mm tank gun and a coaxial machine gun 7.62 mm DT; one ex–German armored infantry 2-axle wagon, a typical command wagon (Kommandowagen) of German construction, type BP-42/44 with rifle ports in

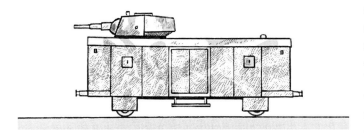

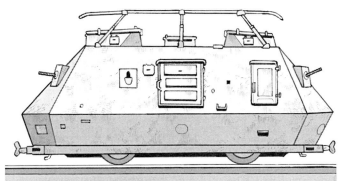

Top: *Polish SOK train No. 4 Blyskawica.*

Middle: *German Steyr Panzer draisine. Original armament consisted of four German MG 34 machine guns, and in Polish SOK service it included one 7.62 mm DP light machine gun and rifles of the crew. The draisine was 2-axle, and was powered by an air-cooled 3.5 l V8 engine Steyr 70 hp, placed centrally.*

Bottom: *Profile, German Steyr Panzer draisine in Polish SOK service. The vehicle had a crew of 5 to 8; a length of 569 cm; a width of 252 cm; a maximum speed of 60 km/h; a range of 400 km; and an armor thickness of 14.5 mm.*

the sides; two flatcars; and one ex–German concrete armored 2-axle car armed with two 37 mm flak guns.

In 1947 the Polish People's Republic (Pol-

ska Rzeczpospolita Ludowa) was established under the rule of the communist Polish United Workers' Party. By 1950 the Soviet Union and Poland had quelled the UPA, although sporadic actions still occurred until the mid–1950s.

FRANCE

After World War II, France was involved into two exhausting colonial wars, in Indochina (Vietnam, Cambodia and Laos) between 1946 and 1954, and in Algeria between 1954 and 1962.

Indochina War (1946–1954)

The railroad network in the French colony of Indochina (comprising Vietnam, Cambodia and Laos) was built between 1885 and 1936. The principal route was (and still is today) the 1,600-km (990-mi) single-track North-South Railroad line, running parallel to the coast between Hanoi and Ho Chi Minh City (Saigon). In Tonkin there is a line linking the port of Hai Phong to Hanoi, and an extension from Hai Phong to Ha Long. There is also a standard-gauge line running along the valley of the Hong River from Hanoi to Viet Tri, Yen Bai, and Lao Cai, and eventually leading to Kunning and Beijing in China. From Hanoi there is a track running to Thai Nguyen, and another local track from Hanoi to Bac Ninh, Bac Giang, Kep, Chi Lang, Lang Son, Dong Dang, and further to Nanning in China. Notwithstanding the poor state of the country's road network, the railroad system did not (and today still does not) make a great contribution to the national transport infrastructure.

Indochina was occupied by Japan during the Second World War, and the railroad system suffered a lot of damage. In order to thwart Japanese movement in the peninsula, the Allied air forces bombarded and destroyed many tracks, installations and bridges. After the war the French thought they could regain their colony, but they faced a strong movement called the Viet Minh, constituted of anti-colonialist Communists and Nationalists fighting for the independence of their country. Waging a guerrilla war, the Viet Minh tried to slow down or stop the French road and train circulation. A fierce "battle of the rail" took place on sections of the lines, such as those connecting Saigon–Nha Trang and Haiphong-Hanoi. Vietnam and French railroad engineers, as well as the French army, developed their own technique to meet the emergency. In early 1948 the French were obliged to protect their railroad transport with escorting forces due to constant Viet Minh guerrilla attacks and sabotage.

Soon there were five French armored trains operating in Indochina. One of them was the armored train Lucas, manned by soldiers of the Foreign Legion's 2nd Régiment Etranger d'Infanterie (REI, the 2nd Foreign Infantry Regiment). Another was a train manned by the 1st REC (Régiment Etranger de Cavalerie, the Foreign Cavalry Regiment). There is no point in describing in detail all French armored trains. The focus on one of these trains blindés (TB = armored train), nicknamed La Rafale (Burst), should indicate how the French use their armored trains in the conflict. La Rafale TB was designed by engineer Labrice and by Foreign Legion Chief-Corporal Kaunitz, and built in six months by the foreign legionaries themselves. Designed to be both a cargo carrier and a mobile surveillance armed unit, the train was completed in November 1948. Manned by about 50 native

Radhes auxiliaries and 96 foreign legionaries of the 2nd Foreign Infantry Regiment, the train was placed under the leadership of Captain Raphanaud, Lieutenant Novack, Lieutenant Lehiat, and Adjudant-Chef Parsianni.

La Rafale TB soon started to operate in the reconnaissance and protection role on the railroad line between Ninh-Hoa and Suoi-Kiet with sidelines to Phan-Thiet, Nha-Trang, and Phan-Ry, a stretch of about 290 km. The train was composed of one flatcar at the front with sentries who watched for obstacles and eventual mines; two locomotives with armored cab, and tenders containing fuel and water allowing an endurance of 72 hours; a command/radio car for the officers; eight armored troop quarter/combat cars (provided with loopholes and each housing about 15 men); a supply car; a field kitchen car; a field infirmary car; and two cars transporting rail material in order to repair destroyed tracks and bridges if necessary. The crew-served armament included eight twin Reibel model 31 machine guns; one 40 mm Bofort gun mounted in a turret; one ex–German 20 mm quick-firing twin flak gun; four 60 mm and four 81 mm mortars; and numerous light machine guns (British Bren and French FM 24/29) and grenade launchers. The walls of the cars were reinforced with masonry bricks, concrete, sandbags, and metal armor plates. This makeshift protection represented a considerable weight, reducing the train's maximum speed to 20 km/h in straight portions of the line, 10 km/h in the curves, and only 4 km/h at night. Before any tunnel and any bridge with a length of more than 6 meters, the train was stopped and a patrol was sent ahead to check for sabotage.

The Rafale and the other French armored trains (in combination with fortified posts placed every 25 km all along the tracks) proved rather effective weapons, which took part in numerous actions in the war in Indochina and particularly in Southern Annam. The rail network was of crucial importance in this territory, for it formed the most

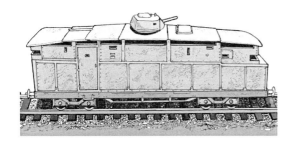

Left, top: *Insignia, French armored train. The insignia bore the mention* Train Blindé (*Armored Train*) *and the Latin device* Aes Triplex Deo Juvante (*Showing Great Courage with God's Help*).

Left, middle: *French armored train La Rafale in Indochina.*

Left, bottom: *Armored train La Rafale car with tank turret.*

Right, above: *French Foreign Legionnaire, Indochina.*

convenient mode of communications between Tonkin and South Annam. The mobile fortresses, with their large payload, armor protection, and firepower, were placed at the service of the railroad system, and undertook missions of all kinds: on the track (repair and maintenance), supporting outposts and isolated garrisons (in defense and resupply as well as evacuation of casualties), and with other trains (escort and support duties). The trains participated in operations planned by the military staffs, and were rather effective in the struggle against the guerrillas, generating a climate of insecurity around the railroad line. Constantly in action, by day and night, they surprised Viet Minh forces in several occasions through a combination of flexible maneuver by the troops they carried on board and the firepower of the train's guns. Viet air attacks were obviously not feared, but the

French armored trains were however extremely vulnerable to ambushes and sabotage of the tracks.

The adventures of the Foreign Legion's armored train La Rafale have been vividly related in Paul Bonnecarrère's book *Par le Sang Versé* (Anthème-Fayard 1968): for example, the release of the fortified post of Phu Hoi; the deer hunting of the legionaries in the forest; a spectacular ambush in late April 1949 when Rafale was immobilized, trapped and ambushed in a meander of the Song Cat River; and the capture of a Viet supply party near Tang Phu in August 1950.

Algerian War (1954–1962)

France was politically and militarily defeated in 1954 and the colony of Indochina was lost. At the same time, yet another even more atrocious colonial war started in Algeria, North Africa. On November 1, 1954, the nationalist FLN (Front de Liberation National, or Front of National Liberation) launched the rebellion against the French. During that conflict the Algerian freedom fighters waged guerrilla warfare in the countryside and terrorist actions in the cities. In order to disrupt French communications and create a permanent state of insecurity, one of their targets was the railroad network.

The Algerian rail network had been built by the French starting in 1857. In 1945, the network included some 5,000 kilometers of standard and narrow-gauge tracks connecting the most important cities and ports of Oran, Algiers, Constantine and Bone (aka Annaba), as well as local tracks connecting regional towns like Tlemsen, Sidi Bel Abbes, Saïda, Béchar, Tiaret, Tizi-Ouzou, Setif, Batna, Blida, Skidda, and Touggourt. As early as 1955, the French army and the Chemin de Fer d'Algérie (CFA, or Algerian Railroad) used lightly armored vehicles on rail in order to patrol tracks, protect infrastructures, escort convoys, and thwart sabotage. Among other armored vehicles used were CFA draisine Billard, and American World War II vintage surplus such as the Dodge WC 51 and the White scout car M3 A1. These vehicles were lightly armored and armed, and were usually operated by Compagnies des Régiments de Zouaves (Zouave Companies), Compagnies de Circulation Routière (Highway Traffic Companies) and Bataillons du Train (Logistic Battalions). Regular road armored vehicles were also used for patrolling, reconnaissance and escorting trains along the tracks by day and by night. Every morning patrols on foot "opened" the tracks and roads searching for mines and booby traps.

The efficiency of the different methods of track surveillance was illustrated by the number of attacks: 870 in 1957, and only 89 in 1961. However, armored vehicles on tracks played only a small role. The real winning weapons were indeed light and fast armored cars on road, and a new weapon system that combined speed, surprise and flexibility: the helicopter.

In Algeria, the French army won the war on

Dodge WC 51 on rail. Some Dodges were fitted with rubber-coated wheels, allowing driving on the track in relative silence, an important trump against guerrilla warfare.

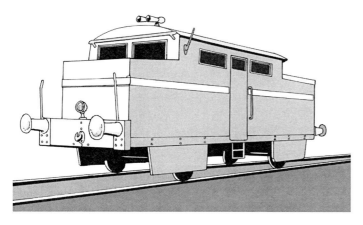

Top: *Armored CFA draisine.*

Bottom: *Sikorsky H-19 helicopter. The French army in Algeria was one of the first armies to use helicopters in combat as rapid troop transport, gunships and medical evacuation in large-scale counterinsurgency warfare. The U.S.–designed Sikorsky H-19 Chickasaw (aka "Happy Elephant") was introduced in 1950. It was a versatile multipurpose machine operated by a crew of two with a carrying capacity of ten soldiers. It had a cruising speed of 135 km/h, and a maximum range of 563 km.*

the ground, but politically the Algerian nationalist insurgents were ultimately the winners. The French government finally granted the independence of Algeria in March 1962.

CUBA

In Cuba the dictatorial regime of Fulgencio Batista (1901–1973) was overthrown by Fidel Castro (1926–2016) as a result of the Cuban Revolution from 1953 to 1959. In January 1959, Batista resigned and fled the country, and Castro took power.

Before being defeated, the regular Cuban army operated a Tren Blindado (armored train). Indeed, one of the biggest problems facing Batista's troops was the country's roads and bridges that were sabotaged by Castro's rebels. To alleviate the problem, an armored train was built. In December 1958 the train, with some 340 officers and enlisted men commanded by Colonel Florentino E. Rosell y Leyva, was sent to repair bridges and tracks near Santa Clara, some 270 km east of Havana. The train was ambushed, and officers and crew surrendered to Ernesto "Che" Guevara (1928–1967), Castro's second-in-command. The train carried a considerable amount of supply and weapons, important booty to Castro's forces, and was eventually used as a basis for further attack. Various reports, however, have suggested that the surrender of the train was prearranged, relying on payments made to the crew by Castro's forces rather than on Guevara's military skill. In any case, the capture of the train, and the subsequent media broadcasts from both the government and the rebels, proved to be a key tipping point in the Cuban Revolution. Despite the next day's newspapers hailing Batista's "victory" at Santa Clara, contrary broadcasts from Castro's rebel forces accelerated the succession of army surrenders.

Today a monument created by the Cuban sculptor José Delarra commemorates the battle. It is made up of a large 22-foot bronze statue of Ernesto Guevara, and a mausoleum with the remains of "el Che" and some of his followers. A few blocks further, near the depot of Santa Clara station, there is an open park commemorating the battle around the Tren Blindado. This consists of sculptured symbolic elements representing the actions that were carried out, the Che Guevara Obelisk, the bulldozer used to rip out the train, and original wagons of the derailed convoy housing a museum with weapons, photographs and artifacts of the event. It was declared a national monument in 1990.

SOVIET UNION

Armored Trains

The 1960s were years of the Cold War, but also a period of tension between the two largest Communist nations, China and the USSR. Facing the threat of Chinese cross-border raids during the Sino-Soviet split, the Soviet Union developed armored trains in the 1960s and early 1970s to protect the Trans-Siberian Railroad. According to different accounts, four or five trains were built to deter any possible Chinese attack. Every train included ten battle tanks, two light amphibious tanks, and several AA guns, as well as several armored personnel carriers, supply vehicles, and equipment for railroad repairs, all mounted on open platforms or in special railcars. Different parts of the train were protected with 5–20 mm thick armor. These trains were used by the Soviet Army to intimidate nationalist paramilitary units in 1990 during the early stages of the Nagorno-Karabakh War (also called Artsakh Liberation War, from 1988 to 1994) in Azerbaijan. They were also used in both Chechen wars in the 1990s and early 2000s.

Although the use of armored trains was greatly reduced after World War II, the Soviet Army still employed vehicles for railroad line patrolling. A common type used between 1969 and 1991 was the BTR40A (ZhD), a standard armored scout car fitted with retractable flanged steel wheels at the front and back, allowing for riding on rails. The vehicle was primarily deployed within the borders of the USSR, notably in Far East regions.

Nuclear Weapons

During the Cold War, both superpowers developed railroad-based ICBMs (intercontinental ballistic missiles). These mobile rail-based missile launchers had the obvious advantage of mobility over the static concrete silos used for most of these weapons. The Soviets deployed the SS-24 missile mounted on armored trains in the late 1980s. The SS-24 was a nuclear-armed rocket with a payload equal to 550,000 tons of TNT and capable of reaching the United States with its range of 6,000 miles. The missile launchers were innocent in appearance, disguised as a convoy of refrigerator cars pulled by two or three M62 diesel locomotives, but each fake refrigerator car had a hinged roof that would open to deploy the missile. The control car was disguised as an ordinary caboose, and the train further included an electrical power generating car, and several accommodation cars for the crews.

Soviet RT-23 Molodets (front view).

Top: *Soviet RT-23 Molodets. The RT-23 (NATO name SS-24 Scalpel) was a Soviet ICBM in service between 1987 and 2008. It was a three-stage solid-fueled missile carrying a nuclear MIRV (multiple independently targeted re-entry vehicle) warhead with a range of about 10,000 km. It could be either silo-based or rail-based. At the time of the Cold War, a typical Soviet missile launch train included: three standard diesel/electric M62 class locomotives; a power plant car; a command car; various support cars; and three missile launch vehicles. The missile launcher had the shape of an innocent refrigerator car, and the service cars had the appearance of civilian passenger carriages.*

Bottom: *Soviet BTR-40. Manufactured by GAZ (Soviet State Factories) in the 1950s, the armored scout car had a crew of two and could transport eight passengers. It weighed 5.3 tons (10,600 lbs), had a speed of 80 km/h (26 mph), and an armor thickness of 6 to 8 mm (02–0.3 in). It was usually armed with one 7.62 mm or a twin heavy 14.5 mm KPVT anti-aircraft machine gun. BTR was the acronym for "Brone-TRansporter" (Russian for armored transporter). The BTR-40 existed in several variants for fulfilling the roles of APC (armored personnel carrier), scout vehicle, fire support/antiaircraft vehicle, chemical reconnaissance vehicles, mobile command post, and rail scout car. In all some 8,500 units were produced. During the Cold War many were also exported to Soviet allies, including East Germany, Poland, Hungary, Egypt, China, North Korea, North Vietnam, and Cuba.*

This deployment system would allow the Soviet military to launch missiles and then move the launchers at a moment's notice to protect them from retaliatory strikes, all in perfect disguise. This made the trains' detection practically impossible, and kept the Western military and intelligence services seriously nervous for several years. It is unclear how many such trains were ever built.

Budget costs and the changing international situation led to the cancellation of the program, with all remaining railroad-based missiles finally being deactivated in 2005 and the trains eventually scrapped. One of the RT-23 Molodets missile trains is today preserved in Saint Petersburg, where it is displayed at the Vashavsky Rail Terminal Museum.

GREAT BRITAIN

Between 1948 and 1960, Great Britain was involved in a conflict known as the Malayan Emergency. It was an insurrection and guerrilla war fought between government forces and Malayan communists and nationalists. The uprising was an attempt by the Malayan Communist Party to overthrow the British colonial administration of Malaya. It started in response to the murder of three British planters in northern Malaya. It had its roots in postwar economic and political dislocation in Malaya, in particular the disaffection of the Chinese community.

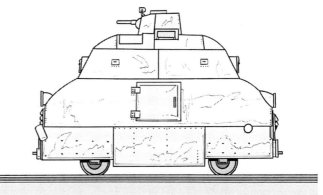

The guerrilla campaign mounted by the military arm of the Malayan Communist Party, which in 1949 became the Malayan Races Liberation Army (MRLA), soon confronted the British authorities with difficult and serious security problems. The state of emergency entailed the revocation of many civil rights, the granting of special powers to the police, and other measures aimed at the suppression of left-wing political movements, especially the Malayan Communist Party (MCP). It started shortly after the Japanese withdrawal in 1945 and extended at least to the signing of the peace treaty between the communists and the government of Malaya in 1989.

During the Malayan Emergency, Britain, just like the French in Indochina, employed counter-guerrilla methods, notably the use of self-propelled armored rail cars fitted with weapons for reconnaissance, convoy escort duties, rail traffic security, deep penetration patrolling, and ambushing guerrillas along the

Top: *British self-propelled armored rail car used in Malaya during the so-called Malayan Emergency in the period 1948–1960.*
Bottom: *Profile, British rail car.*

tracks. Just like the French in Indochina, British troops in Malaya were often unable to tell the difference between enemy combatants and noncombatant civilians while conducting military operations through the country, due to the fact the guerrillas wore civilian clothing and sometimes had support from the sympathetic civilian population. These instances led to war crimes committed by both sides.

UNITED STATES

In 1947 in the USA, an American Friendship Train operation was launched to travel through the States and collect money, supplies and foodstuffs for the people in need in

France and Italy. In 1949, as a response to the supplies collected by the Friendship Train, millions of people in France and Italy donated for the creation of the so-called Merci Train (Thank-you Train), aka the Gratitude Train. Composed of 49 cars filled with pieces of art, gifts and presents, the Merci Train was shipped across the Atlantic and arrived in New York City in February 1949. It was then divided amongst the 48 U.S. states with the remaining car shared by the District of Columbia and Hawaii.

Following World War II, the United States of America emerged as one of the two dominant superpowers, the Soviet Union being the other. The awful threat of nuclear weapons inspired both optimism and fear. Nuclear weapons were never used in warfare after 1945, as both sides drew back from the brink and a "long peace" characterized the Cold War years. There were, however, regional and "conventional" wars in Korea and Vietnam.

Korean War (1950–1953)

The Korean War began as a civil war between North and South Korea, but the conflict soon became an international "Cold War" conflict when, under U.S. leadership, the United Nations joined to support South Korea. On the other side, the People's Republic of China entered the fray to aid North Korea. In September of 1950, UN forces led by U.S. General Douglas MacArthur managed to regain lost ground in South Korea and push north. After landing at Inchon near Seoul, MacArthur's troops quickly moved to cut off the advancing North Korean army from its supply lines. By the end of the month, UN forces were approaching the 38th parallel, had liberated Seoul, and had restored the status quo that existed before the war. With authorization from Washington, UN forces pressed north, and by October 1950 had nearly reached the Yalu River, which marks the border between China and North Korea. Chinese officials viewed the U.S.-UN forces approach-

ing the Chinese border as a genuine threat to their security, and late in 1950 they sent Chinese forces into North Korea. The U.S. and UN had grossly underestimated the size, strength, and determination of the Chinese forces. As a result, MacArthur's troops were quickly forced to retreat behind the 38th parallel.

In many respects the Korean War was an old-fashioned and conventional conflict, fought with infantry, armor, and artillery supported by air cover, and even at times involving armies entrenched in static warfare. In fact, the Korean War was fought with exactly the same weapons that had been used to fight the Second World War—of course, with the exception of nuclear fire.

Railroads again played an important role during that conflict, as the North Koreans were supplied from Chinese Manchuria by train. That led the Americans to launch two massive aerial campaigns (coded Operation Strangle and Operation Saturate). Despite being supplemented by a naval blockade and gunfire from warships, the bombing air attacks proved ineffectual. The North Koreans managed to keep their train transport operating because railroad lines were difficult to destroy only from the air, and because the damage done was rapidly repaired. The U.S. and UN forces also used railroads for transferring supplies and troops from Inchon to the front lines, depots, and bases. For these purposes they had shipped in boxcars and locomotives—an efficient and well-prepared operation.

In July 1953 an armistice was signed agreeing to a new border near the 38th parallel as the demarcation line between North and South Korea. Both sides maintain and patrol a demilitarized zone (DMZ) surrounding that boundary line since then.

The Korean War had long-lasting consequences for the entire region. Though it failed to unify the country, the United States achieved its larger goals, including preserving and promoting NATO interests and defending Japan. The war also resulted in a divided Korea and complicated any possibility for accommodation between the United States and China. The Korean War served to encourage the U.S. Cold War policies of containment of communism by force, setting the stage for the further enlargement of the U.S. defense perimeter in Asia, notably in Vietnam.

Nuclear Weapons

Just like the Soviet Union during the Cold War, the United States made attempts to provide mobility by train to a part of their nuclear arsenal. Between 1953 and 1957, the St. Louis Car Company built an armored "White Train" for the United States Department of Energy. It was used for transporting nuclear weapons from the Pantex Plant near Amarillo, Texas, to various locations throughout the continental United States. It consisted of armored transport, escort and support cars. The armored escort cars mounted heavy machine guns and carried armed security couriers from the Office of Secure Transportation. The train was initially painted white. Individual cars were subsequently repainted into different colors to make them less conspicuous, but it continued to be known as the White Train. It was withdrawn in 1987 and replaced with newer vehicles, which could be marshaled into any freight train. Some of the White Train cars are now preserved at the Amarillo Railroad Museum.

In the 1980s the United States made a plan for the so-called Peacekeeper Rail Garrison Car, consisting of a mobile railroad missile system to deploy fifty MGM-118A Peacekeeper intercontinental ballistic missiles. The railcars were intended, in case of increased threat of nuclear war, to be deployed onto the U.S. rail network to avoid being destroyed by a first-strike counterforce attack by the Soviet Union. Each train was planned to consist of two locomotives, two cars for housing security forces, two launchers each holding a single missile, a launch control car, a fuel car, and a mainte-nance car. Each launching car would carry one missile in a tube that, upon the receipt of an authenticated firing command, would elevate to fire the missile from the bed of the car. The plan was canceled as part of defense cutbacks following the end of the Cold War. As a result, all 114 Peacekeeper missiles produced were installed in former Minuteman silo launchers instead. Following termination, the prototype rail garrison car was delivered to the National Museum of the United States Air Force at Wright-Patterson Air Force Base, near Dayton, Ohio, in 1994 for public display.

Vietnam War (1955–1975)

After the defeat at Dien Bien Phu and the total withdrawal of the French from Vietnam in 1954, the Saigon-Hanoi railroad that ran parallel to the coast was in a bad shape due to years of maintenance neglect and repeated destruction. When the Americans started to arrive in large numbers in the early 1960s, the 600-mile-long Saigon-Hué line, close to the border on the 17th parallel, regained importance. Consequently the track was rebuilt, and new ports were created, developed or extended to allow the deployment of U.S. Army depots in South Vietnam (notably at Saigon-Newport, Cam Ranh Bay, Qui Nhon, and Da Nang). However, the rail network was often difficult to use properly due to constant attacks, sabotage and ambushes by Viet Cong guerrillas. At times long sections of the line had to be abandoned, and road transport (although often primitive) became the principal way of communication for the U.S. and South Vietnamese armies. Along with the use of trucks, the Americans employed barges and landing craft on waterways in the numerous rivers and wet zones. In places not reachable by trucks and boats, they made use of fast but extremely expensive helicopters and transport cargo airplanes.

When the war escalated, the U.S. Air Force frequently attacked North Vietnam from the air, attempting to destroy its economic and communication systems. Again, air raids on the whole proved less efficient than expected, and many sections of railroad in North Vietnam remained in use owing to quick repair. Besides, transport by rail was only a secondary way of transport for the North Vietnamese. In order to supply the guerrillas in the South, war matériel was sent along the famous strategic Ho Chi Minh Trail, a series of pathways allowing for infiltration by heavily loaded bicycles, pack animals (including elephants), mule and ox carts, and porters. The trail gradually became a logistical network of metaled roads able to take transport vehicles supplied by Communist China and the Soviet Union. The Ho Chi Minh Trail, used from 1959 to 1975, was extremely well camouflaged under the triple-canopy jungle and dense primeval rain forests. It meandered through sparsely populated territories along the Annamite Range—the rugged forested mountains 500–2,400 m (1,500–8,000 ft) high, at the border between Laos and Annam (Central and South Vietnam). The whole system represented a formidable engineering achievement. By the end of 1966, the North Vietnamese had completed 2,959 kilometers of vehicle-capable roads, including 275 kilometers of main roads, 576 kilometers of bypasses, and 450 entry roads and storage areas. By 1973, the North Vietnamese logistical system consisted of a two-lane highway, paved with crushed limestone and gravel, that ran from the mountain passes of North Vietnam to the Chu Pong Massif in South Vietnam. By 1974 it was possible to travel a completely paved four-lane route from the Central Highlands to Tây Ninh Province, northwest of Saigon. Although many times attacked from the air, the Ho Chi Minh Trail was a significant success, which helped enable the general and final all-out offensive to take all of South Vietnam in April 1975.

Yugoslavia

The Yugoslav Wars were a series of armed conflicts fought during the breakdown of Yugoslavia in 1992–1995 between the independents movements that sought sovereignty on one side, and the central government in Belgrade on the other side that wanted to keep large parts of their territories under its control. The issues were extremely complex -characterized by bitter ethnic conflicts among the peoples of former Yugoslavia, mostly between Serbs (and to a lesser extent, Montenegrins) on the one side and Croats and Bosniaks (and to a lesser degree, Slovenes) on the other; but also between Bosniaks and Croats in Bosnia (in addition to a separate conflict fought between rival Bosniak factions in Bosnia). The entangled conflicts brought about long-lasting resentment and hatred on all sides (resulting from many casualties, numerous atrocities, ethnic cleansing and war crimes), as well as massive economic disruption to the successor states. The war ended in various stages and the creation of several new sovereign states.

All factions involved in the secessionist insurgencies designed a number of improvised weapons. Both Serbs and Croats used armored trains. An improvised armored train named Krajina Ekspres (Krajina Express) was used in Croatia in the early 1990s by the army of Republika Srpska Krajina (self-proclaimed Republic of Serbs living within Croatia that sought to remain in Yugoslavia). The Serbian train was probably the last time such a weapon system was employed in combat ever. It was towed by a diesel locomotive, and included several railcars armed with two 9K11 Malyutka missile launchers; a Bofors 40mm gun—later replaced by a Soviet-designed 76mm gun; and a pair of M-53 7.9mm light machine guns. In 1992 the train's armament was reinforced with other armored cars mounting two 20mm cannons; two Zastava M84 machine guns; a twin 57mm multiple rocket launcher, and a WWII vintage M18 Hellcat tank destroyed gun. Some anti-aircraft heavy machine guns and guns were added to ward off Croatian aviation—mostly converted civilian light airplanes used as bombers. The main battle in which the train became involved was the three-year siege of the Bosnian city of Bihac. It was reportedly touched on a few occasions with antitank grenades. However the damage was minor as most of the cars were covered with 25 mm thick sheets of metal, reinforced with rubber and gravel, which caused the explosive to detonate too early to cause real harm. The train was finally sabotaged by its own crew to avoid capture during the decisive Croatian offensive Operation Storm, which overran the Serbs in August 1995.

CONCLUSION

For about a century, from the Crimean War (1853–1856) until the Korean War (1950–1953), railroads were a crucial part of logistics in warfare. In the long history of warfare, which is as old as humanity itself, the military railroad age represents a very short period, but it is a century characterized by several of the most devastating and bloodiest wars in history (e.g., the U.S. Civil War and the two world wars of the 20th century). This is no coincidence. The railroad enabled the deployment of millions of men and enormous quantities of weapons and ammunition, resulting in unprecedented carnage. From the primitive railroad line at Balaklava in Crimea in 1853 to the large UN logistic organization in Korea in 1953, it was the railroad that was the determining factor for the nature, length, amplitude and size of war.

The age of railroad also coincides with the golden era of colonialism. Indeed, railroads (together with the steamship, the telegraph, and modern weaponry) were instruments that enabled European powers to subdue huge numbers of people and establish worldwide colonial empires.

Between 1853 and 1953, railroads were inseparable from war, but with the demise of mass industrial-scale warfare, they are no longer the only means of military transportation. The Second World War and, to a lesser extent, the Korean War are likely to be the last conflicts in which railroads were extensively employed as offensive weapons. The lesson is taught about their vulnerability, and the obvious success of motorized armies has led to a great decrease in their use for military purposes.

Military railroads started by being regarded very dubiously and many said they would never replace the horse. They were only seized upon after their efficiency had been thoroughly proved. They became indispensable adjuncts to any army's lines of supply, but soon the seeds of their downfall gradually appeared. Attempts to use them offensively with armored trains and rail borne artillery were foiled by the inherent disadvantage of any railroad: the permanent, fixed and vulnerable track. Any rail system represents an enormous infrastructure (e.g., tracks, bridges, tunnels, stations, sidings, signaling, locomotives, carriages and so on) that requires enormous investments to build, maintain, repair and modernize. The railroad also requires numerous and skilled personnel to operate. The whole thing is a complex system of specialized equipment, which must be fairly utilized to produce a result. Its strength, as well as its weakness, is summed up in the name of its basic component, the "permanent track." What is permanent is also necessarily rather rigid and vulnerable. As already said, all conflicts since 1945 have clearly demonstrated that transport railroads can only be used with success when strategically operating through friendly-held zones and without threat of attack from the air. Armored trains and heavy artillery mounted on rail cars no longer have a place in the tactics of contemporary armies.

As we have seen above, armored trains, armed draisines and armored road cars used for rail use could remain useful weapons for scouting, patrolling and securing railroad lines for anti-partisan and anti-insurgency warfare, but the day of the heavy rolling rail fortress bristling with weapons has passed.

Tunnel. Once trucks, tanks, armored personnel carriers and other military vehicles became more effective and possessed sufficient firepower, the days of the military combat train were numbered. The trains, installations and tracks they operated on had become extremely vulnerable to attack from the air, despite their protection, and the tracks could still easily be sabotaged with explosives.

As a consequence, military interest has sharply declined. The railroad training grounds of Longmoor (UK) and Claiborne-Polk (USA) have been closed and railroad troops have been disbanded. Inevitably, a large part of military transport has been taken over by flexible motorized vehicles.

However, the military transport railroad has not disappeared altogether. It remains an important means of transportation, although only in friendly territories. During and since the Cold War, railroad represented and still represents a determining factor of strategic mobility due to the problems of supply on long distances. It takes dozens of heavy trucks, numerous drivers, and large quantities of fuel to carry the load of one single train. But tactical and operational mobility on the battlefield now belong to gasoline-engine armored fighting vehicles, cross-country troop carriers, jet ground-attack airplanes, and transport and combat helicopters. Although strategic mobility on land still depends largely on the railroad, the heyday of the military railroad as an efficient offensive and combat weapon is definitely over.

Bibliography

Alcazar, Alfan. *Trenes Blindado en la Guerra Civil.* Barcelona, Spain: Revista Carril, 1985.

Arthurs, Elaine, and Felicity Jones. *Wartime GWR Serving the Nation During Two World Wars.* Shepperton, UK: Ian Allan, 2014.

Balfour, G. *The Armoured Train: Its Development and Usage.* London: Batsford, 1981.

Bishop, C., and A. Warner. *German Weapons of WWII.* Rochester, NY: Grange Books, 2001.

Bishop, Denis, and W.J.K. Davies. *Railways and War Before 1918.* London: Blandford Press, 1972.

_____. *Railways and War Since 1917.* London: Blandford Press, 1974.

Blockmans, Wim. *Oorlog door de Eeuwen heen, De Wording van Europa.* Weert: M&P Uitgeverij, 1992.

Bonnecarrère, Paul. *Par le Sang Versé: La Légion Étrangère en Indochine.* Paris: Arthème Fayard (Livre de Poche), 1968.

Cecil, R. *Hitler's War Machine.* London: Salamander Books, 1976.

Clark, John E., Jr. *Railway in the Civil War: The Impact of Management on Victory and Defeat.* Baton Rouge: Louisiana State University Press, 2001.

Claudel, Louis. *La Ligne Maginot Conception-Réalisation.* Lavey-Village, Switzerland: Association Saint-Maurice, 1974.

Connor, W.D. *Military Railways.* New York: Fredonian Books, 2002 (originally published by the War Department in 1916).

Corvisier, André. *Dictionnaire d'Art et d'Histoire Militaires.* Paris: Presses Universitaires de France, 1988.

Creveld, Martin van. *The Art of War.* London: Smithsonian Books, 2000.

Cruickshank, Dan. *Invasion: Defending Britain from Attack.* Basingstoke and Oxford: Boxtree, 2001.

Day, John R. *Trains.* London: Hamlyn, 1969.

DeNevi, Don, and Bob Hall. *United States Military Railway Service.* Toronto: Stoddart, 1992.

Drogovoz, Igor. *Fortresses on Rails: The History of Armored Trains.* Kharvest, 2002.

Ducasse, André, Jacques Meyer, and Gabriel Perreux. *Vie et Mort des Français, 1914–1918.* Paris: Hachette, 1962.

Engelmann, Joachim. *Deutsche Eisenbahngeschütze.* Dorheim: Podzun-Verlage, unknown date.

Farrington, Selwyn Kip. *Railroads at War.* New York: Coward-McCann, 1944.

Ferrari, Pierre, and Jacques Vernet. *Une Guerre sans Fin: Indochine 1945–1954.* Paris: Lavauzelle, 1984.

Finnish Army 1918–1945. http://www.jaegerplatoon. net.

Fleischer, W. *Feldbefestigungen des deutschen Heeres, 1939–1945.* Wölersheim-Berstadt: Podzun-Pallas Verlag, 1998.

Foot, William. *The Battlefields That Nearly Were: Defended England, 1940.* Stroud: The History Press, unknown date.

Ford, B. *Duitslands Geheime Wapens, Hitlers laatste hoop.* Antwerp: Standaard Uitgeverij, 1990.

François, Guy. *Les Canons de la Victoire,* tome 2: *l'artillerie lourde à grande puissance, collection Les matériels de l'armée française.* Paris: Histoire & Collections, 2008.

Funcken, L., and F. Funcken. *L'Uniforme et les Armes des Soldats de la Guerre, 1939–1945.* Tournai: Editions Casterman, 1972.

Gordon-Douglas, S.R. *German Combat Uniforms, 1939–1945.* Edgware: Almark, 1970.

Harding, D. *Weapons: An International Encyclopedia from 5000 B.C. to 2000 A.D.* London: Diagram Visual Information, 1980.

Heimburger, Donald, and John Kelly. *Trains to Victory: America's Railroads in World War II, Including Foreign Theater Operations.* Forest Park, IL: Heimburger House, 2009.

Heuzé, Paul. *La Voie Sacrée.* Paris: Renaissance du Livre, 1919.

Hilberg, Raul. *The Destruction of the European Jews.* New Haven: Yale University Press, 2003.

Hodges, Robert R., Jr., and Peter Dennis. *American Civil War Railroad Tactics* (Elite 171). Oxford: Osprey, 2009.

Hogg, Ian. *The Guns of World War II.* London: McDonald & Jane, 1976.

_____. *A History of Artillery.* London: Hamlyn, 1974.

_____. *Twentieth-Century Artillery.* Rochester: Grange Books, 2000.

Hooper, Colette, and Michael Portillo. *Railways of the Great War.* Ealing, UK: Bantam, 2014.

Howard, Michael. *War in European History*. Oxford: Oxford University Press, 1976.

Huurman, C. *Het Spoorwegbedrijf in Oorlogstijd 1939–45*. Amsterdam: Uquilair Uitgeverij, 2001.

James, Lawrence. *The Rise and Fall of the British Empire*. London: Abacus Books, 1994.

Judd, Denis. *The Boer War*. London: Granada, 1977.

Keegan, John. *A History of Warfare*. London: Hutchinson, 1993.

Knipping, Andreas. *Eisenbahn im Krieg*. Munich: GeraMond Verlag, 2005.

Knipping, Andreas, and Reinhard Schulz. *Reichsbahn hinter der Ostfront, 1941–1944*. Stuttgart: Transpress, 1999.

Kopenhagen, Wilfried. *Armored Trains of the Soviet Union 1917–1945*. Atglen, PA: Schiffer, 1996.

Krijthe, E. *Spoorwegen in Nederlandse Indie 1862–1949*. Utrecht: Nederlandse Spoorwegmuseum, 1983.

Leavy, Michael. *Railroads of the Civil War: An Illustrated History*. Yardley, PA: Westholme, 2010.

Malmassari, Paul. *Les Trains Blindés, 1826–1989*. Bayeux: Editions Heimdal, 1989.

_____. *Les trains blindés français, 1826–1962: Étude technique et tactique comparée*. Saint-Cloud: Editions Soteca, 2010.

Marcus Wendel's Axis History Fact Book. http://www.axishistory.com.

Martin, Paul. *European Military Uniforms*. London: Spring Books, 1967.

McInnes, Colin, and G.D. Sheffield. *Warfare in the Twentieth Century: Theory and Practice*. London: Unwin Hyman, 1988.

Miquel, Pierre. *Mourir à Verdun*. Paris: Editions Tallandier, 1995.

Molina, Jacinto M. Arévalo. *Los Trenes Blindados Espanoles*. Gijon: Trea Ediciones, 2003.

Montgomery, Bernard. *A Concise History of Warfare*. Ware, UK: Wordsworth Editions, 2000.

Parker, G. *Warfare*. Cambridge: Press Syndicate of the Cambridge University, 1995.

Parker-Lamb, J. *Perfecting the American Steam Locomotive*. Bloomington: Indiana University Press, 2003.

Paxton, Robert O. *La France de Vichy, 1940–1944* (French translation by Claude Bertrand of *Vichy France: Old Guard and New Order, 1940–1944*). Paris: Éditions du Seuil, 1973.

Piekałkiewicz, Janusz. *The German National Railway in World War II*. Atglen, PA: Schiffer, 2008.

Pratt, Edwin Augustus. *The Rise of Rail Power in War and Conquest*. London: P.S. King & Son, 1915.

Pratt, Hugo. *Corto Maltese en Sibérie*. Tournai: Éditions Casterman, 1975.

Robbins, Michael. *The Railway Age*. Harmondsworth: Penguin Books, 1962.

Ronald, D.W. *Longmoor Military Railway*. Newton Abbot: David & Charles, 1974.

Ropp, Theodore. *War in the Modern World*. Cambridge: Cambridge University Press, 1959.

Sawodny, Wolfgang. *Die Panzerzüge des Deutschen Reiches, 1904–1945*. Freiburg: Eisenbahn-Kurier Verlag, 1996.

Trinquier, Roger. *La Guerre Moderne*. Paris: La Table Ronde, 1961.

Wahl, Jean-Bernard, and Jean Metz. *Chemins de fer militaires à voie de 60 cm, du système Péchot à la ligne Maginot*. Ostwaldt: Editions du Polygone, 2002.

Waller, Peter. *Rail Atlas, 1939–1945*. Shepperton, UK: Ian Allan, 2014.

Weber, Thomas. *The Northern Railroads in the Civil War, 1861–1865*. Bloomington: Indiana University Press, 1952.

Weltner, Martin. *Die Eisenbahn im Dritten Reich*. Munich: GeraMond, 2008.

Westwood, John N. *Railways at War*. London: Osprey, 1980.

Wolmar, Christian. *Engines of War: How Wars Were Won and Lost on the Railways*. New York: Public Affairs, 2010.

Wright, Quincy. *A Study of War*. Chicago: Phoenix Editions, 1965.

Zaloga, Steven, and Tony Bryan. *Armored Trains: New Vanguard No. 140*. Oxford: Osprey, 2008.

Filmography

La Bataille du Rail, directed by René Clément, 1946.

The Bridge on the River Kwai, directed by David Lean, 1957.

Der letzte Zug, directed by Joseph Vilsmaier, 2006.

Doctor Zhivago, directed by David Lean, 1965.

The General, directed by Buster Keaton, 1926.

The Great Locomotive Chase, directed by Frank D. Lyon, 1956.

Lawrence of Arabia, directed by David Lean, 1962.

North West Frontier, directed by J. Lee Thompson, 1959.

Once Upon a Time in the West, directed by Sergio Leone, 1968.

The Railwayman, directed by Jonathan Teplitzky, 2013.

Von Ryan's Express, directed by Mark Robson, 1965.

The Train, directed by John Frankenheimer, 1964.

Union Pacific, directed by Cecil B. DeMille, 1939.

Index